D1296613

# Drift Boat Fly Fishing

## A River Guide's Sage Advice

Neale Streeks

Illustrations by: Richard Bunse

Frank Amato
PORTLAND

# Float Fishing

Sport fishing from boats is an ancient practice. Reed rafts, birch bark canoes, Adirondack guide boats, and a host of other craft have been utilized for fishing through the ages. Perhaps no other boat, however, conjures up romantic images of rivers and trout, of distant lands and wild mountainous country as does the river dory or drift boat. With its origins of design in ancient European waters, the dory was transplanted and modified to meet the demands of running boisterous west coast rivers. Zane Gray's adventures on the Rogue River in the 1920s helped build the romantic image of western rivers. By the 1950s drift boats were becoming well-established around the Rocky Mountain region. Today the drift boat is a symbol of western waters and large trout.

Rafts became popular after the World War II era. First used to run white water rivers, they soon found a niche as portable boats for pursuing trout. Today a wide variety of inflatable craft for every conceivable use is on the market. Rafts used for rowing anglers are immensely popular.

Just what is float fishing? Float fishing is many things to many people. To some it means drifting on a scenic lake, looking for risers in the shallows. For others it is merely a means of transportation, a way to get to remote areas of a river where they can camp and get out to wade fish the hot spots. The float fishing *Drift Boat Fly Fishing* deals with is of another sort. It is where rower and angler work as a team in pursuing river trout cast to from the boat. The rower positions and slows the craft, putting the fisherman in the best possible location on the river so he can cast to visible or imagined fish. The angler takes advantage of the boatman's oar work in covering the best water, which is often inaccessible to wading fishers. It is teamwork, maximizing the skills of both parties, that produces the best results. In this way remote waters, and rivers that are too large to be waded can be thoroughly fished. The problems of tree impaired back casts are eliminated. Miles of rugged terrain can be covered without working up a sweat. And many a mile of spectacular scenery flows into your memory.

Float fishing is beautiful rivers, surprised wildlife, ever-changing weather patterns, and journeys through geological time periods. It is cobbled runs, willowy banks, soaring swallows, clear waters, and precious large trout. Float fishing means dirt roads, small towns, cowboys, range cattle, and burly guides. Along the route you may sample many cafes, saloons, riverside camps, steaks, griddle cakes, and blackened coffee pots. Not least of all float fishing means a camaraderie rich in characters and full of life; one that transcends social barriers, wealth and poverty, politics and religion. The river beckons, chides, enthralls, and provokes. Its soothing flow makes all men revert to their primeval reverence for the richness and mystery of life. It turns men into children again, lost in the wonderment of a living river valley. They are often seen returning to the "real world" with a smile on their tanned faces, and Humpies, Royal Wulffs, Girdle Bugs, PMD's, and Trico's adorning their travel-weary hats.

To fully enjoy float fishing, there are skills to be learned and ideas to be grasped. It is a different game than wade fishing. Opportunities are more, but they go by fast. There are others within touching distance to avoid hooking. Once you've honed your float fishing skills, your success and enjoyment keep growing. Learning can be full of aggravation and tangles. Like anything, a little research ahead of time will smooth the road. While some of the following information may lack literary graces, hopefully the bare bones approach will mean more room for usable knowledge to aid in enhancing your float and wade fishing abilities.

Copyright 1995 by Neale Streeks
ALL RIGHTS RESERVED. No part of this book may be reproduced without the express written consent of the publisher, except in the case of brief excerpts in critical reviews and articles. All inquiries should be addressed to:
Frank Amato Publications, Inc., P.O. Box 82112, Portland, Oregon 97282

Printed in Hong Kong

Photos by Neale Streeks
Illustrations by Richard Bunse
Book Design: Charlie Clifford

Softbound ISBN: 1-57188-016-X
UPC: 0-66066-00204-4
3 5 7 9 10 8 6 4 2

# Table of Contents

**Float Fishing** 4

**Introduction** 6

Chapter 1
**Welcome Aboard** 7

Chapter 2
**Boat Fishing Basics** 11

Chapter 3
**Special Casting Techniques** 18

Chapter 4
**Float Fishing Tackle** 29

Chapter 5
**Float Fishing Tactics** 34

Chapter 6
**Freestone Rivers** 44

Chapter 7
**Tailwater Rivers** 54

Chapter 8
**Fighting and Netting Fish** 67

Chapter 9
**Unhooking Yourself** 70

Chapter 10
**Seasonal Conditions** 73

Chapter 11
**Crowded Fishing and Peace of Mind** 80

Chapter 12
**Guides** 86

Chapter 13
**Hatches and Trout Fare** 94

Chapter 14
**The Flies In My Vest** 100

Chapter 15
**The Perfect Day** 108

# Introduction

Wooden oars creak in their locks under the guidance of sun weathered hands. The clear and powerful currents of the Yellowstone heave against the stern, and lap pleasingly against the drift boat's aging wooden hull. A relentless river sweeps the dory on downstream, rocking with the waves in a most relaxing cadence. The magnificent panorama of the Absaroka Mountains, still shouldering a mantle of snow, unfolds as if the boat were standing still and the spectacular landscapes were marching by on their own. It's no wonder they call it "Paradise Valley."

Along the river's bank shimmering cottonwood trees wave in crisp blue afternoon breezes. Billowing thunderheads build in the distance and stride lazily across the sky. Cattle and sheep lounge in the shade, retreating from the arid heat of a mid-summer's day. Only the river seems vibrantly alive and in full motion.

The banks are an endless avenue of roundly eroded stones, each telling a history, born in the tumultuous depths of a lost time in Yellowstone Park. The high water mark is clearly in evidence above the summer level. The grinding of ice during spring thaw insures that much of the shoreline is open of brush. Somehow the stalwart willow survives the crushing grind of tons of ice, and each summer delicate mayflies and caddis return to them to rest, molt, and prepare for egg laying. Could there be a greater contrast than the raw power of an ice jam ripping the banks of a forceful river after a severe winter; compared to the unlikely fragility of a mayfly...molting on a surviving willow's bough on a warm and still summer's eve? The trout are thankful.

Trees that survive spring's thaw are well-scarred by ice. Now, during the interlude of summer, they lean peacefully out over a less threatening flow. Their shade cools, and their limbs drop terrestrials into the stream like a hatchery man scattering pellets. Perennial river keepers are they. Here and there tough old tree roots snake down to the water's edge, supporting undercut banks and cavernous lairs.

All of these stones, willows, trees, and cut banks create excellent pocket water where trout are known to reside. Suspended in the amber and jade flow, secreted among the ancient stones, are unseen trout, fish finning in wait for a hapless summer morsel.

"Here comes one of my favorite runs," chirps the boatman. (Aren't they all?) "Lay your fly in that seam along the bank."

Standing with legs locked in the bow knee braces, you work out a long and graceful line. Having no obstacles behind allows a freedom of casting unfamiliar to many small stream anglers. The swish of the line amongst the glory of the setting is pleasure enough. But down splats your hopper of almost obscene proportions. And on down the seam it bobs and spins.

"Good cast," blurts the boatman, always being one to keep spirits up and anticipation high. "Why last week we caught a five pou...Whoa! Here comes a good one!"

Up drifts a plump brown trout, with that lethargic rise that could almost be a yawn. Stripping slack line to be in a good hooking position, you watch its broad snout suck in your $3.00 hopper look-a-like. Down he goes and you hit him firmly.

"Alright!" yells the boatman as he leans to on the oars, "I told you we'd get one there! Why last year..."

As the trout makes a mad dash for midriver, you unconsciously absorb the beauty of the mountain valley drifting past, inhale the sweet smell of cottonwood groves and sage, and stare down through the clear waters flowing under your hull to the golden gravel below. Smiling in one of those rare moments of perfect contentness, you might even hum to yourself that age-old grade school melody which may have never meant much to you until now:

> "Row, row, row your boat
> gently down the stream.
> Merrily, merrily, merrily, merrily
> life is but a dream."

Such are the pleasures of float fishing for trout in western waters. An abundance of clean, large rivers; spectacular scenery of all descriptions; and of course excellent trout fishing add up to what has become almost a way of life for many.

For touring anglers, taking a guided float trip is often part of a fishing itinerary and almost a ritual of visitation on a first western trip. With more rental equipment available today, anglers can also choose to row themselves and extend their enjoyment of float fishing western rivers.

Many resident fishermen find a drift boat or raft to be almost as standard a piece of equipment as a rod and reel. Floating rivers provides easy access to hundreds of miles of blue ribbon fishing waters. With the many campgrounds and boat camps established on western rivers, floaters have the opportunity to go on week-long float fishing vacations along protected scenic waterways.

As a guide with many years experience, I've found that most first time visitors have never thought about the special situations faced when fishing from a drift boat or raft. They may never have tried to fish with two other people in such close proximity, constant tangles with the other caster and everything in the boat are common results. Knowing special considerations ahead of time makes all the difference in the world between having a day of frustrating tangles and one of pleasurable and successful fishing. For the thousands of anglers that visit the west each summer, there are aspects of fly fishing that need to be relearned when fishing from a boat. The first part of this volume deals in depth with skills needed. The second part suggests fishing strategies used in float fishing with the fly rod, fishing seasons, hatches, and thoughts on guides.

It is hoped that the large store of float fishing experience shared here will be of benefit to beginning and experienced anglers alike. Since this is the first book ever applied solely to drift boat fly fishing, touring anglers should find much to accelerate their understanding of the special skills within. Even advanced float fishermen will probably find a few bits of valuable information that might not have occurred to them before. If you can acquire these skills without having to learn every mistake the hard way, then I will have succeeded at my task. Time is too short—especially premium fishing time—to spend making mistakes that are easily avoided with proper instruction. Guide fees are too costly to waste by being tangled all day when taking a float trip. May *Drift Boat Fly Fishing* make easy what so many beginners find annoyingly difficult. Float fishing and guiding have afforded me some of my most pleasant memories and experiences riverside. May your enjoyment of our beautiful rivers be heightened, and your fishing improved by the following culmination of a guide's years on Montana rivers.

*The tubes of rafts can be slippery, especially when morning dew or frost is present. Step over them directly onto the floor for a safe entry. I fell off raft tubes several times last year, into the river and onto rocky banks.*

# 1. Welcome Aboard

## GETTING IN AND OUT OF THE BOAT

Before you can begin floating, you'll have to board the drift boat or raft, something that can be trickier than you think, especially if you don't think about it first! Many an angler has taken a "header" into the drink trying to negotiate an entry or exit from a high-sided drift boat while encumbered by sagging waders.

The first thing to remember is that the boat will move in the water when you put your weight against it. Chances are that it will be floating and not totally stationary, even if anchored or being held. Everyone has seen the old picture of a guy with one foot on the pier and the other on a small boat, the boat pushes away and the guy falls in between them. It's the same principle when entering a drift boat. Commit your weight either to the bank or to the boat, don't balance somewhere in between.

As drift boats have high sides in the front, or "bow", the bow angler usually has a little more trouble entering the craft. The angler in the rear, or "stern," of the boat has an easier time of it as the sides are lower there. He can enter just in front of his seat or even plop right down into it. The boatman or guide usually tries to hold the craft as still as possible while the anglers enter the boat. The boatman generally enters last, giving the boat a shove out into the current. It is nearly impossible for the boatman to hold the boat 100 percent still while the others get in, so as mentioned above, commit all your weight and balance at once when entering. Don't stand there balancing between the two.

There are two common ways of entering a boat. One is by stepping in with one leg, committing all your weight there, and then swinging your other leg up and over the side. The trick here is to avoid hooking your foot on the "gunwale" or uppermost edge of the boat's side when you swing your second leg over. With your full flexibility restricted by waders, this is the point when most accidents happen. Steady yourself by keeping a solid grip on the gunwale while entering the boat. Swing your second leg over the lowest part of the gunwale, that closest to the center of the craft. When exiting the boat, the potential for an accidental plunge increases. We'll talk about that in a moment. Once you've gotten both feet in, expect the boat to rock a little. Hold on to a seat or gunwale while making your way to your seat. The second angler should wait until the first is seated, otherwise he will rock the boat and possibly cause the first angler to take a spill, much like a bus driver taking off while you are still walking down the aisle. Be sure to keep rods out of the way when entering and exiting as this is the prime time to break one.

The second way to enter a boat is by turning your back towards it, putting both hands on the gunwale, and sitting up on the side. Again, commit all your weight at once. The angler in the bow position can then either swing his legs over and stand up, or sit down on the thwart (cross section that the front seat is located on) and swing his legs over while remaining seated. From there he can shift over to the seat. The stern angler can, depending on the design of the boat, often sit directly in his seat by turning

The boatman can help lower the entry side of the boat for the less agile by positioning himself on the opposite side and lifting up on it. At the same time, his body will help stop the boat from moving as the fisherman enters. The third party can help steady the craft too. The less boat movement, the less chance of an accidental spill. I've seen plenty of them too!

When entering a raft one should expect the tubes of the raft to be slippery. While you might see experienced boatmen dancing about on top of the tubes, it is best for a novice to either step over the tube (inflated side of the raft) onto the floor of the raft, or to sit down on the tube and then swing his legs in, from there making his way to his seat. Rafts have lower sides than drift boats and don't rock much at all. On the whole they are easier to enter and exit.

If you are getting in or out of an unanchored boat in the middle of a river beware of boat movement. It is hard to hold the boat perfectly still so expect movement in response to your entry. Commit all your weight at once. Avoid entering or exiting the boat on the downstream side as it can drift and knock you down. This is one of the most common ways of taking a spill, and is potentially dangerous in swift rivers and those with obstacles like downfall trees and boulders. Enter the boat at the sides or stern and do so in a quick determined fashion.

While exiting the boat is much like entering, there is an added complication. Not only do you have to negotiate the high sides of the drift boat, you are stepping down to a lower point than the bottom of the boat. When you get out, the boat will buoy up as your weight is removed. Stepping down and swinging your leg over is noticeably more difficult than stepping up and doing so. This is where anglers are most likely to fall in the river. From the bow especially the step down is a long one. For some it is almost impossible to swing the second leg over the gunwale once the first foot is on the river's bottom, the common dunking occurs when the angler in this position irretrievably hooks his second foot on the gunwale. Now off balance, and not helped by the boat buoying up and rocking after he has removed his weight from it, he finally takes the backwards plunge and comes up sputtering mad. Some anglers get so upset and embarrassed by this that they let it ruin their day. On days of extreme cold and wind the threat of hypothermia is also very real, as is the possibility of breaking or spraining bones, ankles, knees, and wrists.

The best way to avoid such a spill is either to move to the lowest edge of the boat with the shallowest water (or the bank) underneath before disembarking—usually the center, or use the sitting technique. If you are stepping out one foot at a time, hold on to the gunwale and brace yourself. Expect the second leg over to take more of a stretch than it did getting in. Maintain a sure grip on the gunwale throughout your exit and have the boatman steady the boat as it will rock and buoy up as you remove your weight from it. It may be best to let the boatman exit first and then get out next to him as he holds the boat, that way he can give you a steadying hand at the critical moment.

The sitting method calls for swinging both legs over the gunwale as you sit upon it. With both feet dangling in the water, push off with both hands landing on the river's bottom with both feet at the same time. As you do this, one hand remains firmly gripped on the gunwale, your body turns towards that side as you basically jump into the river. This exit is much like a gymnasts dismount from the parallel bars, but on a much less acrobatic scale. It is best to leave your rod on board during this maneuver, picking it up once you're safely situated.

There are a few things to watch for when making this sitting exit, especially if the water is more than shin deep. First, make sure the gunwale is smooth so that rough wood, fiberglass, or a sharp bolt don't rip your

Deck

Bow knee brace

Bow angler seat

Stern knee brace

Stern angler seat

Gunwale

Thwart

Rower seat

The bow angler sits up on the gunwale and then swings his legs in. He holds the gunwale for balance as boatman and second angler stabilize the craft. Stow rods safely when entering and exiting boat.

it sideways towards him before entering (pivoting seat). One fatal error to avoid is leaning on the boat excessively before entering. It is very easy to start pushing the boat away from yourself when doing this back to the boat, sitting entry. By leaning on the boat and trying to back onto it, rather than a jump up and sit maneuver, you might push the boat away and end up sitting in the river instead. It's best to have the boatman stand on the opposite side, holding the boat still as this sitting entry is made. This may be the best way for aged or less agile anglers to enter a drift boat.

## Entering the Boat

Entry side lowers         Rower lifts

The boatman can lower the angler's entry side by lifting up on the opposite side. At the same time, he helps stabilize the craft. This makes entering the boat easier for the bow angler.

## Getting out of the Boat

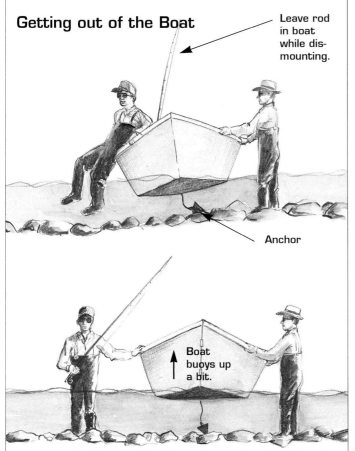

Leave rod in boat while dismounting.

Anchor

Boat buoys up a bit.

One way to exit a drift boat is by sitting on the gunwale, with both legs dangling in the water, then sliding/jumping in while turning to the side and keeping a firm grip on the gunwale. The rower stabilizes the boat.

waders. Second, make sure the water isn't too deep, or that the bottom isn't too slippery or soft to jump onto. Also avoid jumping off the downstream side of the boat, it could drift down as you're exiting and knock you over. Boats lightly pulled up on shore have a tendency to drift downstream a bit just after their human cargo has been removed, even if anchored. Removing several hundred pounds from a drift boat buoys it up several inches, sometimes causing it to drift free of the bank, pivoting on its anchor rope and potentially knocking down disengaging or unwary anglers. If possible have someone hold the boat still and offer you a hand. This method is for rivers with slower flows and easy footing.

Whether getting in or out of the boat, it is helpful to get a hand from someone for support. Whenever feasible, parking the boat in the shallowest and slowest water is a great help. If the boat is actually beached (usually

stern first), you can then walk down the length of it and step right out on shore.

## KNEE BRACES

*Knee braces in drift boats and some rafts allow anglers to stand and fish with stability. Some find casting easier when standing, and you are braced against the motions of both rower and river.*

Most drift boats and even some rafts are equipped with knee braces or yokes. Originally seen only in the bow, or front of the boat, today knee braces are common in both the bow and stern. These are designed for anglers to wedge themselves in by slightly spreading their legs while leaning into them. They comfortably brace the angler and keep him from being thrown about and taking a fall due to movement of the boat. The effect of the boatman pulling back on the oars, especially during a pivoting move, is enough to knock over a standing fisherman if unbraced. Knee braces overcome this problem and make standing to cast from the drift boat a pleasure.

Directly in front of the bow knee brace is a deck. It is here that the caster attempts to strip his extra line when fishing, much like a stripping basket. If the deck is kept uncluttered fewer tangles will result. As every fly fisherman knows, anything that can tangle a fly line eventually will. This includes the knee brace, seat, any gear around his feet, or a beverage on the deck. When fishing from the bow you can also strip line overboard. Since the boatman is backrowing to slow the boat down, the fly line will drift out in front of the boat safely, unless there is a tie down ring on the outer bow of the craft that sometimes grabs the line. The stern angler doesn't have this benefit and must either hold his fly line in neat coils (which is best though seldom done), or strip it on the floor in front of him. If the stern angler is overloaded with duffel, he'll soon find himself constantly tangling his stripped line amongst it unless he is one of those rare individuals who has perfect line control. There are few such anglers among the living. If you are used to using a stripping basket of any kind, bring it along.

There are a few other things to consider when positioning yourself in the boat to float fish. If in a drift boat, keep your weight in the center of the craft so that it floats with an "even keel." A drift boat tilting sideways because someone is constantly leaning on one side is most difficult and very annoying to row. The boat no longer rows properly. Keep your weight centered as much as possible.

Another practice that seems to appeal to anglers in the stern of the boat, be it drift boat or raft, is dragging one foot overboard in the water. This has an amazing effect on the boat's handling, all detrimental! It makes the boat several times harder to row, with the foot acting as a sea anchor. Keep your feet in the boat if the rower is trying to properly put you into the best fishing.

On windy days a standing angler acts as a sail. To help out the rower, who is suffering enough already in battling the wind, sit down and cast whenever possible. I've been on the river many, many times when it was all I could do to keep the boat from being smashed against the shore by wind. A novice rower wouldn't stand a chance. Last summer we experienced winds of 90 miles an hour in one furious western thunderstorm! Having a fisherman sit and cast makes quite a difference when handling the boat in a howling wind, but extra attention to the height and safety of the back cast must be applied!

When fishing from a raft be aware that raft floors are vulnerable to puncture when it drags over rocks, if there is weight on the floor. It's OK to stand on the floor of a raft and lean your legs into the "tubes" or inflated sides of the boat for a knee brace. If, however, the raft is about to go over shallow rocks or gravel, sit down and take your weight off the floor. It can then stretch upwards with little or no damage as it scrapes over the river's bottom. Don't wear metal boot cleats in a raft either, they damage the floors.

## WHAT TO BRING WITH YOU

Drift boats and rafts have moderate amounts of room, allowing you to bring enough gear to be ready for any weather or fishing contingency.

The first thing to plan is a full array of clothing and outer wear suitable for your trip. Since weather in the western mountains can change rapidly at any time, you need to be prepared. This is particularly true in spring and fall. I've seen the temperature drop 60 degrees in ten minutes, and have been snowed on in July and August. The sun is very intense in the mountains too. You'll want to be geared up for sunburn and heat, yet ready for near freezing rain and snow.

Have appropriate clothing for the anticipated weather, i.e. light shirts in mid-summer plus a heavier one, a jacket, and raingear. During spring and fall include a turtle neck to keep those ever-present chill winds out, a warm coat, hat, gloves, and again, raingear. I always carry a warm scarf to stop the wind from blowing down my collar, and find the plugging of that hole to be a great boon to my comfort. Even in summer, a warm hat and

gloves can come in handy. A cold thunderstorm can chill you more than you'd think, especially when accompanied by the usual high winds. Neoprene waders are essential in all but the mid-summer period of late July and August, you may well want to have them along then. It's a good idea to check on the water temperature of the river you're planning to fish, as this can vary quite a bit. Polarized sunglasses should top the list of every angler's wardrobe.

Have sunscreen and lip balm handy to combat the arid heat of summertime in the Rockies. I find it necessary to carry a volume of skin cream too, to be applied during and after a day on the river. Fishermen who haven't been out in the sun much tend to burn quickly and on specific parts of their anatomy. The forearms and wrists are conspicuous burn zones on fly fishermen, the face is also subject to burn if your hat isn't providing enough shade. Float fishermen wearing shorts and wading shoes or sandals, a common summer combination, get burned on their knees, top of the thighs, and top of their feet from sitting in a boat all day. When fishing from a standing position in the knee braces, the backs of your calves can get a good scorching. Keep these parts of your body well doused with sunscreen if you don't want to be suffering the next day!

On cold days you might want to bring a thermos of coffee and some extra snacks to keep your energy up. Don't forget any special medications, and of course your camera. Naturally you'll want to have a full array of flies, rods, reels, and your regular fishing paraphernalia.

To keep all these clothes and accessories handy, a medium size duffel bag (or two) is useful. There are bags on the market that are totally waterproof, which is a much better choice than the old water absorbing canvas type. Usually items in a boat end up getting wet one way or another even if it doesn't rain, so obtain the best designed waterproof duffel you can find. You may have to check some of the white water river equipment suppliers, though many of the big mail order houses carry them these days.

When it comes to rods and reels, most anglers bring along two—one for lighter dry fly work, and one for heavier nymphing, streamers, and wind casting. Having two rods rigged saves you from having to cut leaders and change flies as different fishing situations arise when floating down the river. Instead, you can just switch rods. Some anglers get by very well with just one rod, say a 9' 5-6 weight, while others bring an arsenal of half a dozen or more! Two, or three at the most, will suffice for most any fishing you're likely to encounter, presuming you've checked out the specific river you'll be floating.

*An after-dinner drink in the wilds follows a hard and memorable day's fishing.*

The new rod cases that allow you to keep the reel attached are handy for float fishing, knowing that you will want to change rods occasionally. Keep a watchful eye on your spare rods if unsheathed in the boat! Many are broken and lost each year. Getting in and out of the boat are perhaps the most dangerous moments for your rods, though I've seen them break in every imaginable way.

Once you've accumulated all this gear for your day on the river, pack it in the most space-saving way you can devise. Drift boats and rafts aren't luxury liners. Remember that everything you bring with you will be something to tangle your line on. If you can't carry all your gear at once, it might be too much. Multi-day camping trips are an exception, where you would have extra luggage consisting of sleeping bag, extra clothes, and perhaps a bottle or two of your favorite aperitif or "medicinal cure." (For nonfishing spouses who might be reading this, the last point is merely an angling legend. I have never verified river camp boozing with my own two eyes, not that I remember with a clear mind anyway!)

*Taking turns casting, and casting in parallel planes, helps in avoiding tangles. Here, the bow angler (front of boat) is letting the stern angler cast to a rising fish.*

# 2. Boat Fishing Basics

Float fishing requires an adjustment of wade fishing skills, and a relearning or unlearning of your present casting habits. There are specialized casting and fishing tactics used in float fishing, which become art in themselves. This is especially true if you're used to fishing small streams and making most of your casts directly upstream.

Perhaps the biggest adjustment an angler needs to make is casting in close quarters with the boatman and another angler. You can no longer be unconcerned about the direction and control of your cast. It now becomes a matter of teamwork, with the anglers and rower working together for a harmony of special techniques when fishing from a boat. Each party must not only think about the fishing, they must consider at all times what the others in the craft are doing. A consciousness of the path of fly lines and safety of crew must develop.

The boatman slows down the boat, keeping it at a proper distance from the target water. He will do his part to give the fishermen a platform from which to best cover the water or rising fish. Not only does he keep the boat well positioned but, if he is any good, he will do it in a smooth way so

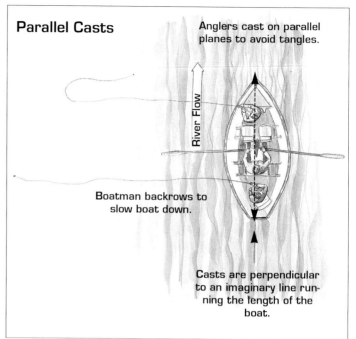

Anglers cast on parallel planes to avoid tangles.

River Flow

Boatman backrows to slow boat down.

Casts are perpendicular to an imaginary line running the length of the boat.

*Getting untangled is part of the float fishing game. Learning the proper skills will minimize "down time," the greatest inhibitor to catching fish.*

that anglers aren't jostled about by exaggerated oar strokes. This is what separates good boatmen and guides from the crowd of part-timers. Not only will a good guide keep the boat in the best position, he also looks ahead for trout—both rising and under water—planning his upcoming rowing route, ducking errant casts, tying on flies, getting beers from the cooler, and making suggestions on presentation and pattern...all at the same time! Such is the calling of the vocation.

The anglers worry about catching fish. If they are new at the floating game, they'll probably spend much of their time getting untangled—from each other and their duffel. The stern angler will be untangling from the oars as his line is swept into them. Both fishermen are getting used to an unfamiliar situation.

Experienced float fishers are quickly and efficiently shooting out accurate casts, picking the pockets, hitting the seams, using specialty casts...all with a precision, speed, and lack of wasted time unfamiliar to a more contemplative wade fisher. And they will catch more fish.

But this float trip is for the beginner. Let's head on downstream...

# PARALLEL CASTS

The first rule float fishermen need to bear in mind is that their casts must be parallel with each other. (We are presuming that there are two anglers per boat.) In order to avoid frequent tangles with each other, this rule must be consciously followed. This is not to say that all casts will be exactly parallel, certainly they won't. To consider where your back cast is going, and on what plane in relation to your fishing partner's line it's traveling, is of the utmost importance in avoiding tangles.

The moment two fishermen in a drift boat begin casting in different directions, their back casts are sure to intercept each other...or worse. Someone may get hooked by accident. Anglers can cast parallel with each

other at most any angle and direction. If they cast in the same direction that the ends of the boat are pointing, their fly lines are then traveling the same path and can tangle. While this is an unusual casting situation, it can be managed by having the anglers lean out on opposite sides of the boat to space the paths of their parallel casts.

On the whole, your casts should be perpendicular to a line running the length of the boat. In actual practice you'll find that a cast slightly in front of or behind the perpendicular line will give the longest drag free float to your fly, depending on current speed and how energetically the boatman is back rowing. For starters however, think perpendicular to the boat, and parallel with the other caster.

# TAKING TURNS

In order to deviate from parallel casts, reach back upstream for a second cast to a hot spot, or make long downstream casts to spooky fish, it can become necessary to take turns casting. While parallel casts allow casting any time you like, to capitalize on every opportunity and whim of the current requires added teamwork. When you're about to break away from parallel casts, take turns casting in the following manner.

One of the best ways is to announce when you are about to cast, if it is out of parallel with your fellow caster, this way he knows not to pick up his fly line until you're done with your cast. In these cases fishermen should watch each others casts and maintain a consciousness of what is transpiring in the boat. Verbalizing your intent is one of the safest ways to go about it.

Another method is to put the burden on the stern angler since he is facing forward and can easily watch the bow man's casting. The stern angler watches and waits, timing his casts after the bow angler's. This insures that only one angler is casting at a time and helps immensely in avoiding tangles. This is most important when anglers are not casting "in sync," not casting on parallel planes with each other. Some anglers keep up a running dialogue on their casting intentions throughout the day. Surely this is the safest way to go about it, especially if you are new to the game.

Another situation that calls for taking turns is casting to rising fish. The novice's usual reaction is to both cast to the same rise at once. Two lines fall, one over the other, creating quite a disturbance in front of the

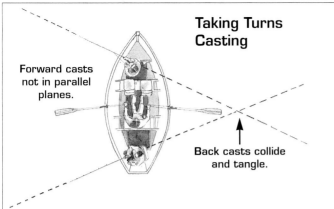

**Taking Turns Casting**

Forward casts not in parallel planes.

Back casts collide and tangle.

If anglers deviate from casting on parallel planes, tangles will result. In these cases, the fishermen must consciously take turns casting to avoid tangles. The stern caster (back of boat) can watch the bow man's (front of boat) casts, and purposely alternate casting timing. Fishermen can also announce when they're about to cast, to help avoid tangles.

befuddled trout. There are some rivers where float fishermen can spend much of the day seeking and pursuing rising trout from the boat. On such waters it becomes necessary for anglers to take turns on these fish, unless there are so many fish they can all cast to different trout at the same time. While it may seem that each angler is losing fishing time when taking turns on risers, there are ways to turn this time to profit. If the trout are being fussy, anglers can experiment with different patterns, tying new ones on while the other fisherman is trying his luck on the riser. This is also a good opportunity to get action photographs, and to look for the rises of trout coming into range. Taking turns in this fashion also gives you an opportunity to critique each other's casting style, which can be beneficial and fun, often resulting in day-long duels between sharp tongues and agile wits.

## KEEPING CASTS UP HIGH

A major concern when float fishing is keeping your casts high enough in the air so as not to hook any of your boatmates. The lazy side armed and low level casts you might be used to making when wading aren't always possible from a boat, and can cause serious injury by hook-

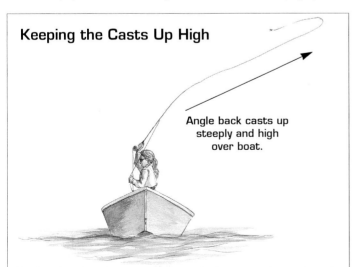

**Keeping the Casts Up High**

Angle back casts up steeply and high over boat.

For the safety of your boatmates, angle your back casts steeply up and over the boat. Pull in all slack on the water before making your back cast to ensure good power transmission. On windy days, make back casts extra high and powerful.

ing your companions. Indeed, longer rods of 8 1/2 to 9 foot are favored boat fishing lengths. These keep lines higher in the air and out of harm's way. As wind is usually a companion on western rivers, your back casts don't always go where you planned them to, often ending up over the heads of your boatmates. Thus longer rods provide a measure of safety in a boat.

One of the most common mistakes anglers make when in a boat is not pulling in all their slack before making a back cast; they get used to the current doing it for them when wade fishing. This lazy habit, which is magnified when you are floating along with the current, results in dangerously low back casts which often "rake the boat amidship with hook fire." To keep casts high and well above the boat you must strip in all your slack before making a back cast. As guides, we've gotten highly skilled at telling how low a back cast is going to come overhead before the angler has even carried out his first motions. If an angler starts their back cast with any slack on the water, we hit the deck! A tight-lined back cast and long rod add up to a safe cast when float fishing.

Shooting your back cast at a high angle or imaginary target 20 to 30 feet over the water helps in keeping your line and fly up in the safety zone. In a severe wind, make your back cast almost straight up in the air, over the boat. When you guide all summer long, you see a lot of flesh wounds from low soaring flies.

This is not to say that you can't use a short rod when float fishing; but when you consider the wind, larger flies, bigger rivers, and the safety of those in the boat, you'll find that a short rod requires greater concentration in meeting the special conditions of float fishing. It's lots of fun to catch large trout on your favorite 7 foot, #3 weight rod when conditions allow, and you'll have opportunities to get out of the boat and use it when wading. For the first time float fisherman, however, a longer rod makes it easier. An 8 1/2 to 9 foot, #5 to 6 weight outfit is a good all-around choice.

## DUELING WITH THE OARS

The angler in the stern, or rear end of the boat, finds himself doing constant battle with the oars if he is not careful. As the stern angler's fly line sweeps downstream in his presentation, and the rower dips his oar back upstream for the next stroke, they overlap in a zone of entanglement. Here again, the benefit of a long rod becomes obvious. What the stern angler needs to do is subconsciously keep track of the oar strokes, and lift his rod and line up to allow the 9 to 10 foot oar to pass underneath. This becomes habit with experience. A short rod in the stern is much more likely to have trouble with oars than a 9 foot rod. If a short rod is used, the angler will have to concentrate on overcoming this inherent problem all the more. The stern angler should not interrupt the rower's oar strokes if he can help it. A good boatman puts forth a great effort to keep the boat in perfect position. His computer-like rowing mind is plotting all moves and adjustments in advance, each stroke is calculated to keep the craft on an upcoming course. Any interruption of his rowing cadence disrupts this work.

Another occurrence for the stern angler to avoid is trailing his line in the water when undoing tangles, removing weeds from flies, or landing fish. This trailing line always ends up getting tangled around an oar! Any time you have to attend to such details, *reel all your line in*. This also relieves you of further tangles that generally ensue from having excess line about the boat or in the water. Make a habit of reeling up excess line whenever you find yourself burdened with it. It's better for your long term peace of mind!

I also find that anglers who leave their fly in the water close to the boat while undoing a tangle end up snagging something. In rafts particu-

## Dueling with the Oars

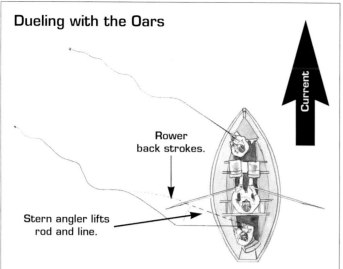

**Rower back strokes.**

**Stern angler lifts rod and line.**

Current

The stern angler must be aware of the boatman's back strokes, and lift his rod and line slightly to allow the oar to pass under them. Obviously, a longer 8-1/2 to 9 foot rod makes the subconscious task easier.

larly, which often have safety ropes around their perimeters, your dangling fly *will* get caught up somewhere. The rope is the most common catch. Barbed flies are difficult to remove from tightly woven ropes. Seams, in the raft and under it, also catch their share of flies. If nothing else, the fly will eventually get caught up in the oars. Make a point of getting line reeled in and your fly safely stashed when working on tackle. T.L.C. (Total Line Control) is a very important time and nerve-saving aspect of float fishing!

Anglers who routinely tangle in the oars become a real thorn in the side of a boatman and his concentration. His usual good natured disposition is slowly whittled away. Soon he is muttering ungracious epithets and dreaming of a smoky saloon and a cold draft beer. Don't let me make this sound worse than it is, but it is something the stern angler will have to add to his casting concerns.

## LINE CONTROL IN THE BOAT

Of all the intricacies and facets of fly fishing, excess line control in the hands and boat seems to be the least mastered of any skill. In my experience as a full-time guide, only one angler in a thousand controls his stripped in line with finesse. It is understandable that most fishermen are used to dropping their stripped line in the river and letting the current take it away untangled when wading. In a drift boat or raft, however, the

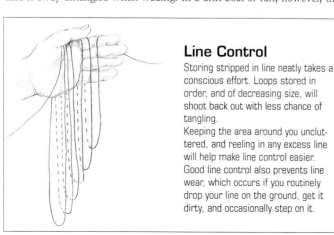

### Line Control

Storing stripped in line neatly takes a conscious effort. Loops stored in order, and of decreasing size, will shoot back out with less chance of tangling.

Keeping the area around you uncluttered, and reeling in any excess line will help make line control easier. Good line control also prevents line wear, which occurs if you routinely drop your line on the ground, get it dirty, and occasionally step on it.

line tends to get tangled on everything in the boat. The distance caster's practice of keeping neat loops of excess line coiled in hand is highly desirable. Even though the bow position of a drift boat has a stripping deck, the line still seems to get tangled around feet, drinks, tackle and what have you. I've seen many anglers spend half their day, for which they paid dearly, untangling line from both the other fisherman's rod, and from around their own feet and gear.

Line should be held neatly in your noncasting hand, stored in loops of ever decreasing size. Then as you shoot line on the next cast, release the loops one at a time, much as line peels off an open face spinning reel. With practice you can feel them escape your loosely touching finger tips one loop at a time. This helps prevent tangles. Throwing out all your loops at once often results in a bird's nest of line at your stripping guide. Only by constantly practicing this skill will you reduce those endlessly maddening tangles, but rest assured that everybody has some tangles, even the "pro's." This is one of those problems that takes relentless attention to overcome. In addition, keeping the area around you in the boat as uncluttered as possible will make a noticeable difference in cutting down on your tangles per day, as will reeling in any excess line you're not fishing with or shooting out. One could even make a netting to cover much of the boat to keep line from tangling in it, sort of an extended stripping basket.

## THE EFFECT OF ROWING ON CASTING AND FISHING

The rower has a great effect on fishing from a drift boat. Not only does the boat's position to target water play a role in the ease or difficulty of presentation, the boat's speed of progress in relation to the current also influences the way you must cast.

Let's say you are float fishing a swift river. If the boatman floats along with the current, rowing only enough to keep the boat an even distance from the bank and to avoid obstacles, your line will float right alongside the boat. Only slower water eddying along the shore will cause much drag, pulling your line to the stern. This makes for leisurely fishing and calls for fewer back casts to readjust your fly position, though you'll only get one good shot at any piece of water. It makes for a very lazy day of casting compared to wade fishing the same water. Many miles will be covered, but not in the most thorough way.

On the other hand, if the boatman is back rowing like mad, bringing the boat to a near standstill, it will be more like wade fishing. You'll have to cast, mend, recast at a much quicker pace as the river runs swiftly by the almost stationary boat. Casting at a slightly upstream angle to the perpendicular with a big reach cast might prolong your drag free presentation, whereas casting a bit downstream of the perpendicular is preferred when floating along with the current. If fishing from the stern position, you'll have more problems tangling with the oars if you're not careful (as mentioned previously). If you're in the bow you're in an ideal position to fish every pocket thoroughly, but quickly. Progressing slowly down the river allows better coverage of the water, but calls for a faster pace for rod work.

The progress of the boat's drift relative to current speed depends on many factors. If you have many miles to go and fish are everywhere, you might just "go with the flow." If you have fewer miles to travel, and want to capitalize on every pocket and undercut bank, you might go down the river at a crawl. The rower's ability and desire will also dictate the pace. As a guide I find that some anglers want to see a lot of the river and prefer to float extra miles. Others would rather cover fewer miles,

## Casting at an Upstream Angle

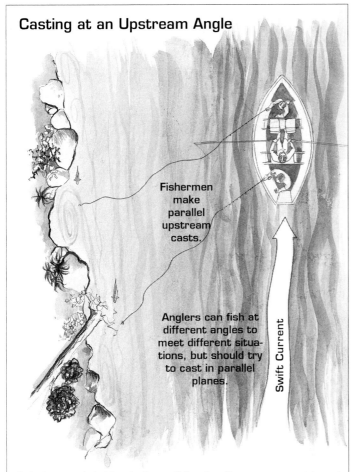

Fishermen make parallel upstream casts.

Anglers can fish at different angles to meet different situations, but should try to cast in parallel planes.

Swift Current

If the boatman is holding the boat still in a fast flow, you may want to cast upstream, as when wade fishing. Tuck casts, reach casts, slack line casts, and mends will be necessary to achieve drag free floats.

and get out to wade fish every inch. A swift river like the Madison calls for a different pace than a slow, smooth one like the Missouri.

In any case, you don't have the leisurely advantage of a wade fisherman who can make as many casts as he likes to a rising fish or likely spot. When float fishing you may only get one, two or maybe three casts at a target. Speed in casting, accuracy, and a minimum of false casts become desirable habits in keeping your fly on the best water most of the time. The angler who is most successful is the one who can put his fly on a dime, in a second, without waving a lot of pretty false casts in the air. He is fast, mechanical, and accurate. At first glance you may think that this takes some of the art and pleasure out of casting, instead you'll find a certain grace in the perfection of efficiency. Float fishing is an art in itself. You may find out just how much valuable fishing time you might have been wasting with your fly in the air instead of over fish.

If the boat is drifting at or near current speed your casts will want to be either perpendicular, directly in to the bank, or downstream of the perpendicular, both executed with a reach cast (see page 20). Your casts need to be parallel with the other caster's to avoid tangles. Since current speed along the banks is usually slower than that of mid-river where the boat is, casting slightly downstream of the perpendicular tends to give you a longer drag free drift. This is particularly true when you're trying to drop dry flies in a bankside eddy. Since the boat is out in the swifter water, it's more difficult to cast back upstream very far and still get a good drag free float. The swift water near the boat and angler will drag your line almost immediately, even with a good tuck and reach cast and the proper mends. When float fishing, forget water you've passed and concentrate on what's coming. The only routine presentation that can be effective when casting way back upstream is throwing streamers. Fish seem to like the down-

stream swim of a streamer.

Casting downstream of the boat can be taken to extremes with spooky fish or when drifting with swift flows. The bow angler shoots out a downstream cast to a visible fish, rise, or likely eddy, and then mends and strips in his line as the boat approaches the slower target water. This also allows nymphs and streamers to sink deeper or circulate in an eddy longer, provided the proper mending is employed in keeping the fly line out of the grips of the main current where the boat is. Experienced float fishermen routinely use this dodge to maximize the duration of their presentations. Extreme downstream casts can only be performed by the bow angler.

The maximum angle you can safely cast either up or downstream from the boat is limited by where your back cast starts to cross your companion's positions. Generally speaking, you will seldom be casting at such an angle, which is almost in line with the length of the boat. Most casts will be closer to the perpendicular (the boat's length). If you do find yourself about to cast either straight up or downstream, be sure to announce your intentions and watch your back cast for safety reasons. Anglers excited about shooting another quick cast to a missed opportunity seldom think about the consequences of their back cast. Moments of excitement tend to block out such concerns. Learning to keep your back cast safely up and away from your boatmates at all times is one of the most important basics of float fishing.

One practice that doesn't work well, whether float or wade fishing, is radically changing the direction of your cast. Anglers often try to pick up their line from the downstream angle the water has carried it, and with no false casts, deliver it quickly at an upstream angle. Fishermen in a boat try this for the sake of speedily getting off a cast to a hot spot passing by. They don't take the extra second to make the one quick false cast needed when changing directions. Changing directions radically in one cast usually means a loss of transmission of power and a collapsing, sloppy delivery. The danger is that the cast will come low over the boat and hook

## Casting at a Downstream Angle

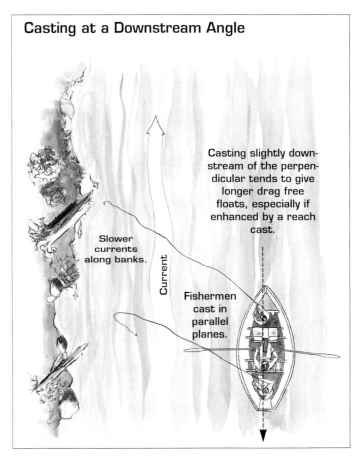

Casting slightly downstream of the perpendicular tends to give longer drag free floats, especially if enhanced by a reach cast.

Slower currents along banks.

Current

Fishermen cast in parallel planes.

## Extreme Downstream Casts

Reach Cast

Swift Midriver Current

Anchor

Extreme downstream casts are used when casting to sighted rising fish that can't be stalked from below. By hugging the bank with the boat, the angler is kept out of heavy midriver flows that would make exacting drag free drifts of a fly difficult. This is a "bow only" presentation. The stern angler reels in and sits out the action. If a number of bank huggers occur in such situations, the anglers can switch positions in the boat. Such fish often require repeated casts, finesse, and good slack line reach cast presentations.

someone. While you want to minimize false casts to keep your fly on the water, you do need to make some when changing the direction of your cast and to dry your fly. As a last note, when float fishing you can't get a cast off to every likely spot. It's better to achieve good line control and presentations and miss a few pockets (the other angler can try the pockets you've missed), than to try to rush out of control and sloppy casts everywhere.

## DIVVYING UP THE WATER

When float fishing, each angler has his own zone to cast in. While there is no hard and fast rule (maybe there should be), the oars or oar lock position makes a good dividing line for starters. The stern angler should restrict his casts and drifts to as far upstream as he can cast without his back cast passing over his companions, to the oarlocks about mid-

## Divvying Up the Water

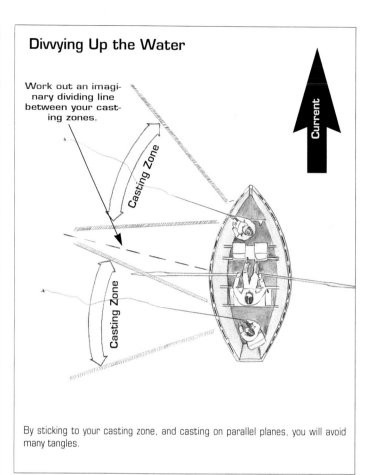

Work out an imaginary dividing line between your casting zones.

Current

Casting Zone

Casting Zone

By sticking to your casting zone, and casting on parallel planes, you will avoid many tangles.

boat. The bow angler should restrict his casts to the oarlock position, on downstream as far as he likes up to the point where his back cast becomes a hazard. As previously mentioned, any time the two fishermen's casts deviate from being parallel they should take turns casting and announce their intentions.

For some unknown, but inherent, reason the following scenario is typical on a float fishing trip. The stern caster constantly casts further and further downstream into the bow angler's water (perhaps he's jealous of not having first crack at the best water); and the bow angler casts further and further upstream into the stern angler's arena. Switch their places in the boat and they'll do the same thing, crossing each other's lines! It's hard to explain, but every guide is familiar with this occurrence. That is why you must bear in mind each casting position's proper zone of water to cover. The oarlock position is a good divider to start with. If fishermen remember to cast parallel with each other, perpendicularly to the length of the boat, each sticking to their zone of fishing water, they will have fewer problems of entanglement during the course of the day.

One other bad habit the stern angler often has is constantly casting back to spots he's missed. Soon all his casts are behind the boat. If fishing a dry fly he will seldom be making good presentations, as the fly zips out of eddies in no time. The odd fish will take skating dry flies and high speed nymphs, but the majority won't. When the stern angler continues casting backwards to missed spots, his back casts also begin to cross those of the bow angler, causing unnecessary tangles. Always keep an eye out for good spots coming up, don't shoot back for opportunities already gone by.

*Facing Page: Your pace traveling down the river will depend on mileage to be covered, current speed, the presence or lack of rising fish, and the party's personality. Each river and these combined elements will dictate an optimal fishing pace.*

**Above:** *The double haul cast is being executed here to help shoot a streamer across a big eddy line.*

**Left:** *Working a beautiful freestone run on Montana's Smith River. It's all in the line control!*

While several of the following casts are covered in many angling books, I include them here since I see so few fishermen using them when I'm guiding. I guess most anglers would rather fish than read about it. Such is the way in which old techniques and fly patterns, originated even in the last century, are "reinvented" and thought to be cunning bits of "modern" development.

The following are specialized casts I find most useful from a drift boat or raft. Before going on let me stress again the importance of casting safety—of stripping in all your slack line on the water before making a back cast. This insures that your back cast winds up well over the boat and safely over the heads of your boatmates. Low back casts due to starting with too much slack on the water are perhaps the number 1 cause of hook injuries when float fishing. Keep that back cast high and taut!

# THE REACH CAST

The reach cast is the simplest and most effective way to get long drag free drifts. Every angler should know this cast, which is highly beneficial in many moving water fishing situations, be it wading or from a boat. Once you learn it, you'll use it routinely in dealing with the intricacies of currents.

To begin, make your normal forward cast slightly higher and a little more overpowered than usual. As the line straightens in front of you, keep the rod tip held high, above your head. When your higher than normal, overpowered forward cast straightens out in front of you, it will spring back a bit, giving you some slack line. Just as your line extends and begins to turn over, reach your rod, arm, and body upstream as far as you can, and drop your rod tip and line to the water. This should be a very smooth, continuous motion. Ideally your line and fly should fall upon the water at the same time. Now you

have a long drag free drift as you follow the line downstream with your rod tip held low, mending when necessary. Follow the line with your rod tip from the upstream reaching position, until you're reaching and leaning downstream with the rod at the maximum downstream position. You can even feed out slack line to extend a good drift. Not only does the reach cast give you about three times as long a drag free drift, it also presents your fly before the leader, which is often preferable for wary trout.

Reach casts are just as beneficial from a boat as they are when wading. They also allow weighted nymphs and streamers to sink deeper, or circulate in a bankside eddy longer. You'll notice a great increase in your fishing success once you've mastered this essential cast. It takes a little practice to put the fly "on a dime" when you first try it, but if you "reach" smoothly it won't take long to perfect your style.

By casting downstream to an eddy with a slack line reach cast (see page 21), your fly can sit in the eddy till your line comes even with it. Drag sets in as your fly line passes it, and is washed on downstream. Adding a powerful tuck cast (see page 23) gives a longer float yet. Feeding out additional line from your rod can also extend the drift, but you want to be alert for strikes and take up slack and set the hook quickly.

Casting downstream to achieve a longer float seems sacrilegious to most stream-bred anglers who tend to work directly upstream. This is perhaps *the* major difference between float fishing and wade fishing presentations. Consider that the wade fisher is often in slower water near the banks casting upstream into fast water. Float fishers are generally out in faster water casting to slower water plus they are moving downstream at the same time. In both cases the angler gets a drag free float by way of what we'll call the accordion effect, for lack of a better term.

Successful wade fishing presentations are most often made upstream from slower water up into faster water. As the line floats back towards the angler, slack is created, sometimes folding up accordion fashion. This slack must then be stripped in as it floats back towards the fisherman in order for him to be in a position to set the hook should a trout rise to his fly.

The drift fisherman works on the opposite principle, usually casting slightly downstream from fast water into slow. The boat is slowing down but still traveling downstream. The angler needs to drop his line on the water aiming down and across, and landing it like a compressed accordion. His line and leader will straighten out as the current grabs it and his fly heads for its intended target. The position his line lands in, and the timing of both his cast and the downstream progression of the boat, are crucial in achieving perfect presentations. Traditionally, the serpentine cast would have been prescribed for this maneuver, but is not as easy and efficient as the slack line reach cast (see page 21). The downstream-angled cast has the added benefit of placing your fly out in front of your leader which fools more fish.

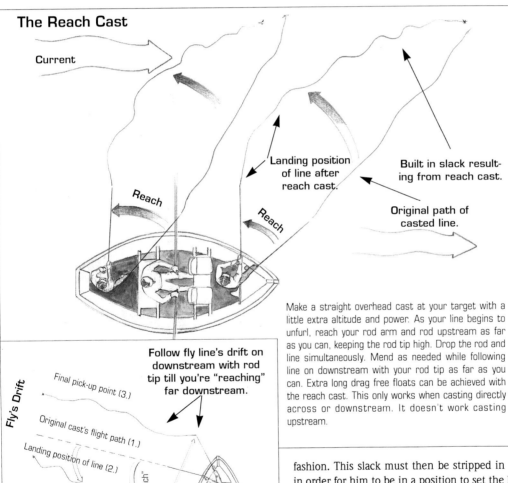

**The Reach Cast**

Current

Landing position of line after reach cast.

Built in slack resulting from reach cast.

Reach

Reach

Original path of casted line.

Make a straight overhead cast at your target with a little extra altitude and power. As your line begins to unfurl, reach your rod arm and rod upstream as far as you can, keeping the rod tip high. Drop the rod and line simultaneously. Mend as needed while following line on downstream with your rod tip as far as you can. Extra long drag free floats can be achieved with the reach cast. This only works when casting directly across or downstream. It doesn't work casting upstream.

Follow fly line's drift on downstream with rod tip till you're "reaching" far downstream.

Fly's Drift

Final pick-up point (3.)

Original cast's flight path (1.)

Landing position of line (2.)

"Reach"

Current

"Reach" upstream as far as you can smoothly while your fly line is still in the air on your forward delivery.

## Wade Fishing Presentation

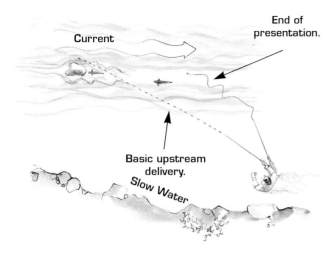

Current

End of presentation.

Basic upstream delivery.

Slow Water

In most wade fishing situations the delivery is with a straight cast. The line slackens as it drifts back towards the wade fisherman. The angler casts from slow to fast water.

## Float Fishing Presentation

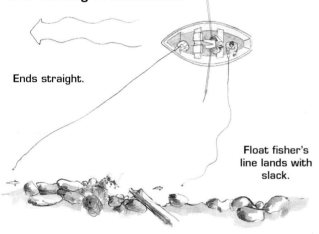

Ends straight.

Float fisher's line lands with slack.

The basic float fishing presentation is made from fast water into slow, and cast at a slight downstream angle. The angler's line needs to land with slack on the presentation, and then straigten as it approaches its target.

# SLACK LINE REACH CAST

Traditionally, the serpentine cast was used to cast downstream or across in an attempt to achieve longer drag free drifts. This delivery is made by casting at your target and wiggling your rod tip from side to side as the line extends forward and turns over. The result is a series of side to side curves in your line, which add slack, thus allowing longer drag free presentations. I believe this effect can be improved by wiggling your rod tip up and down, vertically, rather than side to side, horizontally.

With the serpentine cast, there can be a tendency to make the side to side curves in the line too extensive and widespread, this increases the amount of line on the water and thus can increase the water's effect on it. The serpentine cast can end up giving you serpentine drag. This is not always noticeable to anglers at water level. Some fishermen have a problem putting the fly where they want as well, as the side to side motion tends to deflect the fly from its

intended course. (Experienced anglers overcome these problems.)

Using a reach cast with a vertical serpentine application can give a better overall result. This is what I call a slack line reach cast. The reach cast gives an excellent start to maximizing drag free drifts, the addition of a vertical rod wiggle adds more slack yet. Since you're wiggling the rod tip up and down, slack curves in your line tend to be closer together than when shaken from side to side. Ultimately, this gives the current a little less to grab hold of, resulting in somewhat less line and fly drag. Feeding out more slack from your rod after the cast and before drag sets in lengthens your drift even more. Do this by peeling more line off your reel and flicking small "mends" or loops of slack line towards your fly, using the same basic up and down wiggling of your rod tip.

## Slack Line Reach Cast

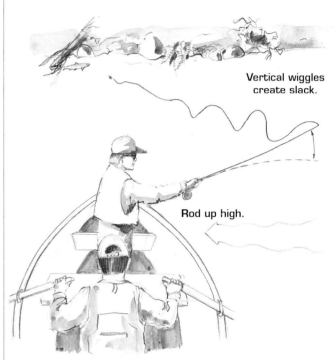

Vertical wiggles create slack.

Rod up high.

A slack line reach cast is made by wiggling the rod tip up and down vertically, while "reaching" with the rod upstream. This is done while the line is still in the air. The sooner you begin this vertical shaking after the forward casting stroke, and the more you wiggle the rod tip, the more slack will be built into your final presentation. As the fly is about to land, drop your rod tip and line to the water, and follow the line downstream with the rod tip.

# MENDING LINE

Since a drift boat is usually out in heavier currents, you can expect to have to "mend" your fly line often, especially the line nearest the boat. The trick to most mending situations (maneuvering your fly line to reduce drag) is in performing them *before* drag actually sets in. They should be planned before drag occurs, not as a last minute rescue attempt for your now dragging fly.

My wife has been an excellent student in this regard. When float fishing she now lays out an extreme slack line reach cast every time, and then immediately mends the line nearest the boat knowing it would soon begin to drag. Often she'll stack mend extra slack as well (see page 22). Her casts are right on the money, as reach casts

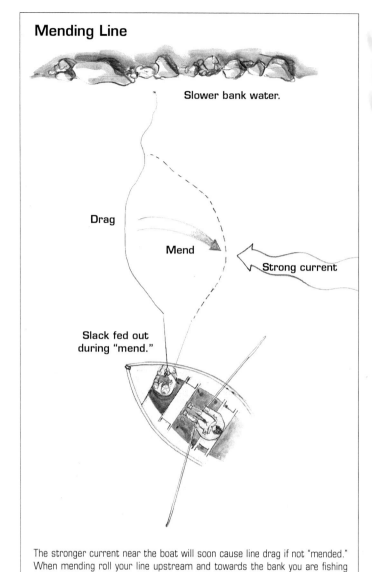

## Mending Line

Slower bank water.

Drag

Mend

Strong current

Slack fed out during "mend."

The stronger current near the boat will soon cause line drag if not "mended." When mending roll your line upstream and towards the bank you are fishing to. Feed out slack from your line hand while doing this so as to keep your fly from moving. Mend before line drag starts moving your fly for best results.

To make this mend without moving your fly, you want to employ two concepts. The first is to roll your line, or mend it, outward from the boat a bit, upstream but also towards your fly. The second maneuver is to feed slack line out of your rod and line hand while making the mend. This few feet of fed out line absorbs line tension the mend creates, which would otherwise move your fly. If you wait till your fly is dragging before you mend it, chances are the mend will drag your fly too, taking it out of its intended path and not producing the desired result. Try to figure out both your fly *and* your line's path of travel on the water, and mend *before* drag actually sets in. Anticipate having to mend your line as soon as you lay your cast across the water, even if you've performed a perfect slack line reach cast. On a long drift, two, three, or even more mends might be necessary. These are quick easy motions that will improve your success noticeably, especially when combined with the reach cast.

## STACK MENDING

Stack mending is a technique usually employed to help nymphs sink very deeply in runs. It can also help achieve long drag free floats of your fly from a boat. It is a useful ploy when working downstream to a rising fish, or when trying for extra long drifts with either dry or wet flies fished blind. We often use stack mending when floating big hoppers, and for indicator nymphing and "worming" deep, just above weed beds.

It is best to start off a stack mend presentation by casting well upstream of your target, but downstream from the boat. Begin with a reach cast and immediately mend your line as described in the previous chapter. If you recall, the mend is made by rolling the fly line upstream and out a little towards your fly. Slack line is fed out of your rod and line hand to keep from moving the fly during this procedure. To stack mend, merely repeat this mending process several to many times, feeding out more slack with each mend until a pile of slack line is layed out upon the water beside the boat. This is done in anticipation of needing or wanting an extra long drift, whether to rising or imagined fish. This slack unfurls as your fly and line drift further and further downstream from the boat. Sometimes the boat is drifted at current speed rather than back rowed, to maximize such drifts.

It will become obvious that if a fish takes the fly before expected, you'll have a hard time pulling in enough slack to set the hook during a stack mended presentation. Of course you can strip in line like mad, while rearing back on your rod as far as possible. But there is another way that can help.

Instead of trying to strip in all your line, you can try mending the slack out of it. From the bow try making a big power mend upstream and towards the middle of the river. Use all the rod and "body english" you can muster in rolling the line away from the boat and out towards the heaviest current. This takes but a second or two. Your elevated position in the boat helps you in performing this. If your mend is strong enough, you might be able to remove all the slack from your line *and* set the hook in the same motion. If the fish is hooked, keep your rod pointed low towards mid-river and reel in line till you have direct contact with the fish. In the meantime, the fish will be fighting your line which is kept taught by the main current. It will usually stay hooked. If you still haven't set the hook, you can try power mending again and/or strip in line and rear back on the rod too. Of course a percentage of fish will be lost through your momentary inability to strike, but you'll find that mends and rod manipulations can be used for more practical maneuvers than are

allow you to pull back on your delivery to fine tune its landing spot. Her drag free drifts are long and efficient. She casts quickly and keeps the fly in front of fish, not in the air. She catches trout.

When mending, the main goal is to not move the fly during the operation. How many times have I seen anglers place the fly in the right place, say right along an undercut bank that trout won't come out far from to take, and then make a big mend, pulling the fly several feet out and away from its intended path. The fly was in the right place for one second and then is never in the right place again. This goes on all day, reducing their chances of success to but a fraction of what it would be if they could mend the fly *without moving it*. This, by the way, is another situation where the reach cast helps, a good reach cast eliminates the need for an immediate mend. The line lands pre-mended.

The usual mend entails rolling part of your fly line upstream when you first detect or even suspect a "belly" is forming in your line. (This is when a faster current makes a downstream bend in your line, as it moves faster than the fly.) To ward off this dragging belly of line, make an upward rolling motion with your rod tip which in turn rolls the bellying line back upstream, thus thwarting drag a little longer.

## Stack Mending

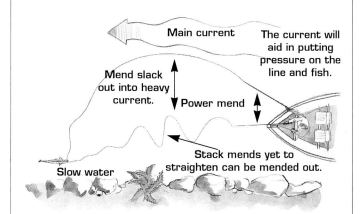

Current

Mend

The angler has made repeated, or stack mends, in order to get an extra long drag free drift with his fly. This is often performed when fishing hoppers and attractor patterns on the surface, or with deep riding indicator nymphs.

Main current

The current will aid in putting pressure on the line and fish.

Mend slack out into heavy current.

Power mend

Slow water

Stack mends yet to straighten can be mended out.

If a fish takes your fly before your stack mended line has straightened, try power mending it out into the main midriver current. This alone can set the hook. Repeat while stripping in line rapidly.

usually employed by fishermen.

From the stern of the boat, you can only power mend out such slack by rolling the line upstream and towards the shore, considering that there are others in front of you.

As previously mentioned, stack mends are usually used either to get nymphs down deep for long drifts, or to prolong surface drifts with hoppers, salmonflies, or other large attractor patterns. Both of these are generally "fishing the water" tactics as opposed to targeting rising fish, and maximize the time your fly spends on the water where fish can get it.

The big exception is when the drift boat is being held or anchored above a bank eddy in which fish are rising. In many cases holding the boat in near the bank while feeding slack line downstream to such fish is the best presentation. (In other cases it's better to land below the fish, get out of the boat, and stalk them.) By holding the boat in close to the bank, the angler is relieved of having to fight the stronger currents that his presentation would encounter if held further out in the river. We've picked off many a bank feeder by holding above them and feeding slack downstream. It always seems to be those eddy fish that demand a caster's greatest skills!

# THE SKID CAST

Here is a dodge that's simple, yet works well in targeting rising fish, especially for beginners. The only necessity is a good floating fly, one that won't sink when dragged across the surface.

To begin, throw a downstream reach cast above and a little *beyond* the fish's feeding lane. Now lift your arm and rod tip, skidding the fly across the surface until it comes into the path of the rising trout. The higher your rod and arm are in the air, the more slack will be given to your final drift over the targeted trout. Reach your rod upstream a bit during this lift too, at the same angle as a reach cast.

When the fly is in line with the fish, drop your rod tip and line to the water. Then follow it downstream with your rod tip. This usually puts your fly out in front of your leader, right over the fish, with enough slack delivered at the last second for a good drag free drift. Ideally, you should lower your rod tip, providing slack just as the fly enters the trout's field of vision. This could be anywhere from one to six feet upstream of it, depending on the speed and roughness of the current, and character of the fish. Fast water trout tend to be grabbier than slow water fish. Additional slack can be fed from the rod too, for lengthening drifts.

The benefit of this skid cast for a beginner is that they can put a fly right over rising fish without having to be an "on a dime" caster. The cast itself can be sloppy, as long as it's long enough to go beyond the trout's feed lane, and far enough upstream of the fish so as not to spook it. The act of skidding the fly will be the novice's pinpoint delivery. The dropping of the rod tip usually provides enough slack to fool a percentage of fish.

If a beginner can't cast far enough, we'll even move the boat in closer for the cast, then move it out again for the drift over the fish. The beginner can feed out slack, then perform the skid.

I use this ploy if I've over-casted a bit, or if a riser happens to pop up closer to the boat when I already have a fly drifting along the bank. If eddies start to curl up your leader and take your fly off course, a quick skid often straightens out the situation.

Having dry fly crystals on hand (a powdered silicon product) makes it easier to keep your fly high floating. Periodic applications make your fly float like a cork, insuring that a skid cast will not submerge your fly.

The skid cast is indeed a handy fine tuning device and an aid to beginners. Since trout are used to seeing insects flutter on the water, minor drag isn't always fatal. It can even induce trout to make bold rises.

# THE TUCK CAST

The tuck cast is a method of getting your fly to hit its target well before the line and leader does. This is especially desirable when fishing to slower currents and back eddies along the banks from a boat. It allows your dry fly to sit in an eddy a little bit longer, before the main current drags it away, and allows weighted nymphs to sink deeper. Here is another case of overpowering your forward cast with the rod held high. As the fly line reaches the end of its length, the fly turns over and then under, whipping down beneath the line. A tug back on the fly line just before the cast turns over accelerates this action. Now your fly lands before the leader and line, giving a few more seconds of drag free drift in critical situations. You can make

## The Tuck Cast

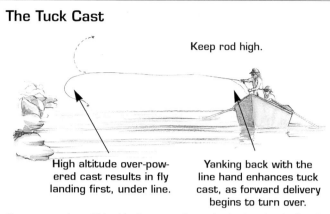

Keep rod high.

High altitude over-powered cast results in fly landing first, under line.

Yanking back with the line hand enhances tuck cast, as forward delivery begins to turn over.

By over-powering a high altitude cast and stopping it abruptly, the fly will "turn over" and then "under" the fly line. The fly will land first, allowing longer drifts in eddies, and helping nymphs sink deeper. Having your fly land before your line is always advantageous.

your fly land forcefully too, which will propel a nymph deeper, or imitate the "splat" of a hopper. Since both deep nymph fishing and bank eddies are common western fishing scenarios, the tuck cast is a valuable tool in improving these specific presentations.

In boat fishing (any moving water fly fishing for that matter) it is desirable to have your fly land before your fly line whenever possible. Those low, lazy "unrolling" casts allow the current to start dragging your line well before your fly has even landed. Put some speed and a tight loop into your casts. Both the reach and tuck casts are great aids in getting the fly to land first so as to achieve maximum length drag free floats. The only flies you'll have difficulty in getting to land first or even at the same time as your fly line are big bushy dry flies that

**INCORRECT**

Lazy casts, where the fly line unfurls across the water before the fly lands, result in poor presentations. The fly line begins to drag before the fly even hits the water.

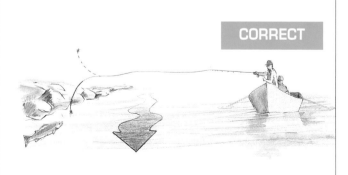

**CORRECT**

Any time you can get your fly to land before your line, you'll get longer drag free floats and better presentations.

have lots of air resistance. They tend to lag behind unless a very forceful tug on the line at the turnover is employed. Even then, they will not tuck as a weighted nymph or trimmer dry fly will.

# Side Arm Casts

Both positive and negative curve casts, which are cast side armed, are effective tools from a boat. There are limitations to when you can use them for safety reasons, depending on whether you're in the bow or stern, whether you're right or left handed, and which side of the river you're fishing.

## Side Arm Cast

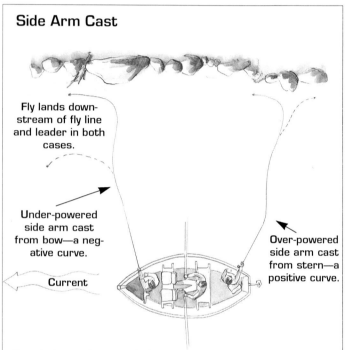

Fly lands downstream of fly line and leader in both cases.

Under-powered side arm cast from bow—a negative curve.

Current

Over-powered side arm cast from stern—a positive curve.

From the bow, anglers can only throw upstream, under-powered or "negative" curve casts. This achieves the same result as a "positive" curve, and can be further enhanced by adding a "reach" upstream.

The "positive" curve is a horizontal application on the tuck cast. Abruptly stopping a strong side arm cast puts the fly in front of the leader, for better and longer drag free drifts from the stern position.

From the stern, positive curve casts will give a fly first presentation and lengthens your drag free drifts. Unless you can cast with either hand, a right handed caster will only be able to use a side arm cast on the right bank, and a lefty only on the left bank, unless you cast across your body.

To achieve this positive curve, the stern caster overpowers a side arm cast and stops it abruptly just as the rod comes perpendicular to the bank. An added tug on the fly line increases the effect. If done with enough extra power, the line will curve around with the fly and leader landing downstream of the fly line, as shown in the illustration. This is the horizontal application of a tuck cast.

The bow angler is limited to negative curve casts, in which he can only make side arm casts upstream. Safety prohibits him from making downstream side arm casts, which would hook his boatmates behind him. The negative curve is performed by underpowering your side arm cast, but from the opposite direction. In other words, a positive curve from the right lands in the same position as a negative cast from the left. In practice, the bow angler will find the reach cast much more practical and easier to perform than the negative curve side arm cast. I find myself, however, often combining these two specialty casts into one continuous motion. When I cast right handed, I can only do this on the left side of the boat (from the bow) and vice versa. The end result is an excellent fly first, drag free presentation, which on some rivers is *the* key to success.

I find that being able to cast with either hand is a great benefit. In this way the stern angler can make side arm curves on either side of the boat. It is also a benefit to the bow angler if the wind is blowing upstream, as he can keep the rod and line as far from the rower as possible by fishing the left bank with the right hand, and the right bank with the left. His casts and wind blown line are then out in front of the boat rather than across it.

The one side arm cast that is valuable for the bow caster (and stern caster too) is used to skip flies under over-hanging willows and brush found on many western rivers. There are those dark shady spots that are oh-so-difficult to hit with an overhead cast, yet promise so great a reward if you can only get the fly under there. Such shady spots are sometimes the only steady producers on hot summer days along some rivers.

The bow angler can only cast side arm on the downstream end of the boat, and the stern angler on the upstream end. The cast to get a fly beneath the willows is made low, and parallel to the river's surface. With a little practice you can skip the fly under particularly low branches, much like skipping a stone. If you can bounce the fly just beneath the lowest bough, it will skip a little further back into those shadows of promise!

*Deceiving a "bank hugger" with that perfect under-the-willows cast—one of those victories an angler remembers at the end of a long floating day.*

## WIND CASTING

One thing about the west—it's windy! It seems like everywhere trout grow large, they are sheltered beneath the wind ripples of powerful gusts. There's no getting around it, you'll have to cast in the wind. Out here a 50 mph wind is not uncommon. You need to be good at wind casting to get the most out of float fishing. This might mean leaving your pet seven foot rod in the case and sparing your partners several hook injuries. It's in the wind that the safety of a longer, hi-modulous or heavier weight rod becomes evident. The right rod and line, and the right techniques make wind casting a little easier than you might imagine, if not quite as graceful or subtle. I remember a day in Yellowstone Park when winds were clocking over 60 mph, and trees were blowing down around us. We fished on. With the right amount of reckless enthusiasm, you'd be surprised at the wind you can manage!

From a boat you have the benefit of positioning yourself so that you seldom have to cast directly into the wind, but more commonly across it. On many rivers, tailwinds are most common, and more easily dealt with. Winds that might seem impossible from one point on shore become quite manageable once you're afloat. The boatman usually seeks out the more sheltered areas to make casting as easy as possible under the circumstances. Be assured of one thing, if you think it's hard to cast in the wind, the boatman will be having twice as much trouble rowing in it!

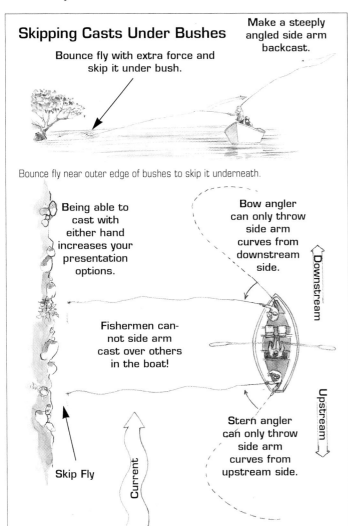

**Skipping Casts Under Bushes**

Make a steeply angled side arm backcast.

Bounce fly with extra force and skip it under bush.

Bounce fly near outer edge of bushes to skip it underneath.

Being able to cast with either hand increases your presentation options.

Bow angler can only throw side arm curves from downstream side.

Downstream

Fishermen cannot side arm cast over others in the boat!

Upstream

Stern angler can only throw side arm curves from upstream side.

Skip Fly

Current

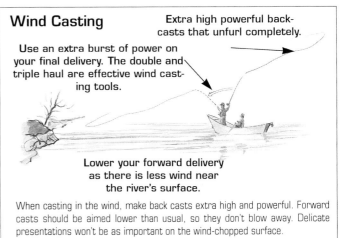

**Wind Casting**

Extra high powerful back-casts that unfurl completely.

Use an extra burst of power on your final delivery. The double and triple haul are effective wind casting tools.

Lower your forward delivery as there is less wind near the river's surface.

When casting in the wind, make back casts extra high and powerful. Forward casts should be aimed lower than usual, so they don't blow away. Delicate presentations won't be as important on the wind-chopped surface.

*Extra high and powerful back casts are sometimes required to fight the wind.*

The wind must be met with extra power, more precise timing, and the right techniques. Back casts must be extra high and thoroughly straightened out behind you. Forward casts must be low, crisp, and powerful, with an extra burst of speed delivered at the very end of the forward stroke.

The main weapon wielded against the wind is the double haul; But let me take you one step further and introduce you to the triple haul. This allows you to punch a cast and make it turn over, even in the stiffest breeze.

## THE TRIPLE HAUL

The triple haul is identical to the well-known double haul, with the addition of a third haul as the final forward delivery is about to turn over.

To begin, strip in any and all slack line on the water in front of you, our usual safety precaution. As you begin your back cast, haul down with your line hand to accelerate line speed. As the line goes back overhead, let your line hand drift back up near the first, or stripping guide on your rod. Beginning your forward cast, haul down again, further increasing line speed. Immediately after this second haul, again position your line hand back near the stripping guide. As the line begins to turn over in front of you, haul down with your line hand a third time. This third haul takes place just a second or two after the double haul. This forces the line to turn over much more

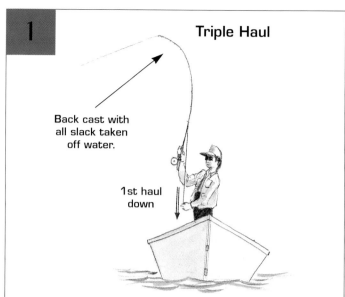

**1** **Triple Haul**

Back cast with all slack taken off water.

1st haul down

First haul accelerates back cast. Line hand drifts back up by stripping guide between hauls.

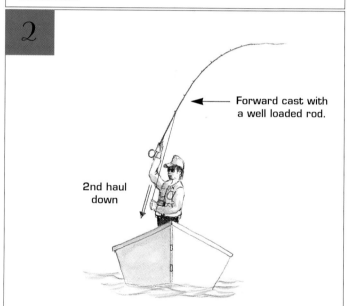

**2**

Forward cast with a well loaded rod.

2nd haul down

Second haul accelerates forward cast. Line hand drifts back up near stripping guide between hauls. Hauls are made in latter half of each casting stroke, after rod is partially loaded.

**3** Third haul, which takes place quickly after the second haul, makes fly "turn over" forcefully and places your fly near its intended target before the wind carries it away.

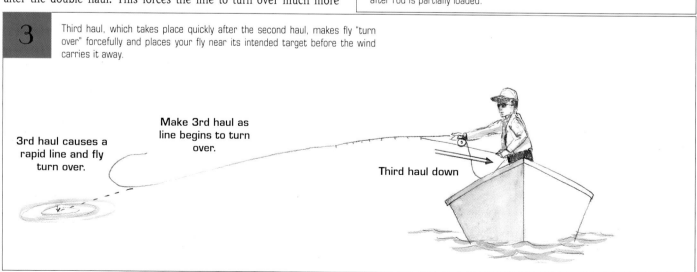

3rd haul causes a rapid line and fly turn over.

Make 3rd haul as line begins to turn over.

Third haul down

quickly and forcefully than it ordinarily does, splatting the fly down on the water. Without this third haul, your fly and leader would normally blow away from where you wanted it to land when in a substantial wind. The double haul gets the line in the air over your target, but allows the fly to blow away at the last second. The triple haul not only gets the line out over the water but also, and more importantly, it forces the fly down to your targeted spot. The third haul is similar to a tuck cast, except that the forward cast of a triple haul is lower to the water to help keep it from getting blown away. A fair amount of practice and perfect timing will be needed to get the feel of this cast. It won't be pretty, nor will it be delicate, but it won't have to be in a ripping wind. The triple haul allows you to fish at times you have found daunting before. In battling the romping and ever-present winds of the West, this technique becomes indispensable if you're to maximize your fishing time and not get blown off the river.

Other ways to fight the wind include using low powerful side arm casts when possible; waiting for lulls to make your casts; fishing the bank that gives you a tailwind; using weight forward lines with sink tips; using flies with low wind resistance; and using flies that can be left in the water longer, such as slowly fished nymphs and streamers. You will want to shorten the leader as well. Weighted flies cast on a sink tip line, using the triple haul have the ability to punch into a pretty fearsome breeze. But woe to the angler that hooks themself with such a rig, for they will be heaving it with all their might, developing high line speeds, and propelling a dangerous projectile that is often out of control. Tailwinds often knock down back casts, and when the now low flying forward haul is made, often it buries the fly in the back of the angler's head. Number two weighted streamers have knocked men for a loop and caused considerable bloodshed!

When casting in the wind, and especially from a boat, you will most likely need to make a higher than normal backcast. A tailwind usually knocks backcasts down, often resulting in much lower than expected forward casts, endangering everyone in the boat. I make my backcasts almost straight up in the air overhead when boat fishing with tailwinds, using a very powerful haul. The forward cast is then made with the casting arm fully extended upwards to keep the cast high and out of danger. The wind will help carry the cast to its full extension.

A strong wind blowing straight down the river will give the stern angler problems. His line will tend to blow into himself, the oars, and even the bow fisherman. The stern angler will need to master the wind fighting tactics mentioned previously, and may at times want to quit fishing altogether, or at least until the wind abates. While such downstream winds make fishing from the stern difficult, the bow angler will find that he has little problem coping with it. The wind merely blows his line safely downstream of the boat, out of harms way, and better yet if he can cast with either hand. While he will have to use extra force getting the fly out where he wants it, the bow caster can manage almost any velocity stern wind. During a day of ceaseless stern winds, the anglers will want to switch positions in the boat, with the least experienced fly fisher given most of the time in the bow where he can handle the wind more easily. A head wind, quite naturally, reverses these problems.

In strong cross winds, the boatman will be having serious difficulties keeping the boat in an ideal fishing position. He may have to row almost perpendicular to the current, tacking against the wind. Drift boats sail very well, like leaves upon the water. It sometimes takes a great deal of effort and profanity to keep a boat tracking properly in a gale, and to keep anglers in ideal casting positions to the banks. This can mean that the stern fisherman will have to quit cast-

## Rowing and Casting in a Cross Wind

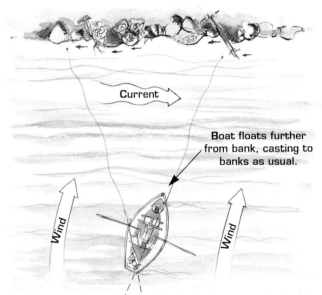

Boat floats near bank or target water.

Wind    Wind    Current

Here, the rower has to go sideways down the river to fight the wind. The fishermen are casting straight downstream, on parallel planes, and fishing different feed lanes. The boatman must angle the boat to fight both wind and current.

Current

Boat floats further from bank, casting to banks as usual.

Wind    Wind

Here again, the boat is sideways fighting the wind. The bow angler is casting directly over the length of the boat. The stern angler is watching and taking turns casting so their lines don't collide. The boat is staying further away from the bank.

ing, or that both anglers will have to cast directly downstream (in front of) or upstream (behind) the boat, which will be drifting sideways. In the first case, the bow angler will be backcasting directly over the boat, this pretty much prohibits the stern angler from doing much serious casting. If both anglers fish downstream, angling in to the bank or target water, reasonable presentations from either position are possible, though the hooking angle is less than ideal. Regardless, have some pity on the rower. He's having the toughest time of all!

There are times when it is so windy that you'll have to quit fishing for a while. The boatman will hardly be able to row. Casting will be treacherous. The best opportunities may be had by finding lee shores and sheltered areas to stop and wade fish. At least fishermen can spread out while wading so as not to hook each other, which is very likely in the boat. Hooking each other in the boat becomes particularly risky because extra power and concentration is being put into delivering the fly, and you start to forget about where your backcasts are going. The wind starts antagonizing you, and soon anger is also propelling each cast. When you do hook someone, it's often with a weighted streamer, casting as hard as you can, with the added impetus of the wind. Anglers always look surprised as their companion in the other end of the boat screams in pain, only to find their fly has traveled far from its imagined path.

Some fishermen try roll casting, both in wind and calm. Roll casting, as it's usually performed, can be dangerous in a boat. When you think of how a roll cast is performed, with the line rolling right beside the angler, and even slightly behind before it rolls out forward, the potential danger becomes apparent. The fly, on its roll, flicks up near the faces of others in the boat, usually the rower's. Roll casts can be performed if the casting arm is way out towards the ends of the boat, and attention is paid to the course the line travels. But my experiences in guiding lead me to hit the deck whenever I see someone unwittingly begin a roll cast, for as often as not that fly will be shooting up by my head before it rolls out to sea. As a routine presentation, it is best to avoid roll casting altogether from a boat.

# The Unsnagging Roll Cast

While roll casts in general aren't prescribed for boat fishing, this adaptation of the roll cast is very beneficial. The unsnagging roll cast, as I call it, helps in unsnagging your fly from rocks and logs along the river bank where you're casting. Instead of having to row the boat over to the snag, or break your fly off, this technique allows you to retrieve your fly from the boat, where you are, about 60 percent of the time.

As soon as you find yourself snagged, pull another couple of yards of fly line off your reel and throw a high roll cast up, over, and

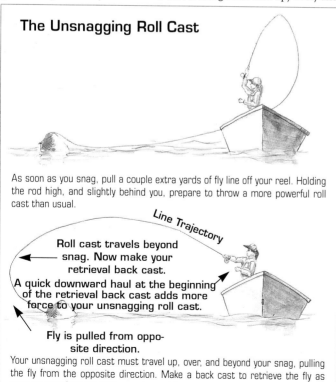

**The Unsnagging Roll Cast**

As soon as you snag, pull a couple extra yards of fly line off your reel. Holding the rod high, and slightly behind you, prepare to throw a more powerful roll cast than usual.

*Line Trajectory*

Roll cast travels beyond snag. Now make your retrieval back cast.

A quick downward haul at the beginning of the retrieval back cast adds more force to your unsnagging roll cast.

Fly is pulled from opposite direction.

Your unsnagging roll cast must travel up, over, and beyond your snag, pulling the fly from the opposite direction. Make a back cast to retrieve the fly as soon as your forward cast goes beyond the snag.

beyond your snag. This extra powerful roll cast results in your fly line actually pulling on the fly from the opposite direction. In most cases, this is enough to undo your snags. It saves fishing time for both anglers, and saves the expense of losing flies or rowing over and through the best fishing water to undo the snag by hand.

There are a few factors in maximizing the efficiency of the unsnagging roll cast. The first is to perform it as soon as you know you're snagged, if the boat floats further on downstream you'll have a hard time throwing the roll far enough to work. This only works on short to medium length casts. Very long casts and sinking lines are much harder, if not impossible, to unsnag with this method, as it is difficult to power the roll up and over the snag. It is essential to get your unsnagging roll cast off while the boat is still even with your snag.

As soon as your roll cast has gone beyond your snag, quickly make a backcast to pull the fly away. If it's still snagged, try it again. If it still doesn't work, either row over to undo do it or break it off, depending on the swiftness of the river and temperament of your rower!

If you snag the branches of a tree, don't use the unsnagging roll cast. Instead, pull slowly and evenly on the line and hope that the fly crawls out of the branches. If you jerk quickly on the line, the leader has a tendency to wrap itself in a myriad of tangles. By pulling slowly, your fly will often exonerate itself of any simple tangles amongst the brush. If the slow pull doesn't do the trick, row over and retrieve it by hand or break it off. If you're using streamers and a heavy leader, you may be able to break small branches by pulling hard enough, and free the fly that way. But always check your leader for nicks and weak spots after such an operation.

While on the subject of snags, let me relate my personal opinion on retrieving them if the unsnagging roll cast doesn't work. A boatman's willingness to row back upstream to undo a snag is often proportional to the number of times that he has to do it! If fishermen are snagging 50 times a day because of inattention to their presentation, I stop rowing to retrieve them except in placid waters. The only exception would be if we were very low on productive fly patterns. Remember that each time the boat has to row over to undo a snag, it ruins the fishing for the other angler, cuts into prime fishing time, and slowly whittles away at the rower's patience and willingness to put out his energies to keep the boat in the best fishing position. It is one thing to repeatedly retrieve a beginner's fly, and another to strain yourself rowing for someone who is skilled, but is just being lazy about casting and line control. You expect to make extra retrievals in the first case, but not in the second. Fishing weighted stonefly nymphs from the boat is one of the worst snagging scenarios. In this case, adjusting the weight and a constant attention to line control is necessary to avoid undue snags. Using the heaviest leader possible is also advised. Casting into heavy bank cover causes plenty of snags too, so bring plenty of flies, leader, and tippet, cast diligently, and expect to lose some flies. It's part of the float fishing game.

If your casts are getting sloppy due to fatigue, stop casting and watch the scenery go by for a while. For some anglers this is about the only time they look around, instead of staring at the water. Don't feel obligated to cast every moment of the day, even though many guides want you to in order to maximize the "productivity" of the day. If your casting arm is tired, give it a break. Few people, besides hard core river bums, can cast twelve hours a day in good form, and without pain. Your enjoyment of the river will be a combination of precision casting and what successes come your way, mixed with perhaps a longer lasting memory of the river's scenery and personality. No two rivers are the same. So if your casting is beginning to fail, put your rod down, let the soothing cadence of the river and scenery displace your irritation, rest your arm, and soon a renewed desire to fish will put your casts back into good form.

*I like to use stout leaders for streamer fishing. Takes can be vicious, trout can run the line through brush, or shake their heads violently, raking the leader with their sharp teeth. When going after larger trout, I like to have the upper hand.*

# 4. Float Fishing Tackle

Western float fishing favors medium weight rods and lines, and 8 to 9 foot rods. The safety factor of keeping the fly well above your companion's head, the often larger fly patterns, and wind all combine in making this length rod in a 5 or 6 weight the best all-around tool.

## RODS

The latest generation of graphite rods are ideal for float fishing. They have the power to shoot long lines with a minimum of false casting. From a safety point of view, they are able to crisply pick up the line from the water on a backcast and power it high overhead. Softer fiberglass and bamboo rods flex mightily under even a short line load and tend to bring the backcast over the boat at a lower, more hazardous altitude. Hence, the power of graphite is triply beneficial when float fishing. Not only does it lift the fly line safely and effortlessly off the water and high above, but the extra power and speed dries off dry flies in one or two quick false casts, which means that your fly is on the water in front of fish more than in the air. Graphite's distance casting ability means you can reach hot spots easily too, with a minimum of time consuming false casts.

Rods of 8 to 9 feet are ideal for most boat work. Seasoned hands can cast shorter and lighter rods, but for the average caster, it's best to stick to the longer rod for actual boat fishing to keep the casts high above the boat. Safety comes first. Bring your favorite short rods along for wade fishing excursions, along with their cases for protection while not in use.

Today's rods are packing more power in less weight all the time. Some of the most expensive models have taken this to extremes. Consider that rigidity + light weight = fragility. In fact, the rods I've seen break most often while just casting, those that have exploded under a low stress load without being mistreated, include several of the brands that are considered most "hi-tech."

In any case, today's 5 weight can throw longer lines with less effort than yesteryear's 5 weight. Consequently, anglers are using lighter weight outfits as their workhorse rods. Once it was not uncommon to see fishermen using 8 weights as standard rods on many Montana rivers. Today, the 6 weight can do it all, and even that is a little heavy for much of the fishing. Add to this a greater emphasis on smaller fly hatches and patterns and it's no wonder that 3 to 5 weights are becoming more common tools through much of the season. If I could only have one rod for the entire season, it would be a 8 to 9 foot 5 weight. From there I would add a shorter lighter rod or a heavier 9 foot model, depending on the river I was planning to fish.

# REELS

To me, the most important feature of a reel is its ability to pay out line smoothly. The biggest demands in this regard are when hot fish are hooked on very fragile tippets, 5X or finer. If a 20 inch trout sips a Trico pattern on a 6X tippet and then wants to run 100 feet in a matter of seconds, your reel must be able to unspool the line smoothly without the tippet breaking. This is the only critical facet of trout reels to consider. Theoretically what you want is a wide diameter reel of medium width, which requires less turns to pay out or reel in the line. The smaller the reel's diameter, the harder it is for it to pay out line quickly. I have a very small Hardy reel which I like, but it is not the tool for hot fish on light tippets. Now when you look at what's on the market, you see the trend is to wide reels of medium or small diameter. In my mind, this is not the ultimate design. I'd much rather have a larger diameter, medium width reel which would not only pay out line very smoothly, but also enables you to reel in line more quickly and efficiently with the same given rachet/drag assembly. The idea with most of today's reels is increased line capacity, which is certainly a consideration but can be achieved in a variety of designs. Many anglers see how much of their fly line they can routinely cast and then cut off the rest to make room for extra backing. This is usually done to weight forward lines only.

Another feature of many of the latest reels are advanced drag systems, which are for the most part unnecessary for trout fishing. Adjusting drag can easily be achieved by a combination of rod attitude, palming the reel, and fingering the line. With the thousands of western trout I've caught, and the many New Zealand trout from 4 to 12 pounds, I've never once longed for or needed an intricate drag assembly, only a reel that can pay out line quickly and smoothly enough. After all, we're talking about 12 to 20 inch fish for the most part, not bluefin tuna! It is handy to have a reel you can palm. Other than that, in my opinion, the high priced super drag system reels

could be considered expensive novelty items for "equipment fanatics."

Consider that as line runs off your reel, the acting diameter of the drum decreases. This makes it harder to pull line off the reel, thus the reel creates its own drag. I've seen reels with drag systems that tighten even more as line pays out, necessitating a loosening of the drag by the angler during the fight. This is something he should not have to worry about during a battle with a hot trout. A quality reel with a basic ratchet drag, one that can feed out line as quickly as possible without over-spooling, is all a trout angler needs.

# LINES

As usual, your choice of fly line depends on your actual fishing conditions. Western rivers vary from the boisterous, with white water runs like Idaho's Salmon, to the serene, where fastidious trout habitually sip emerging midges.

# FLOATING LINES

For many rivers of a swifter and wind-prone nature, weight forward floaters are preferred. For casting a hopper into a Yellowstone wind for instance, they help to "punch" the fly out into the attractive pockets of that scenic waterway. A weight forward, or bug taper, floating line should be part of your arsenal on western rivers.

There are many flat water rivers too, and gentle tailouts of swifter rivers where delicate presentations are a must. With the heavier fishing pressure that grows year after year, light landing casts and small flies are necessary on many waters, especially on tailwater fisheries. In these cases a double taper is advantageous in delivering small flies to demanding trout. On some rivers, the Missouri for instance, where trout become ultra spooky, particularly on bright windless days, stealthful quiet casts are everything. Fish are seen racing away from "crash landing" lines and even bolt from casts in the air over them. It is on such occasions that it pays to have a lighter weight outfit with a double taper line. Study ahead of time the nature of the waters you plan to fish. Inquire about the habits and personalities of the trout you intend to fool, for indeed, the trout in every river show some idiosyncrasies. You can then apply this knowledge to your choice of equipment. As a failsafe, bring both weight forward and double taper lines to meet any happenstance. Extra spools take little space. A 3-5 weight double taper and a 5-7 weight weight forward would be good choices for most waters.

# SINKING LINES

Sink tip lines are popular with streamer fishermen, which are many on western rivers. Larger trout are over fond of sculpins, crayfish, minnows, leeches, and other ample fare. Streamer and wet fly fishing between hatches is a good way to add some larger trout to the catch. When sink tips first came out, it became the fad to use them for nymph fishing. After that usual period of experimentation allotted to new products, many anglers found that it was easier to cast and control nymphs with a floating line and extra weight added to the fly and/or leader.

Care must be taken when casting sink tip lines from the boat, especially if distance casting. Retrieves should be made a good way back in towards the boat so the caster can more easily lift the heavier fly line out of the water and high and safely above the boat on the backcast. Since a sink tip will not lift off the water as easily as a floating line will, extra care and attention needs to be applied when fishing sink tips and weighted flies from a drift boat.

One benefit of sink tip lines is their ability to be driven into strong winds. You can often shoot a sink tip further, when a floating line would be carried off by the wind. Extra caution is needed, however, when powering out big weighted flies on sink tips in the wind. I've witnessed many hook injuries in such cases. Anglers tend to channel their casting zeal, power, and often anger into these high energy double haul exhibitions and begin to lose control. The all too common end is a big weighted streamer hook buried firmly in the back of the head. In a boat you become a serious threat to others on board. When floating you need to restrict your casting to situations you can cast in with control. If it's very windy, you can float closer to the target water, as the trout will be less wary under the broken surface. There is no need to cast great distances from a boat either, you can usually move within easy range of your target. If you have to make long casts, be especially aware of the path your fly line is traveling.

Many anglers prefer to use floating lines for streamer and nymph fishing, adding weight to the fly and leader. This allows easier pick-up of the fly line on the backcast and better mending and line control, while still getting the fly down to the desired depth. For beginners this is a safer and more desirable set up when float fishing. If in possession of a sink tip, bring it along, though it is seldom an absolute necessity for success. Bring a selection of weights and strike indicators too, so any depth level can be achieved and monitored.

Some of the latest interchangeable shooting head systems are effective tools. These have loop to loop connections, where short sink tips of various lengths and densities can be switched to meet the conditions at hand.

Full sinking lines are seldom used in river float fishing, though many float tubers use them in western lakes. While there are possibilities for them, such as fishing very deep runs and pond like pools and eddies, their general use doesn't merit the purchase of one for float fishing applications.

Stretching out and cleaning your fly line each day will help make your casting a little easier. Though few people do it and modern lines require less attention, cleaning and lubricating them will add an edge of smooth, distance shooting ability. If you're up early and putting down that last cup of coffee, and have a little time before the boat takes off, give your line a good stretch and rub down.

# LEADERS

Leaders provoke an endless array of theories and have prompted numerous developments in materials and design. From gut to "bungibutts," braided butts to oval mono, there is always the search for a better way.

For most of my fishing, I use what I jokingly refer to as an "axis power" leader. The butt and midsection are made from stiff German material—Maxima; and the tippet or last 2-3 sections are constructed from softer Japanese leader such as Dia-Riki. The butt section turns over well in the wind, plus you have the benefit of a pliable, narrow diameter, and strong tippet to fool fussy trout. I use leaders of 9-12 feet, plus tippets of 18-30 inches for dry fly and small nymph work.

For larger streamers, shorten the leader up a bit and use Maxima throughout, about 6-10 feet. Some anglers use leaders as short as 18 inches when trying to get large wet flies down to the bottom on sink tip lines. I can't help but think that some fish have to be put off by a fly line dragging right by them, maybe that one really large fish you've been hoping for for years. Rereading the old Ray Bergman classic, *Trout,* gives you something to consider about this subject too, as he experimented with varying leader lengths with streamers and noticed great differences in their fish fooling ability—and this was way back when trout were much less accosted. In murky to average water conditions I use 8+ pound tippet for streamer work, with weight added to the leader as needed. This gives plenty of strength for the savage hits that streamers can elicit from fish, especially larger ones. When that rare hook-up with a really big trout occurs, I want to have the power to set the hook in its tough jaw and bully it out of tangling cover, my way! Maxima also has excellent abrasion-resistant qualities which come in handy when a large trout's teeth rake back and forth across the leader and when it runs you through rocks and branches. Casting heavy streamers on light leaders can weaken the knot eventually, and I've seen lots of nice fish lost on the strike by using too light a tippet in streamer work. Bear in mind also, that streamers cast from boats are often being pitched into the banks from mid-river, where the occasional tangle in streamside brush can be expected. Here again, a stout leader is advisable. The one situation where I use lighter tippet with streamers is when water conditions are very low and clear, fish can be spotted, and smaller, lighter streamers are called for. Low, clear summer flows can mean trout will be harder to fool, as they see everything better and have been fished to a lot. In such cases, you must strike with less vigor to avoid breaking off on the strike. The sharpness of smaller hooks makes a lighter set possible, whereas large barbed hooks have to be set with force or else they don't penetrate deep enough to hold.

For catapulting heavy stonefly nymphs, I use a 6 foot leader constructed of Maxima, plus a 2-3 foot tippet of more pliable 2-3X tippet. The more pliable tippet aids in allowing the nymph to sink and drift naturally, without undue drag. A tuck cast is used to punch the nymph down hard, helping it to sink before drag sets in. A tuck-reach combination gives a longer drag free float. Extra slack can be piled on the water too, for even longer drifts, if you're using a strike indicator. Otherwise the line must be kept semi-taught to feel strikes.

I have never worried about exact leader tying formulas, since the way I cast tends to reduce their importance when it comes to turning over the leader. By using a slightly overpowered reach cast and pulling back on the rod a bit at the end of the forward stroke, the leader is forced to turn over, regardless of precise or imprecise leader segment measurements. Any reasonable taper will do. (This type of casting is used for medium to long casts from the boat and in adverse conditions. Getting out to stalk steadily rising trout upstream at close range in calm weather can call for more exacting tapers.) One learns to do things differently when always faced with the prospect of wind.

I see people having lots of problems with some of the knotless tapered leaders on the market. Some of the Japanese makes are too soft throughout to be good wind casting leaders, people get the most exasperating wind knots in these ultrasoft leaders and I usually end up constructing a new leader for them before the morning is old. On the whole, I find that European leader material is stiff, American material medium, and Japanese material soft. By mixing these materials in your leader construction, you can achieve the results you're looking for in different casting and fishing situations. You may want to use stiffer material for casting large flies on windy days and light, limp material for placid spring creek sessions. There are such multiformulated knotted leaders on the market as well. Be aware, however, that some manufacturers don't recommend joining hard monos to certain soft ones, as the harder ones cut through the softer at leader

*Thin, long leaders are often required to fool selective tailwater trout, tapering down to 5X-7X.*

and tippet knots.

Different types of rivers have different leader requirements, for instance, on choppy freestone rivers with aggressive trout you can get by with shorter 6-9 foot leaders tapering to 3-4X tippets. Large, bushy attractor patterns that would twist ultralight tippets, fish better on medium strength ones. Fast water fish usually have to make quicker decisions and don't see the leader as well.

Slick, spring-fed rivers with selective trout on the other hand, require longer leaders and finer tippet. Twelve to fifteen foot leaders down to 5-7X are used and flies may be in the #16-24 size range. Advanced casting skills are required for constant success. The smooth waters allow trout to see better and more easily detect fraud. The abundance of food allows them the infuriating luxury of being highly selective (an attraction to many). All this is reflected in leader requirements.

In all waters these days, with the growing pressure, using the longest leader you can easily handle means catching a few more wary trout. The days of wholly innocent trout have slipped away. Anglers seek every advantage. On rivers where trout were easy just a few years ago, they now grow discriminating. Long leaders will help.

Loop to loop leader connections are popular, and promoted by manufacturers and writers. I find they increase the occurrence of "wind knots" for the average angler. The long leaders and fine tippets we sometimes use in breezy Rocky Mountain waters seem to find a way of tangling more often around those little loops, than they do around a cleaner connection. Since I untie a lot of these in my capacity as a guide, I prefer, endorse, promote, and pray for epoxy slices, nail

knots, or other clean connections, as opposed to loop to loop joinery.

When I am starting to fish for the day and stringing up my rod, I always stretch my leader. This eliminates the coils formed by being stored on your reel—or "memory" as it's often called. Good leader material should lose these memory coils when stretched once. Start at the butt and work your way down to the tippet, stretching an arms length between your two hands. It will take three or four stretches to cover the full length of the leader. Stretch the leader smoothly but firmly. When stretching the tip of the leader and tippet, you'll be pulling at near its breaking strength (it takes a little practice to know just how much force a light tippet, and especially the knots, can take.) If the memory coils don't straighten with one or two stretches your leader is probably too old. Some anglers carry a piece of rubber to straighten leaders, but I feel that leaders should be replaced if a quick stretch doesn't instantly straighten them out.

While stretching your leader, look for weak spots and abrasions. I try to stretch mine as hard as I think it should be able to withstand. If there's a weak spot, it breaks and I rebuild it from there, this happens often. I feel and look for abrasions and replace those segments too.

Performing these rituals at the beginning of the day makes casting more efficient and minimizes the chances of breaking off a good fish on a bad leader. Continue to check for abrasion and weak spots throughout the day, they are often present—caused by the trout's teeth, tangles in streamside brush, and by accidentally stepping on your leader or getting it caught up in rough edges on the boat.

# NETS

Long handled nets of 2 to 3 feet make landing fish much easier from a drift boat. The bow of many dories can be 3 feet up over the water, making regular trout nets inadequate and troublesome when trying to lean over and net a fish. Since larger trout of up to 26 inches are not unrealistic in many western rivers, a large diameter net is also desirable. Sure a big trout looks impressive when stuck in a net meant for Eastern brookies, but in practical use miniature nets are a bit of a nuisance when continually trying to land trout that are too large for them. A long handled, larger capacity net with a soft (non fish scratching) mesh is ideal, though unfortunately not always available on the local market. The handle is a good place for inch measurements, to record the size of the fish before its release. Fish can also be weighed in the net and the net's weight subtracted. Most float fishermen have one long handled net for the boat, plus a smaller one for wade fishing.

# WADERS

Most anglers wear waders when float fishing, except in mid-summer when both air and water temperatures allow wading in shorts. Since most float fishing trips also include some wading (just getting in and out of the boat may require getting wet feet), and because waders also make great rain gear, consider them standard float fishing equipment.

One consideration for choosing waders for drift boat use is flexibility. You need to be able to climb in and out of the boat and this can require some dexterity. Some of the old, poorly fitting canvas style waders were poorly suited for this, limiting your normal range of movement. Fortunately, the modern neoprene wader (if properly fitted) is ideal. It is flexible, modifies extremes of both cold and heat, and is fairly compact when folded up and stored in the boat if not required.

For some reason, everybody seems to think that neoprene waders have to fit tightly to be effective. This must be a reflection of their wet suit, skin diving origins. I find that neo-waders that are properly fitted, especially regarding inseam/crotch length, but are just barely loose around the body to be ideal. By barely loose I don't mean sagging, I mean just loose enough to allow a slight bit of air transfer, and so as not to stress the seams. This last point I think important in ensuring the longevity of your waders, since seam failure is often the downfall of neoprenes. Most anglers wear their neo-waders so tight that the seams are stressed every second they are worn. Neoprene stretched thin also has slightly less insulation qualities. The well tailored, but slightly looser fit, eliminates this stress and allows easier leg movement when entering and exiting the boat. If it gets cold, you can also add an additional layer of underclothing and tuck a jacket into the waders, both of which are harder to do if your waders already fit like tights! If you feel nervous about a tiny bit of looseness allowing a lot of water to fill your waders should you fall in—wear a belt. In reality, however, if they're properly tailored, and the suspenders connected, this won't happen. Neoprene floats well, and the waders shouldn't be so baggy as to allow much water anyway.

I've always wondered why neoprenes aren't smooth on the exterior, instead of having water retaining woven material. This outer layer of material holds water and the ensuing long process of evaporation acts like an air conditioner, cooling off the waders after you get out of the river. This is of course the opposite of the desired result you want in cold weather! The outer fabric finish also makes leak detection and repair difficult. Perhaps a manufacturer will come up with a superior design in this regard soon.

Don't wear wading cleats in boats. Minimally, they scratch the bottom of the craft and they do extensive damage to the floors of wooden boats and rafts. Be considerate of the finish and structure of any boat you fish out of and ask the boatman if there is anything you need to know, both about the boat's use and well being, and what you need to know about fishing from it.

*Getting in and out of the boat requires waders that allow a free range of movement. Neoprene waders that aren't over-tight are ideal.*

*Above:* Trout can be fanned out across shallow eddy lines and riffles. Such broken water offers them overhead camouflage and is abundantly populated with nymphs.

*Left:* Float fishing can be a very relaxed experience on our scenic waterways. Few, but effective, casts and long drifts catch many trout.

Float fishing requires an adjustment of wade fishing tactics—the approaches are different, usually seeing casts made to the banks from mid-river. You are on the move, without the leisure time to think out a strategy and presentation for each and every fishing situation. On the other hand, you get to cover more good water, that you couldn't wade to, while relaxing and watching splendid scenery glide by.

The following float fishing tactics are geared towards those intense fishing individuals trying to capitalize on every good bit of water and potential fishing action.

For those that enjoy leaning back in the boat and watching their Elk Hair Caddis drift alongside...enjoying any fish which might come their way while enjoying the floating just as much...for the leisurely angler—they too can benefit from these tactics without having to work at it too hard!

# Speed Casting

Casting quickly and accurately is of prime importance when float fishing, presuming you are out to cover as many fish as possible. This kind of effortless fast casting, which works so well with modern graphite rods, allows you to keep your fly on the water most of the time. Every guide has rowed anglers who cast as if they had the softest and slowest of bamboo rods, and false cast endlessly, as though they were trying to catch swallows instead of trout. This is not the best way to catch fish.

As you begin your float, and those enticing pockets begin slipping by, you'll want to get your line out quickly. If you're the efficient sort you will have rigged your rod while the boatman was launching the craft. (And you will have promptly loaded the boat and moved it and the vehicle away from the boat ramp so others might launch without you holding them up.)

After tying on the first experimental pattern of the day, it's time to work out the first cast. The boatman will have lined up, keeping a certain distance from the banks so that you don't have to adjust the length of your cast more than necessary.

To get line out quickly, with little wasted time, begin by holding your fly rod in the center of your chest with one hand, and your stripping hand on the fly line next to the reel in the same locale. Now spread out your arms to the sides, fully extended. There, you

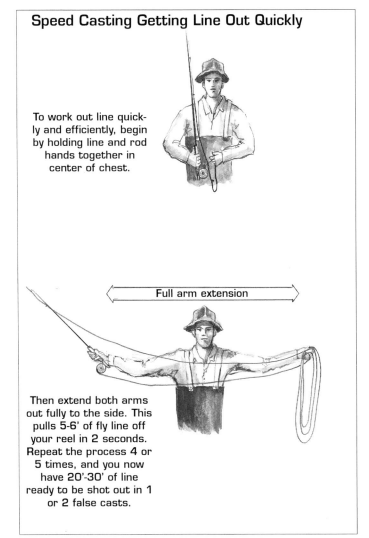

## Speed Casting Getting Line Out Quickly

To work out line quickly and efficiently, begin by holding line and rod hands together in center of chest.

Full arm extension

Then extend both arms out fully to the side. This pulls 5-6' of fly line off your reel in 2 seconds. Repeat the process 4 or 5 times, and you now have 20'-30' of line ready to be shot out in 1 or 2 false casts.

have just ripped 5 to 6 feet of line off your reel in 2 seconds. Repeat the process 6 times and within that 12 seconds you have 30-36 feet of fly line coiled on the casting deck, or by your uncluttered feet. If you're having trouble getting the end of the fly line through the rod's guides, try dragging the leader and fly in the water, to help pull it through, or else have someone in the boat pull it through for you. Now that you have the fly line running free, a couple quick false casts should shoot all that pre-stripped line out. Rip off a few more arm lengths of line to achieve the distance the boatman has set up for you. All this takes very little time.

Compare this method with the more common and time-consuming way of pulling inches of line out at a time, while continuously false casting. The previous method is quick and efficient, the latter slow and time-consuming. It's no harder to do it the fast way, in fact it's easier. If the boatman is working hard to put you on good water, perhaps holding strenuously beside a large fish he's just seen rise, he'll appreciate your being able to get the fly out to the fish in a reasonable (short) amount of time.

With dry flies especially, a quick cast with a minimum of false casts keeps your fly in front of trout. One or two false casts should do it, if any are needed at all. A weight forward floating line will shoot a little more easily than a double taper, thus reducing the number of false casts needed over the course of the day. When drifting by beautiful bank cover and riffles, you'll want your fly on the water as much as possible where a gluttonous salmonoid can procure it! Watching a rapid fire caster is the best instruction. He doesn't use more energy, he uses less since he casts and false casts less often, he just does it more efficiently. You will see how effortless it can be and how it increases dramatically the percentage of time that your fly is in a prime fish-catching position. A properly balanced quality rod and line certainly helps in maximizing your casting efficiency.

Lee Wulff clocked his casts up at around 90 mph. While you may not attain this line speed, you'll find speed casting will catch more fish, if that is your goal. Speed casting also dries your dry fly with half the false casts and helps in punching casts into the wind. The less time your false casts are in the air and over the boat, the less chance you have of tangling with the other angler in the boat. This alone is no small matter when looked at over the course of a day. Indeed, speed casting has many benefits and few faults. While initially you might think it would be more tiring, the opposite is the case, you end up spending less time casting and more time with your fly drifting in a good position. Many modern graphite rods work best when cast at high speeds, especially at short to medium range. With some rods, you have to cast rapidly to load the rod until about 40 feet of line is out. I don't want to make this sound like it's a frantic, competitive venture. In fact, there is a certain passive pleasure in knowing your casts are quick, efficient, and effective; that no wasted energy has been expended. And then there are the extra fish you catch by the end of the day!

With wet flies, speed casting isn't as practical—especially with large, heavily weighted flies. Here, you need a somewhat slower power cast to allow the lagging weighted fly to extend fully at both ends of a cast or false cast. It helps to watch your backcast to see how differently weighted or air resistant flies travel at different speeds, effecting the timing of your cast. Your fly line's loop will need to be a little more open with heavy flies. Too much speed and not enough waiting for the line to straighten behind you results in a weighted fly jerking around on the end of the leader and snapping like a whip. If there is additional weight on your leader, the "bola" effect can ensue, with the fly and weight tangling. This can weaken the knot (to the fly), tangle your line, and ruin your smooth transmission of casting power.

## Varying the Distance of the Two Angler's Flies from the Banks

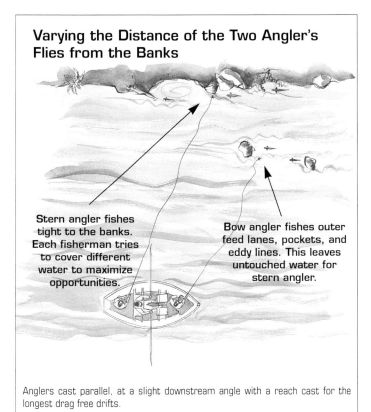

Stern angler fishes tight to the banks. Each fisherman tries to cover different water to maximize opportunities.

Bow angler fishes outer feed lanes, pockets, and eddy lines. This leaves untouched water for stern angler.

Anglers cast parallel, at a slight downstream angle with a reach cast for the longest drag free drifts.

Another element to consider here is that a heavy wet fly can't be whisked up off the surface like a dry fly can. You'll have to strip in a portion of your fly line to bring the fly up near the surface before making a safe backcast. Trying to yank a large wet fly in any other way will mean a dangerously low backcast, probably out of control, with the likelihood of tangling or hooking someone in the boat. Since you'll have to strip in some line you'll probably have to false cast once or twice to work the fly line back out. Remember to keep those false casts up high above the boat for safety reasons.

There is only a certain degree that you can speed up a weighted fly in casting, best learned by experience. Light or unweighted small wet flies on the other hand can be cast almost as rapidly as a dry fly, as long as the power transmission is smooth and not jerky. The only downfall is if you want to retain moisture in your wet fly or nymph, in order to help it sink. In this case, many anglers purposely cast slow to retain that moisture, whereas speed casting flings it off. Using a tuck cast however will help you to both cast quickly and sink the fly, giving the advantage of longer drag free drifts as well.

## COVERING THE WATER

The success and enjoyment of a float fishing trip largely hinges on the two anglers' ability to thoroughly cover the water with their flies. The biggest factors here include:

1. Eliminating down time, not being tangled or otherwise out of commission.

2. Casting quickly and precisely, and keeping your fly on the water in total control.

3. Covering the water efficiently, with the two anglers casting to different pockets or feed lanes, or using different fly patterns fished at different depths.

There is a tendency for both anglers to use similar patterns,

especially if one angler has had some success. There is also a tendency for both anglers to cast to the same spots. As they float by a bank, their minds usually pick the same pockets as looking the most promising.

Think of it as a teamwork situation. The rower keeps you in the best position, slowing the craft down. The bow angler covers certain pockets and feed lanes, the stern angler watches and tries to cover different pockets and feed lanes, perhaps with totally different fly types (i.e., streamers vs. dry flies). A maximum amount of water is covered in the most thorough way. If one fly pattern proves to be the "killer pattern," then both anglers end up using it. In the meantime, think team-work coverage.

## PICKING POCKETS

Many classic float fishing trout rivers are made up of miles of enticing pocket water. A rock here, log there, bank eddy, ripple line, drop-off, undercut bank—each creates a pocket of calmer water that can hold trout. Trout often maintain one or two favorite feeding positions where they can watch food go by, a calm spot where they don't have to fight the current so much. Keeping your fly floating along these series of pockets is the name of the game. On the many western rivers that have 3000 to 4000 trout per mile, every one of these

*There are many likely trout-sized pockets in a river. The anglers make a team effort to cover them as thoroughly as possible, while the rower slows the craft down and positions it advantageously.*

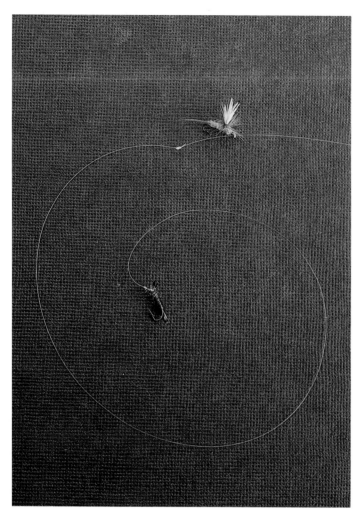

*We find the "two fly system" to be very productive on both freestone and tail-water rivers.*

looked for years. Many big browns cruise shallow, featureless flats. Unseen springs may have large collections of trout. So try even the uninviting water if you have any "hunting" instincts at all!

On larger rivers where both anglers are fishing the same side, you have other options for covering all the pockets. Not only can you alternate pockets, with the stern angler picking up the untouched water, but you can also try different tactics on the same water.

One good approach is to have the bow angler use a dry fly and the stern angler "sweeping" with a nymph or streamer. This is presuming there isn't one "killer" pattern you've found most all the fish are going for. A well presented dry usually doesn't disturb a fish that's not inclined to rise and a nymph or streamer following up will often tempt a fish that didn't rise to the dry. Reversing this order, that is having the bow angler cast the streamer, with the dry fly in the stern, isn't as good an approach. The streamer splatting down has a tendency to scare or alert fish if it doesn't attract them, leaving the dry fly angler in the stern with fewer opportunities. When trout are "turned on" to streamers, however, both anglers can use them successfully. Spring and fall, morning and evening, nasty days of rain and cloud...sometimes find larger trout in the mood to attack streamers. Nothing is more exciting, especially in clear water where you can see the big fish coming!

Another approach is varying the distance of the flies from the bank. The logical pattern here is to have the bow angler's fly several feet (or more) out from the bank and the stern angler's fly right up against it. This way you cover different feeding lanes without scaring fish. This is especially effective along banks that have more graduated slopes, where fish could be lying anywhere, and where eddy lines

good-looking pockets could have a fish in it. It's your job to find out!

When float fishing the idea is to hit as many of these promising pockets as possible, the rower's job is to slow the boat down enough so the fishermen can. The anglers try to hit each pocket, even if only for a few seconds each. On many rivers trout hit almost instantly, while on others they drift up slowly for an inspection. Individual trout have their own feeding personalities too. As a rule, swift rivers with moderate food supplies will have quick rising trout. Slower paced, rich rivers have more selective, slower rising fish.

The bow angler (front of the boat and first going downstream) will have first shot at all the best pockets. He may be able to hit a single pocket several times if the boat is slowed enough. The stern caster should keep an eye on the pockets that the bow angler covers and try to cover untouched water to maximize his chances. While it seems as though the bow angler has all the advantages, I recall many, many days when the "stern gunner" out-fished the bow angler. Usually anglers switch places throughout the day anyway.

On smaller rivers the boatman can guide the boat down the middle of the river, while the anglers cover both banks. The bow angler will cover one side, the stern angler the other. One benefit of this, if you stick to it, is that while fishing "your side," you will inevitably come to some water which might not look good to you. Examples of this might be slow, shallow edgewaters with little in the way of attractive cover, or mud bottom sloughs. Keep casting! In this way you will find, as I have, that trout have personalities and haunts unlooked for, you may begin catching fish in waters you have over-

## Two Fly Leader System

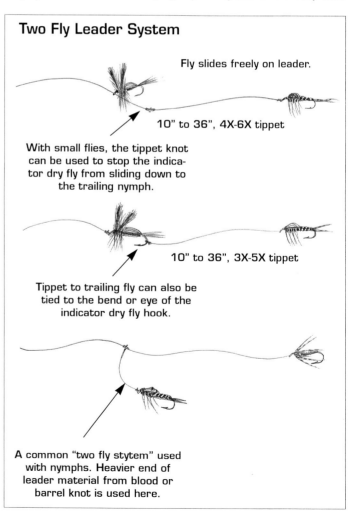

Fly slides freely on leader.

10" to 36", 4X-6X tippet

With small flies, the tippet knot can be used to stop the indicator dry fly from sliding down to the trailing nymph.

10" to 36", 3X-5X tippet

Tippet to trailing fly can also be tied to the bend or eye of the indicator dry fly hook.

A common "two fly stytem" used with nymphs. Heavier end of leader material from blood or barrel knot is used here.

ripple away from the shore and bankside rocks. (Human nature often leads both anglers to cast to the exact same spots, those that look most likely to hold fish, instead of systematically covering the water in a more thoughtful manner.) On deeply undercut banks in swift water, both anglers want to keep their flies drifting right along the edge. They want to experiment with different patterns until the best combination is discovered. It is amazing how many fish won't move more than a couple inches off such a bank to take a fly. Whether their vision is limited, their stomachs full, or whether they know more food will be coming closer so they don't have to go rushing out into the current...many "bank huggers" won't move far for a meal.

Another very effective technique along bank pockets and elsewhere is the "two fly system." This style has waxed and waned in popularity throughout the history of fly fishing and remains a "killing" method. The way we do it is a little different from the traditional "team of wet flies" once used.

The basic idea is to have a visible, buoyant dry fly for a strike indicator and either another dry fly or a nymph as a dropper. With flies of #14 or smaller, we use a free sliding set up that has no extra dropper line and minimizes tangles. The dry fly floats free along the leader just above the tippet knot. When the tippet is knotted on, it stops the dry fly from sliding down any further. Twelve inches to two feet of 4-6X tippet is used, depending on how deep or close to the surface the dropper fly is intended to drift. A nymph, emerger, or sometimes a smaller dry fly (trico, midge, etc.) is attached to the tippet. This casts as easily as a single fly. The dry/nymph combo is especially effective and is often cast to sighted fish. Individual trout may be favoring emergers over duns and you'll have both bases covered. This arrangement is also handy for multiple hatch situations, for example, when both *Baetis* mayflies and midges are hatching simultaneously. I might use a #16 Parachute Adams (which floats well and is easy to see) for the dry/indicator and a #22 emerging midge pupa for a dropper. This particular set up is good on tailwater rivers like the Bighorn and Missouri.

Other two fly systems we commonly use include: an Elk Hair Caddis with a Soft Hackle Caddis Emerger dropper; for swift water streams—a Royal Wulff or Trude with a Hare's Ear dropper; and a big Stonefly dry with a Stonefly Nymph dropper (a little unwieldy to cast!) during stonefly hatches. When trout are on midge adults or small spent wing mayflies, I often have clients use a visible dry fly for an indicator and then trail the smaller, harder-to-see dry that we expect the trout to take as the dropper. The trick here is to know how much tippet you have between the two flies, so you can drop the small fly over the fish—not the bigger one. Many times trout will take the larger one anyway!

When using larger flies with the two fly system, the tippet knot won't stop the dry from sliding over it. Instead, the tippet is tied to the bend of the dry fly hook.

A mid-summer duo we've found to work well, especially on tailwater rivers, is a San Juan Worm hanging beneath a well-greased Hopper. Large trout respond to these morsels, even in the sultry days of August. The fly combinations to meet hatches, multiple hatches and "blind" fishing situations are endless. It's almost as much fun experimenting with fly combinations as it is catching the fish!

Not all pockets are along the banks of the river, some are found upstream of and behind mid-stream boulders, gravel bars, log jams, etc. Out from the banks in the streambed there will be depressions and mini-channels formed in the ever-shifting gravel. Trout love these pockets too. In shallow reaches of river where these are evident, hit the upstream edge of any depression. Hungry trout often push up to the drop-off, watching for incoming nymphs. Trout pick-

ing off dries may drop towards the tail of a big depression. Always aim to cover the entire pocket by making a point of not missing the upstream edge.

Trout seem to like the confinement of mini-channels. Perhaps the food concentration is at its highest there, or trout feel more comfortable in well defined cover. In any case, whenever you see a mini-channel forming, target it. Such channels often form just after the tailout of a preceding pool, marking the beginning of the next run. Some are formed where currents sideslip across a shallow channel of gravel, others are actual side channels around islands or thick weed beds. Look for that darkening of color in the water, where the golden gravel falls off into darker, more mysterious depths. Here trout can stack up, taking advantage of channelized food and slow water pockets in which to hold, feed, and hide from predators.

The thing to remember about fishing any pocket is that the pocket water will be slower or moving in a different direction than the main current. Since the boat is usually positioned in faster water, you are constantly fighting drag. The length of your fly's drift and the frequency with which you have to recast largely depends on your casting skill. This is why you should make the slack line reach cast habitual, add to this the tuck cast and you have made a significant step towards eliminating drag. (Refer back to Chapter 3.) You can also stack mend extra slack on the surface after you cast, as long as you are quick enough taking it back in when a fish hits. You'll probably have to mend the line as well. If you can make these casts routinely, by the end of the day you'll end up doing a lot more serious fishing rather than wasting time casting. The reach cast can float five times longer before dragging than a traditional straight cast, which means you only have to cast 1/5 as often. A straight cast will float properly so many seconds out of each minute you fish, while a good reach cast ensures that there are only a few seconds out of the minute when your fly isn't floating in an alluring fashion. This aspect of float fishing is so important that I hope you'll excuse me in belaboring the point.

# FISHING THE BANKS

Classic western float fishing scenes bring to mind mountainous, arid valleys, a brawling clear river with a drift boat bobbing on downstream. Fishermen donning western hats alternate casts to an endless array of bank cover, where trout are lined up like corralled cattle.

Indeed, this scene hasn't changed much on rivers like the Big Hole, Yellowstone, Snake, and Smith. There are few things in life as pleasant as drifting down a spectacular river, cool waters gliding beneath, and everchanging landscapes slipping by. Pine forests, sage brush hills, snow-laden mountains...the scents, sounds, and images are all sublimely enticing. The river banks pass by like an action movie set and your casting has never felt better! You work out the proper length of line, rip off an extra yard for good luck, and do a little fine-tuning. Your bushy dry fly plops down with authority, twirls in bankside eddies and dances along shoreline riffles. There is no doubt in your mind that free rising trout are in your immediate future! Maybe in that large, foam-specked eddy, or under that cottonwood root...

The good thing about bank feeding trout is that they see a lot of variety in their diet. Their life is an endless buffet...a few spent wings for an appetizer, hoppers for the entree, and maybe a few beetles for dessert. For a late night snack, some emerging Caddis will do just fine. Such trout are often led astray by their palate, being used not only to hatches, but to a broad variety of terrestrials as well. They've

*Hoppers and terrestrials make up a good percentage of a trout's diet from midsummer into autumn.*

Bank fishing streamers is great fun from a boat too. You slam cast after cast as close to the bushy banks as you dare. This precise target shooting alone is amusing. If the fish are really "on", the vibrations of a streamer slapping down will bring them racing over for the attack. Takes will be swift and violent. Use heavy 1X-3X tippet, both to help pull the odd cast out of streamside brush and to take the lunging strikes of big-toothed fish. Trout will likely be holding close to the banks and if you're not snagging bushes occasionally, you're probably not casting close enough. I'm always ready to pull the rod tip back a bit as a brake if I think the cast is going to be too long. Thus the delivery is fine-tuned.

Streamers cast to the banks can also be enhanced by tuck casts and reach casts, this allows the fly to sink a little before you start stripping. Usually trout will hit the fly broadside—excellent for solid hook-ups. Other times it may follow the fly out towards the boat and take it from behind.

When stripping in streamers, keep your rod tip positioned towards the bank, and right down near the water's surface (or even in it). This allows you to feel the take immediately and be in the best hook setting position. If your rod tip is way up in the air with line sagging from it, it is harder to feel subtle takes and to impart forceful enough hook sets. Set the hook on streamers by pulling on the fly line with your line hand (presuming you're using adequately heavy leader). That way, if the trout misses it the first time, your fly will still be in place for him to circle around and go for it again. You will also be in a position to strike again. Yanking back violently with your rod disturbs the water and often brings the fly line and large hooked fly sailing back into the boat. The hand line set is decidedly better for heavy leader streamer fishing.

If the trout seem lethargic, allow the streamer to sink deeper, then strip slowly or even let it dead drift (drift without added movement). This can be more productive at times. You might need to add

sampled the various fruits of life and aren't above tasting something new. And along comes your Humpy!

Bank feeders can be gloriously adventurous about rising. The big fly-big fish theory proves itself time and again. Fly choice and pattern are often secondary to float fishing skills. There's something amusing too, about fishing a fly that's as big and silly looking as a Double Humpy or Girdle Bugger and catching large, supposedly intelligent brown trout!

Bank feeders can be selective too, especially when hatches are thick and the trout veterans. Volumous hatches including midges, *Baetis*, Caddis, PMD's, and Tricos call for finer tippets, exacting casts, and precise imitations. Yet somewhere in the back of my mind, I have faith that some bank feeders will fall back into their omni-gluttonous ways!

In mid-summer, terrestrials make up a high percentage of a bank feeder's diet. This carries on into fall, as hatches are diminishing for the season. Hoppers of course are on everyone's list. Crickets can be superb, as fewer anglers use them over jaded fish. Beetles and ants are numerous in the wild and on the water. The odd damselfly is taken, as well as craneflies, worms, bees, crayfish, and snails.

Give a trout a Humpy, Stimulator, Wulff, or Trude, and let him make up his mind as to what it is. If you're feeling adventurous, try trailing a nymph, soft hackle, or San Juan Worm beneath it. Most trout would rather not put themselves out rising if an easier alternative is at...well—fin. You can often see a flash just before your indicator dry goes under. The nymph has done it again!

## Streamer Fishing

**CORRECT**

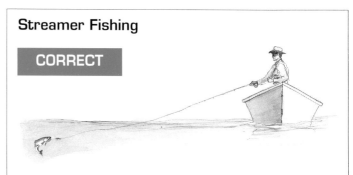

When fishing streamers, use a stout leader and retrieve your fly with your rod tip near the water. Strikes are more easily detected this way and you are in an ideal position to set the hook.

Sagging line makes it harder to detect strikes and set the hook.

Poor hook setting position.

**INCORRECT**

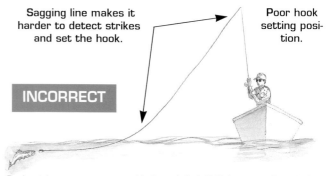

Don't retrieve your streamer with the rod tip held high, or use the rod tip to impart *all* the action to your streamer. It's harder to detect strikes and set the hook.

extra weight and use a strike indicator for this slower streamer fishing. Try shallower, slow water too, as fish can be warming up or lounging there in cold water.

When float fishing your way down a bank, always keep an eye out for the next hot spot. You want to cast to it just before the boat comes even with it in order to get the longest drag free floats. This means that you have to watch your dry fly for a take, plus glance ahead for your next casting target as the boat floats on downstream.

Striking fish that take your dry fly is on a visual basis, you need to see them take it in order to strike them at the right moment. Don't wait to feel them, as they will often shake loose. This goes for strike indicator nymphing too. When wade fishing swift water, the current often helps set the hook for you, but when float fishing you are traveling closer to the current speed, so you need to pay more attention to striking at the right moment. The current is less likely to set the hook for you. Streamer fishing alone (and stripped in nymphing) allows you the luxury of day dreaming and gazing around during the retrieve, as you should feel the take and have a "knee jerk" hook set reaction with your line hand. If you feel like spending a lot of your time looking around at the scenery, and not concentrating so hard on watching your fly, fish a lightly or unweighted streamer. That allows you to make a cast, then strip slowly and gaze off into the sunset. You will still catch occasional fish, and some big ones, without missing all the scenery that's going by.

Not only should you watch your fly and look for the next hot spot, look way ahead for risers too. When fishing the banks, it's easy to mark the location of a rising trout you've spotted by lining it up with a notable bank feature, like a specific rock, bush, or log. Often a fish spotted rising is a fish caught, but you have to constantly keep your eye out for the slightest dimple, swirl, or splash. Many of these will be "one timers," fish that rise once to the odd surface morsel and not steadily to a hatch. These fish can be easy to fool with a variety of patterns and the perfectly placed cast. Naturally anglers with the best eyesight, most concentration and spotting skills, and best casting ability will catch the most fish. The boatman or guide should also be helping in this respect. As he positions the boat, he should also watch for rising fish and alert you to known hot spots. Again, float fishing is a teamwork effort and all this watching, positioning, and casting tallies up results by the end of the day.

Bank fishing consists of many water types—some obvious, others not. Undercut banks, bush, log, and rock cover all provide obvious trout cover. Extensive ripple lines coming off points, gravel bars, or boulders are prime locations too. Even the tiniest ripple or pocket can have a fish. Creek mouths, slough entrances, and large bank eddies all hold great promise. Shade on the water, especially in the heat of mid-summer, can be worth targeting. I've been on rivers where the patches of shade from overhanging bushes and trees signaled where most of the taking fish were. During hopper season, trout may line up along grass banks. You can even cast into soft streamside grass and twitch the fly off it. I've seen trout actually take such presentations before the fly hit the water!

Along richer rivers, weed beds may parallel the shores. Fish can be lined up along and under the edge of these weed beds. The water doesn't have to be deep either, just enough to cover a trout's back. On some rivers, weed beds indicate where springs seep in, during hot and cold weather such spring seepages attract trout.

One mistaken conception many anglers have is that good trout always hold in deeper water, especially mid-day. This may be true of trout well over 5 pounds, but I see many, many beautiful trout to 25 inches holding in just inches of water, even mid-day in the heat of summer. Many browns and rainbows hold and feed in the shallows, even seeming to prefer them if undisturbed. Browns seem fond of

*The slower, inside bends of rivers are home to rising trout. Often the largest specimens will move into the shallowest water, where they can rise without fighting the current. This trout is sipping Trico mayfly spinners.*

shallow riffles, where the broken water gives them a form of overhead cover. They like to sit upstream of bank obstacles too, here they can rise easily or take nymphs without effort. These fish rise to big attractor patterns and hoppers mid-day if your fly chances to go right over them. They are difficult to spot. If a hatch starts, they'll be quickly on it, often becoming very picky. So don't dismiss shallow ripply bank water without overhead cover. The two anglers in the boat should drift their flies down different feed lanes—the bow angler's should be a little further out from the bank, along some seam or drop-off and the stern angler can then cover the bank edge, which will still be virgin water. In this fashion, each angler has a crack at unfished water and opportunities are maximized.

Another type of bank water that might not appeal to you initially are slow, shallow, featureless flats. These are often inside bends of the river. Trout cruise these flats, since there is little current. During a profuse hatch or spinner fall, larger trout may move in and rise since they don't have to fight the current. Often the largest rising fish will be in the slowest, shallowest water—the opposite of what many anglers expect. The trout's rises can be subtle, belying their actual size. Keep an eye out for cruising fish and quiet rises in such water. You may want to pull the boat over during a hatch for a more thorough look, and to stalk these testy fish. If no fish are evident, strip a Woolly Bugger or nymph across the width of the flats or bomb it with attractor patterns, hoppers, or even a damselfly dry. Remember that trout in different rivers develop different feeding habits and personalities. River speed, food availability, cover, altitude, temperature, and fishing pressure all impact trout behavior.

If the lighting is right and the river clear, many bank hugging fish can be spotted under water. This takes some practice, but experienced float fishermen keep their eyes open for such fish throughout the day. A backdrop of trees, a high bank, or thick brush blocks sky reflection and makes it easier to look into the water. Sun on the river's surface illuminates the bottom and fish, this adds up to good spotting conditions. Patchy shade on the water, or gray, windy days make for tough spotting.

Bank huggers that you can see make most interesting prospects. You watch their reaction to your presentation and fly pattern, and see them drift up to inspect or charge your fly. You can also see them spook! Being able to see your quarry is an excellent education in trout behavior and should be taken advantage of whenever possible. A keen eye, concentration, and determination are needed to maximize your float fishing skills.

## Good Fish-Spotting Conditions

Sunlight penetrates water, illuminating fish and bottom.

Dark, or tall trees and hillside block sky reflection, making it easier to see fish under water. A hat and polarized sunglasses help immensley too.

When floating down the river and fishing banks, the rower and fishermen usually come to some agreement on how far the boat should be kept from the shoreline. This depends on the skill of the casters and the nature of the river and fish. You want to stay far enough away so you don't scare the fish, but not so far as to make casting difficult or impossible. Swift, broken rivers usually allow you to float closer to the banks than calm, slick ones do, as the trout's vision is obstructed by the waves.

When I guide, I quickly try to sum up the caster's skills and position the boat accordingly. I tell them it's beneficial to stay as far away as they can comfortably cast. They tell me if I'm a little too far and I try not to daydream, getting too close. People don't realize the concentration it takes to keep the boat just the right distance from the bank for 8 to 12 hours a day. There are wind and current to fight, bad casts to duck, fish to spot, tangles to undo, fly lines to miss with the oars , beers to fetch, sunscreen to put on...all while manning the oars. Consider that a rower might make 5,000 to 10,000 oar strokes a day and you can see that it's no mean feat!

Many small stream fishermen have never cast to their full potential. I might tell them that the average desired cast is 40 to 60 feet, and some think that is too much to handle. But once you're out there with the proper rod (8-9', 5-7 weight) and no trees behind you to interfere with backcasts, you'll find that you can add distance to your

cast quite effortlessly. A drift boat is also an elevated casting platform, instead of being waist deep in water, you're slightly above surface level. This makes picking up and shooting the line easier. If anything is going to interfere, it's going to be wind. It shouldn't be your equipment or attitude that hinders you. The promise of all those good looking bank pockets should be enough to keep your determination up!

## FISHING TO THE MIDDLE

On smaller rivers in the heat of summer, trout often move into mid-stream aerated riffles and rapids for the cooler, oxygenated water. While floating, this may call for the boatman to drift near the banks while the anglers ply mid-river with dries, nymphs, or two fly combo's. (While it's always better to stop and wade fish good looking runs, time and mileage factors sometimes require you to keep floating, especially when current speed is at its summer low.) You often see boat after boat go by, floating the middle and fishing the warming edgewaters. Consider the trout and try different floating approaches. It's easy to get into a "banks only" rut. There will still be good hopper banks, perhaps with cooling spring seepages as well. There will also be many mid-river boulder runs, gravel bar drop-offs, and converging currents that hold more fish. This is when you want to float near the edges and cast to mid-river, or even float mid-river sideways and cast directly downstream.

On larger rivers there are also highly productive mid-stream locations—these are usually gravel bar drop-offs, depressions, boulder gardens, extended ripple lines, converging currents, and foam lines. Broad tailout flats can have many rising fish during a hatch, sometimes all the way across the river. Tailwater rivers usually have expansive areas of weed beds with medium paced flows of 1 to 5 feet depth. Here trout are spread throughout. If not rising to a hatch, anglers float over these weed beds dead drifting nymphs, scuds, or San Juan Worms with added weight and strike indicators. This type of mid river float fishing is very effective, if not particularly appealing style-wise. Many western guides have their clients fish this way throughout the day in non-hatch periods, as it can be the most consistently productive. Woolly Buggers, streamers, and crayfish patterns

*Deep nymphing down the middle of the river from the boat has become a common technique, especially on the tailwater (dam-controlled) rivers. Anglers use extra weight on their leaders and rely on strike indicators to decipher takes, as extra slack is often "stack mended" on the water to achieve long drifts. Boatmen drift over known fish hangouts, usually weed bed areas of moderate-paced currents.*

can be fished across these broad expanses too. Cast these patterns as far as you comfortably can, let them sink near the bottom, then retrieve them all the way back to the boat. Vary the retrieval speed until a winning combination is found.

When floating the edgewaters and fishing the middle of smaller, swift streams, working the water will be more like wade fishing. The boat will be in the slower shallows, while you cast to the swifter stream center. You have to cast upstream more than usual when float fishing, mend and follow your fly on down with the rod tip. Next, you have to change the direction of your cast back upstream. This requires an extra false cast or two, and extra care so as not to tangle with the other rod in the boat. A conscious coordination should be observed between the bow and stern angler. A bushy attractor pattern with a nymph or beetle dropper is an excellent choice in such circumstances.

## Spotting Fish

Spotting fish, whether rising or beneath the surface, takes on an added dimension of difficulty when on the move in a boat. With experience, however, it becomes second nature and a good way to pick up additional fish throughout the day.

When no hatch is on, a fish seen rising is often a fish that will be caught, with the right cast. As you float along with your fly out there bouncing along, keep an eye out for rises in every quarter. Glance back and forth, from your fly to upcoming pockets, eddies, riffle lines, and feed lanes. Put your peripheral vision to the test! By spotting that one rise 100 feet ahead and pinpointing its position in your mind, you'll find a great many of these casual risers to be eager for any reasonable pattern. This takes a continual effort of concentration and good eyesight, but in a day's sport, it adds up.

On large rivers, someone may want to keep an eye on the far bank, or along the great eddy lines formed by bends in the river, points, gravel bars, and islands. Members in the boat can divvy up the river when it comes to looking for risers. As I guide, I always watch for risers as far as 100 yards away. Often I'll ferry the boat from side to side in a broad river, checking out every likely swirl. Since most anglers would rather cast to rising fish, and since actively feeding fish are most likely to take, this hunting of fish can be the best way to keep up the action. In between rising fish, you continue to blind fish the water. There are days of course, when the whole day is spent blind fishing. Such days can be just as productive as sight fishing.

Since many big rivers are slow paced, it is easy to bring the boat to a standstill in order to spot and fish to risers. You can also drop the anchor and work them, though it occasionally scares fish when it hits bottom. Hooked fish sometimes get tangled in the anchor line too. On some rivers you can spend the whole day spotting and fishing exclusively to risers. On these banner days it becomes necessary for the anglers to take turns casting to fish from the boat. It won't do to have both anglers crashing casts simultaneously into the same fish. One angler sits out one fish, while the other angler sits out the next. If the rising fish are steady and wadable, then of course you'll want to pull over and work them, though there are cases where the trout are less spooky when approached from the deep side by boat. Float fishing combined with wading is usually the most productive way to fish a river.

Seeing fish underwater takes even more practice, unless the lighting conditions are perfect. For instance, on slow stretches or giant eddies, it can be very easy to spot underwater fish if you have trees or a hill facing you  If the fish are a contrasting color or tone compared to the water or streambed, so much the better. Even in swift runs, fish can be spotted if the lighting is right. Spotting and stalking trout from a boat takes a coordinated effort of skillful rowing, concentrated searching with polarized sunglasses, and precision casting. A stealthy approach into casting range is necessary, treating the fish for what they are—wild animals. In calm water, make a point of false casting away from the trout, so they don't see your line in the air or the spray that comes off your line and fly. Lead the fish well in the current and have a gentle landing with your fly line. When it all works and you see every stage of the game, there is little to top it for excitement. The fish sees the fly and swims over for an inspection, its mouth opens for the take. You pause a fraction of a second before setting the hook. With a head shake of bewilderment, the trout tears off with the reel harmonizing. Yes, when you can find it, trout stalking from the boat is a real treat!

On freestone type rivers, most trout spotted will be single fish in a pocket, eddy, inside bend, shallow riffle, depression, tailout or along a bank. Their rises can be seen most anywhere and quiet ones can be difficult to see in swift waters.

Big tailwater rivers, on the other hand, are another story. During a hatch, whole schools of trout can be found rising in force. Up to 100 trout in tight formation can be working eddy lines, tailouts, back waters, and feed lanes where tens of thousands of insects drift with the currents.

We'll discuss these two river types in detail, as the nature of the fishing can be so different. No two rivers are just the same though, and there is always some novel fishing approach to discover on each and every river.

*Looking for risers should become habitual when float fishing.*

# 6. Freestone Rivers

**Above:** *The large rubber-legged nymphs catch a lot of big western trout. This brown took a weighted Bitch Creek Nymph during the golden stonefly emergence on Montana's Smith River.*

**Left:** *The Madison, a classic freestone river.*

Freestone rivers are where the classic pictures of float fishing are painted, on a living canvas of swift dancing waters and picturesque mountain vistas. This is the old western image which lives on, of aging wooden boats and anglers flicking out big attractor patterns to a procession of swirling pockets and overhung willows, in search of quick rising trout. The joys of blind casting to likely waters and "element of surprise rises" are major factors in freestone river float fishing. The ever-changing scenery and lively river flow give a renewed passion to an angler's life.

A combination of things cause freestone rivers to fish differently than tailwaters. The uncontrolled flow of a freestone river and it's variability are main factors. Seasons, altitude, river speed, bottom configuration, temperature fluctuations, hatches, remoteness, and fishing pressure all effect angling possibilities.

Many freestone rivers are relatively high altitude, swift running waters, flowing over boulder, cobblestone, and gravel streambeds. Their temperatures vary seasonally from an ice-covered mid-thirties to the upper 70s, and daily changes can be over 10 degrees. Water levels too vary, sometimes in the extreme. When the winter snows melt off the Rockies in May and June flooding can occur. Rivers can be expected to run high and murky in this time period. This happens to coincide with some of the most dramatic hatches of the year. Come mid-summer, rivers become quite low and warm up. Irrigation practices suck off large volumes of water and sometimes return murky warm water back into the river. During drought years, some rivers are almost sucked dry.

*Freestone rivers react to the vagaries of nature. Hitting them when they first drop and clear for the summer is a prime time. Pictured here is Montana's South Fork of the Flathead River in the Bob Marshall Wilderness.*
***Inset:*** *The renowned salmonfly, largest aquatic insect of its kind, hatches from mid-May into July, depending on the river and altitude. This hatch, above all others perhaps, is the trademark of freestone rivers.*

All of this variance effects the fishing, especially when combined with the swift flow rate and large cobble type bottom configuration. The end product is a diverse series of hatches that tend to come and go in a dramatic fashion compared to tailwater rivers, where the hatches tend to be less diverse—smaller flies in astounding numbers over long time periods; freestone hatches feature a broad array of insect types, from the largest to the smallest, each with their own relatively short period of emergence. These hatches include the giant salmonflies and golden stoneflies of renown, numerous medium sized fast water mayflies, a wealth of caddis species, plus midges, sculpin (a small bottom feeding fish and trout favorite), snails, and other trout fare. During the lower pre-run off flows (March - April), and again in autumn, midges, and small blue wing olive (*Baetis* and *Pseudocloeon*) mayflies can be numerous. The great white mayfly *Ephoron* hatches in autumn too, in rivers with some silt bottom. During mid-summer low flows, Tricos can be locally important. The hopper and terrestrial fishing is well known. Many of theses hatches come and go quickly, lasting only a couple of weeks. Being on the river at the right time of year is important, but any time has its own special promise.

Not only do the usual (and unusual) seasonal variations affect fishing, so does the weather. A prolonged cold front chills the river down. In summer this can improve fishing, in spring and fall it can slow it down. Heavy rains can bring the river up quickly. This often causes a brief feeding glut by fish, including the largest ones, but can soon after make the trout more difficult to catch. Prolonged periods of summer heat can make fish sluggish and unresponsive. Since many hatches are believed to be triggered at least in part by water temperatures, you can see where the vagaries of nature will affect your fishing on a freestone river. Banner days can be exceptionally good—100 fish days on big gaudy flies—and the lows can be discouraging. The in-between days are just fine though, and you are at the mercy of nature when on-stream. This is part of the pleasure of fishing freestone rivers, you must meet the challenges that the river and trout hand you on that day.

Don't get the idea that big attractor dry flies always work on freestone rivers either. Certainly they don't. Water level, hatches, and fishing pressure all effect the trout's gullibility. The high murky flows of May and June's snow melt or run off can mean that big Stonefly Nymphs and Woolly Buggers work best. These can be atrocious to cast, but appeal to the trout. As the waters lower and clear in early to mid-summer, hatches proliferate. This is when the top water action can be fast and furious. Number ten to fourteen Wulffs, Humpies, and Trudes fool countless fish throughout the day. Match the hatch patterns work better at times. Come mid-summer and lots of fishing pressure, the trout grow hard to dupe. Small nymphs can win the day, fished in drop-offs, rock gardens, and pockets. Two fly combos are effective. Evening hatches at twilight may be your best dry fly bet. Even on true wilderness waters where native cutthroats are reputed to be pushovers, I've seen them avoid attractor patterns and medium sized nymphs and only go for midge pupa imitations and ants. As with all waters, the angler who is prepared to experiment and go small and deep when necessary will usually prevail.

Much of the fishing on a freestone river will be from the boat. The boatman's rowing skills add greatly to the success of anglers. His cowboy hat stuck full of Girdle Bugs, Sofa Pillows, Humpies, Bitch Creeks, and Elk Hair Caddis bear testimony to the local patterns and techniques in favor. The #22 Tricos, latest PMD emergers, and chironomid pupa of the tailwater rivers may remain in the fly box here (but not always). Rather than the intense concentration of spotting and working on selective tailwater trout, or staring at a strike indicator all day, the freestoners are ideal for leisurely watching your Royal Wulff bob along the eddy lines, or for slapping a Woolly Bugger down against an undercut bank. It is most relaxing and down-right fun, especially when you've worked out the nuances of float fishing.

Compared to the tailwaters where much of the fishing is done out of the boat, wading and stalking the high and selective fish populations, a freestone float usually sees long days of steady casting to good looking water, largely from the boat. Fish populations are somewhat lower, so more miles are apt to be covered. Less time is spent stalking choosy risers. Never-ending pockets are your targets.

Casting coordination with your boatmate should be fine-tuned for maximum enjoyment. Remember to keep casts parallel and well controlled. You won't want to leave any slack on the water before you backcast, especially when using weighted stonefly nymphs and streamers. A taut line makes a safe backcast. The stern angler might want to alternate casts with the bow angler to avoid tangles, keeping an eye on the bowman's casting rhythm. The stern angler will also be working to keep his line from tangling with the oars. The boatman, who is busy positioning the boat into ideal casting positions, shouldn't have to worry about the stern angler's fly line drifting into the path of his oars. Once underway, with your float fishing skills straightened out, the fun begins. The current sweeps you downstream to new vistas, the oars flex and groan, and casts of promise unfurl.

# FREESTONE TACTICS

Float fishing a freestone river could be simplified to this generalized rule: Keep your fly in the most likely looking position all the time, without undo drag.

While there are many promising water types, some less obvious than others, keeping your fly on the water and riding properly is the most important factor of all for success. Cast crisply, without undo false casting. Use reach casts to obtain long drag free floats—be it dry fly, nymph, or streamer. Mend as needed. You can get amazingly long drifts from a boat. On the other hand, whirling eddies may only allow a few seconds drift before the current zips your fly away. (Let your fly drag for a second or two, it attracts some fish.) Pick up and cast quickly again.

Dry fly fishing from a boat relieves the angler of much of the drag he encounters when wade fishing the same stretch. The float fisher only gets a couple of quick shots to any one target though, before the boat drifts on down stream. The trick again, at the risk of being redundant, is to cast quickly and accurately with a minimum of false casts, hitting as many good looking pockets and seams as possible, if only for 5 to 10 seconds each. A bouldery stretch of river, full of gulping pockets, might sink your dry fly every five feet, requiring quick and constant recasting to keep a dry fly neatly cocked. The properly balanced rod and correct casting style makes this quite effortless and when you can get those long drag free floats, so much the better. It makes for some very relaxed fishing. If your object is to catch more fish, doing whatever it takes to keep your fly constantly in front of trout will help achieve this. In this regard, float fishing casting skills should be your priority consideration.

# FREESTONE NYMPHING

The large weighted stonefly nymphs so commonly used on freestone rivers in the early season call for some casting modification.

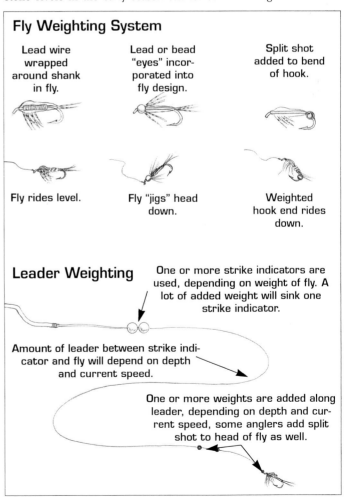

**Fly Weighting System**

| Lead wire wrapped around shank in fly. | Lead or bead "eyes" incorporated into fly design. | Split shot added to bend of hook. |
| --- | --- | --- |
| Fly rides level. | Fly "jigs" head down. | Weighted hook end rides down. |

**Leader Weighting**

One or more strike indicators are used, depending on weight of fly. A lot of added weight will sink one strike indicator.

Amount of leader between strike indicator and fly will depend on depth and current speed.

One or more weights are added along leader, depending on depth and current speed, some anglers add split shot to head of fly as well.

Being heavy, often with added weight to the leader, they require slower casts, yet still with the aim of keeping your fly in a good position as much as possible. In addition to slower casts (to give the heavy fly more time to turn over and straighten out behind and in front of you), the tuck cast, reach cast, and downstream curve (from the stern only) aid significantly in getting better drifts (as discussed in Chapter 3). "Better" in this case means drag free drifts that allow the nymph to sink to the proper depth, where it begins attracting bottom-hugging trout. The immediate drag that many novice anglers get when fishing these nymphs usually means a greatly reduced catch rate. Only by getting enough controlled slack, allowing the nymph to sink to the fishes level, will you maximize the potential of your nymph fishing from a boat.

Most anglers use a shortened leader of 6 to 9 feet when casting these #2-8 weighted nymphs. This makes them easier to cast. Tippets of 3X-1X are utilized, as heavy nymphs stress the knots and fish can take hard. The deeper the water fished, the longer the leader should be, with extra weight added to the leader, though this makes it all the harder to cast. Floating lines give you the best control when it comes to mending and maintaining drag free floats. Short sink tips are used as well, often with shorter leaders. These ultimately give you less line control, since once they've sunk, your mending has less effect.

As your nymph reaches the bottom and you feel it occasionally bouncing off rocks, pull in any excess slack so you can feel takes by fish. It's a good idea to use a strike indicator as well. If you're snagging the bottom constantly, you'll need to adjust the added weight to your leader or choose a lighter nymph. You can also strip your nymph in very slowly, just enough to keep it from hanging up. This kind of fishing takes a lot of attention to detail if you want to do it right. There is nothing worse, as a guide, than rowing anglers who heave out their weighted nymphs, let them sink, and then daydream. They snag every five minutes and expect you to row back *upstream* against a river's highest flows of the year. If you see a shallow bar or boulder coming up, you may have to raise or remove your nymph from the water to avoid snagging on it.

When guiding, I find that many anglers just toss their nymph out anywhere and figure it's OK. You still want to be looking for and hitting the hot spots, except that you have to put your fly there a little earlier since it's not really working until it has sunk to the proper depth.

The success rate between a good nympher and a novice can be quite astounding. I recall a day on Montana's Smith River when I had an experienced angler in the stern who gave the preferred bow position to a novice friend. This was during the golden stonefly emergence, one of the best hatches of the year. The river was up and murky but fishing well with nymphs. The experienced angler outfished the beginner 30 to 1, even though they were using similar rigs and the novice had first shot at the water. This was because the more experienced fisherman placed his fly in the most likely positions as they presented themselves, and he controlled and mended his line in a way so as to eliminate drag and allow the nymph to sink to the fishes level. At that point he paid a great deal of attention to any nudge, bounce or pull on his nymph, striking with his line hand whether a fish or a rock actually struck. Only then are you fishing.

Care must be taken when casting these heavy nymph rigs, for they are prone to coming low across the boat, losing altitude every second they are airborne. It is best to pull your line in until the fly is near the surface before making your backcast. There must be absolutely no slack on the water before you start the backcast. These weighted rigs have the most potential for injury in a boat, so conscious control, including watching your backcasts to make sure they are high enough, is essential.

Always expect to lose some flies when deep drifting nymphs. If you're not getting down to the bottom or close enough to undercut banks, you'll miss out on lots of fish. You'll snag every so often, and the boatman won't be able to row back to retrieve all of them. If you snag too often, he won't be inclined to go back for any of them! If you're breaking off a lot of flies, go to a heavier tippet. The water will likely be at least slightly discolored during the stonefly season and trout won't be leader shy. Some Western anglers use 8 to 20 pound leaders for this kind of fishing! This is leader that you can turn over rocks with when snagged. It works! Always be prepared to lose 6 to 12 flies a day, minimally. Careful attention to line control and nymph depth will cut your losses.

Since most stoneflies crawl out of the river and up the banks to emerge, this is where float fishermen concentrate most of their efforts during May, June, and early July on freestone rivers. Fishing the banks with the heavy stuff is the rule. When the leading edge of the hatch moves up the river dry flies may be effective, depending on water levels. Number two to eight air resistant dries are flopped down beneath willows, in eddies, and along seams. Takes will be aggressive and exciting. Getting top action in a really good salmonfly hatch happens only once every few years for most anglers. Other seasons turn up mediocre dry fly fishing, but if you hit it right, expect numerous and large trout to be as gung-ho as you'll ever see them. Many anglers make special trips to try to hit the salmonfly hatch just right on rivers like Big Hole, Yellowstone, and Madison. Traffic jams on the river occur and there is no solitude here! It's a social affair, with legions of drift boats roaring down dirt roads, spitting gravel on the way to boat ramps. Cafés that were filled at opening time, empty out quickly, with only a few ranch hands left, shaking their heads at the show. Boats run over wading anglers, waders curse at inept boatmen. Countless fly lines wave in the air with an array of hugely ludicrous fly patterns. Prospects may be high, results can be low, but the bars fill up later regardless of the outcome. Tomorrow will bring renewed hopes, different stretches of river to float, and another greasy breakfast at the local café. It's a parade worth participating in till you finally hit it right.

Naturally you'll want stout rods to propel such large flies. A 9 foot 6-8 weight is about right, with plenty of backbone. Modern graphite rods are ideal, though some are a little too rigid in the tip for the smooth transmission of power and wider loop necessary for casting heavy nymphs and streamers. Some anglers even fish two large flies at a time with such outfits which can be more productive, but certainly more cumbersome to cast. You might want to work out your

*A golden stonefly nymph with a fanciful imitation. These large stoneflies hatch after the famed salmonflies, and often provide better fishing opportunities.*

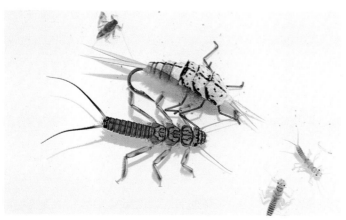

*Cased caddis graze together on a sun-drenched mid-summer rock. When hatches are thin in late summer, trout will pick them off.*

the tan to dark brown color spectrum. While those huge rubber leg nymph patterns still turn fish—and some big ones—it's smaller imitations of these abundant mid-summer nymphs that provide the most consistent action.

Patterns of hare's ear and pheasant tail, of peacock herl, muskrat, and soft hackle should be danced through drop-offs, current edges, and runs. Fish often move into swift rocky channels for added oxygen and cooler water. Their fleeting shapes are hidden within from the eyes of predators. Here nymphs are swept by their summer holding stations, which by now have become settled residences.

Boatmen will likely float shorter stretches of river at low water, stopping frequently at the numerous drop-offs and idyllic wade fishing runs. After possible morning hatches of Tricos or PMD's, mid-day nymphing will likely keep the action going. Strike indicators come to sudden stops, zipping under water. Flashes are seen amongst streambed boulders. Gem-like fish are brought to hand for admiration and release. It might take extra weight, and long, light leaders to probe the depths, but fish are there for the prospecting.

This is when fishing the middle can be more productive than

*A colorful mid-summer trout that fell for a nymph pattern. Browns like this settle into swift water runs, drop-offs, and pools for the low water summer season. Others hide under grass banks, cliff edges, and around spring seepages.*

*Floating anglers stop to wade-fish promising runs in summer and autumn. Here, a beautiful "mini-channel" supports many fish. The foam lane, slowing current, and deepening color give it away as prime trout territory.*

casting arm before fishing several days with a heavier rod on the river. The muscles used are different than those utilized in daily life and many fishermen wear out in half a day of nonstop casting. Of course, there's nothing wrong with sitting back and watching the scenery go by either. Some anglers fish so hard that I doubt they see much of the view all day long. It's only those colorfully spotted salmonoid shapes that interest them!

When freestone rivers drop into low summer flows, a different scene greets visiting anglers. Waters are bubbling clear. Many edgewaters are shallow and warming under the afternoon sun. Green weed beds wave and glow amongst the golden cobble bottoms, where cased Caddis can be seen milling around. Depressions, dropoffs, and channels become clearly evident.

Most giants of the streambed have emerged and left the scene. Gone are the largest stoneflies, though their multi-year nymph broods can be found by digging down into the bottom rubble of swift water runs. The big brown and green drakes have flown away. Of the many hatches left, most are in the small to medium size range and in

*This wide* Epeorus *mayfly nymph, with its expansive gripping legs and gills, is typical of many found in swift freestone rivers. #16-10 Hare's Ear type nymphs are good "generic" imitations when tumbled along the bottom.*

fishing the banks. Pay special attention to where waters are channelled, drop-off, scour boulders, and fan out. Trout will be hovering in bottom eddies and darting out of current edges to seize mid-summer nymphs.

Towards evening, Caddis and mayflies may begin to hatch. Soft hackled wet flies can fool many trout picking off emergers. These are cast down and across from the boat and allowed to swing on downstream. The pulse of the oars adds movement, as your fly swims beneath a broken surface. You can even take time to glance around as the evening light paints a scene of surrealistic beauty over the river valley. The trout's take will be decidedly bold, to the point of breaking off some of your flies! Like streamer fishing, takes to soft hackle nymphs can be felt, with the lunging trout often hooking themselves. Eventually dry flies might become the best bet again, a fitting finale to a glorious summer's day float.

These smaller nymphs in sizes #10-18 help keep summer freestone days productive. As mentioned before, dangling one beneath a bushy attractor pattern or hopper makes a good combination, while keeping you in that enjoyable dry fly realm.

As summer slips into autumn, hatches wane in number and duration. The fish however are looking all the harder for nymphs and food is getting scarcer. Some large Caddis and mayflies still emerge, such as October Caddis, and *Paraleptophlebia, Ephoron,* and *Siphlonurus* mayflies. Also present in larger numbers are smaller *Baetis* and *Pseudocloeon* mayflies (tiny blue wing olives), and midges. Hatches occur mid-afternoon and evening now, as temperatures drop and ice rims still waters on frosty nights. By this time many anglers are heaving large streamers in hopes of chance encounters with angry spawning browns.

The well known October caddis hatches in autumn from rivers across the west.

# FREESTONE STREAMER FISHING

Streamer fishing from a boat is very effective on freestone rivers. Sculpin, minnows, crayfish, and young trout and whitefish are important food items for large trout. Even those of us who prefer dry fly fishing to anything can't help but get excited about the prospect of big, sometimes visible trout slamming your streamer on the retrieve.

Sculpin are populous in freestone rivers and in some tailwaters. They hug the bottom, feeding on nymphs. Big trout love them. A Woolly Bugger is a good imitation, there are many patterns tied specifically to imitate them as well. All should be weighted and fished near the bottom.

Since most western rivers have produced 20 pound trout and have numerous 3 to 5 pounders, one can realistically expect to catch more big freestone trout on streamers. When rivers are clear, you can often see these fish charging your fly—exciting stuff indeed!

Float fishing with streamers has certain advantages over wade fishing. Going with the current allows your fly to sink deeper if desired and you have access to deep banks and other areas you couldn't access wading. By casting directly into the bank and stripping the fly back, your streamer is presented to the trout broadside, a much better hooking angle than the usual down and across wading presentation. Floating also allows you to easily cover miles of water a day. You may not be able to fish every inch thoroughly when floating, like you can wade fishing, you fish more river and pluck out the most aggressive trout.

Much of this streamer fishing is similar to heavy nymphing, with the addition of fly movement. The same rods and leaders are used. Sink tip lines can be an advantage, especially if there is much deep cover. They also punch out better in the wind. Size #2-6 streamers and Woolly Buggers are favored most of the time—big flies for big fish.

Fishing to bank cover is most common. The accuracy called for in repeatedly hitting these pockets without snagging streamside foliage is an enjoyable challenge in itself. Cast, let the streamer sink, strip 6 to 10 times, and cast again...this is the pattern. Hits are usually solid and forceful. Don't use tippets less than 3X!

The banks certainly aren't the only likely streamer water on freestone rivers. Mid-stream boulders, drop-offs, and eddy lines deserve exploration, especially good-looking boulder garden stretches can have promising water from bank to bank. Sometimes it's best to cast far and strip your fly all the way back to the boat. Other times you might want to hit boulder eddies for several seconds each and then hit another eddy, in an effort to get as many as you can. If the fish are turned on they'll respond almost instantly. If the center of a run looks the best, pull the boat over and wade fish it thoroughly. Often shallow riffles contain several good fish. Keep an open mind to approach and presentation, don't be a slave to bank fishing unless it's definitely working better for you. Think trout habitat and thoughtfully adjust your float fishing to it.

Depending on the trout's mood, different rates of retrieve will vary in effectiveness. If the fish are being lethargic, due to cold or hot weather for instance, a dead-drifted streamer can be more productive because trout don't have to go out of their way to chase it. Your fly will also sink deeper, as the trout may be lounging near the bottom and refuse to rise up much to take in the currents. The current alone adds enough life to the streamer.

Just before and during a salmonfly hatch, dead drifting Woolly Buggers can be very effective, as they do a good job of imitating a stonefly nymph tumbling down the river. Keep it drifting along rocky banks, where stonefly nymphs emerge and trout line up to eat them. Fish lying along undercut banks in swift water are usually reluctant to move far into the current to chase food. Keep your Bugger up as close as you can with a long drift, again, the reach and tuck casts will aid you in this. A strike indicator may live up to its name here. If the water gets shallow, strip the fly in. It's hard to lose with a Woolly Bugger, regardless of how you fish it!

When trout are in an aggressive mood, and sometimes it seems that they all are at the same time, medium to fast stripping works best. You cover more water this way, trout don't have time to look your fly over too well, and their instinctive aggressiveness comes to the fore. They hit the fly hard and often hook themselves, as your line is tight.

I find it best to strip in not too jerky a fashion. Use smooth strips with pauses or a steady pull. Fast and erratic stripping sometimes causes the trout to miss the fly just as its mouth is closing around it. Make it easy for them! Strip at a good but smooth pace. If a trout does miss the streamer, let it sit a second and then commence stripping. Many hungry fish will have another go at it if you haven't set the hook too wildly and jerked the fly out of the area. You certainly want to recast quickly to a missed trout, they'll likely be looking for the escaped baitfish if not spooked off.

The best way to fish a streamer is with your rod tip down, almost touching the water, and pointed towards your fly. Use a strong leader of at least 6 pound test. Eight to ten pound is better yet. There are big trout out there and it's rather disappointing to break one off on the take after you've worked hard to entice him. It takes a quick and solid strike to set a large barbed hook. I've seen oh so many lost due to late and underpowered strikes, as well as to understrength tippets.

## Streamer Fishing Hand Positions

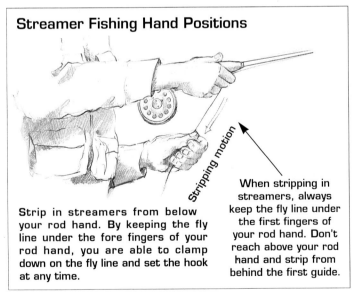

Strip in streamers from below your rod hand. By keeping the fly line under the fore fingers of your rod hand, you are able to clamp down on the fly line and set the hook at any time.

When stripping in streamers, always keep the fly line under the first fingers of your rod hand. Don't reach above your rod hand and strip from behind the first guide.

When you're stripping in line while fishing a streamer, always strip from behind your rod hand and not from in front of it. In this way you are prepared to strike no matter when a fish hits by simply tightening your rod hand on the fly line and rearing back on the rod (the impulsive way), or preferably by pulling back solidly with your line hand while lifting the rod tip only slightly. The latter technique leaves the fly in the same area should the fish miss it the first time, the trout can then find it again for a second take. If you strip from in

front of your rod hand, up behind the first stripping guide, you'll have an awkward moment of line transfer from line to rod hand in which it's nearly impossible to set the hook quickly when a trout takes. This is a very important detail of streamer fishing, whether from a boat or wading.

One mistake many anglers make is using the rod tip excessively to impart action to the fly, instead of stripping. The fatal error is using the rod tip for all the action. The angler twitches the rod back further and further, giving the fly movement with the same length of line out. Towards the end of his drift, he has the rod worked all the way behind him with line sagging in the air. Now when the fish hits, he has little or no ability to set the hook, or even feel the fish take. The fish of a trip might boil at the fly and let go before the fisherman can get all his slack out and be in a position to solidly set the hook. I've seen it a hundred times! Keep the rod tip low, pointed towards the fly or at a slight angle from it, and strip in your streamer. In this way you can strike with all the force needed whenever you like. The larger the fish and the barbed hook, the more force it will take to drive it into a big trout's tough mouth. Pinching down the barb will make it easier to set the hook, but fish are sometimes lost during jumps or if you loosen tension on the line, be it the fishes or your own fault. This commonly occurs when fish run at the boat and you can't take up slack quickly enough. The micro barbs now available on some hooks are the best alternative.

When float fishing with streamers on rivers with lots of promising pocket water, you'll want to explore every nook and cranny you can with your fly. The stern angler can keep an eye on where the bow angler has fished and target different pockets. On a smaller river you might want to fish both sides, experimenting with varying water types. Don't forget that many large trout cruise shallow riffles, flats, sloughs, and tailouts, so try some casts in these waters as well as along the more obvious undercut and rocky bank cover. Unless the river is very swift, and trout are known to hold very tight to the bank, strip your fly in back towards the boat. Some fish will follow a distance before taking, or will be laying out in mid-river. The two anglers in a boat would do well to experiment with different colored flies and different depths and rates of retrieve until the most productive rig has been ascertained. We sometimes fish two streamers per line, of contrasting colors. This gives the effect of small fish chasing each other, which can entice large trout into joining the fray! Using two different colors, say yellow and brown, gives them a choice.

Don't be afraid to try something outlandish, especially if a local suggests it! In fact, seek out local advice and don't get hung up on your old favorites if they're not working. As a guide, I've learned not to say no when a guest angler asks me if a certain pattern he has might work. Everything works sometimes! On the other hand, don't let a more experienced angler's skill make you think that it's only his fly pattern that's letting him catch more fish than you. He will be thwarting drag, placing the fly where he wants it and at the right depth, and in all ways maximizing his streamer fishing potential. Even streamer fishing calls for good line control if you want routinely good results. This good line control carries over in to the safety realm too, as those big hooks are dangerous. Pay special attention to how high your casts go over the boat, especially on windy days. Keep your sunglasses and hat on as armor against wayward casts!

## FREESTONE DRY FLY FISHING

Fishing dry flies on freestone rivers automatically brings to mind Royal Wulffs, Humpies, Trudes, Hoppers and other large attractor pat-

## Trout Laying Upstream of a Rock

Feeding trout often hold upstream of boulders. There is a calm pocket there, where they can linger and watch food come by.

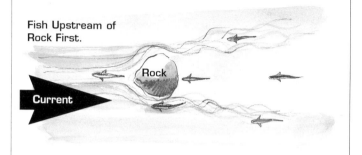

Fish hold upstream, beside, and under rocks, and in the eddy lines that peel off them. Fish these spots first, before tossing your fly in the eddy behind the rock, as is usually done.

*Attractor patterns fool fish that are used to seeing a wide variety of hatches that can occur simultaneously. On freestone rivers this is often the case and is where such flies are frequently plied. During periods of sparse hatch activity, hungry fish like this wilderness cutthroat may pounce on any reasonable pattern that drifts by.*

terns. The river's currents are swift, dancing in sunlight, and ever-changing. These flies ride high and are visible to trout that mistake them for the broad array of stoneflies, mayflies, caddis, and terrestrials that make their way into the seaward flow. The angler can see them too, always a pleasure, especially as the years go by. Such attractor patterns are usually in the #10-14 size range, fished on 3X-5X tippets. Trout have to think quickly and grab what comes by, this is what makes a premium day float fishing a freestone river so much fun.

Banks are often the targets, with their undercuts, rocky lairs, overhung foliage, and rippling eddy lines. Fish are occasionally seen rising or underwater and then are cast to. During late summer, any streamside grass can have terrestrial oriented trout lined up along it. Mid-river boulders, rock gardens, drop-offs, and seams call for attention too. While most anglers seem to think that trout always hold downstream of rocks (which of course many do), just as many hungry trout sit upstream from them. There is a quiet pocket of water just upstream of a boulder that allows trout to sit in front of it without fighting the current. Here they can watch for food. On many rivers, the upstream side of rocks will be among the most productive pockets when it comes to aggressively feeding trout.

*A brown drake spinner, one of the larger mayflies found on western freestone rivers. Locally, brown drakes hatch in late June to early July, in afternoons and evenings. In Michigan, the same hatch occurs closer to darkness.*

Big attractor patterns don't always work on freestone rivers though. On some rivers, the fish have seen too many of them and they work on but a fraction of the available trout. Sometimes just going smaller in size is enough to do the trick, we usually carry these patterns down to #20. It's amazing how well the smaller sizes can work, even on tough tailwater rivers. Of course, there will be times when trout won't rise at all. That is when a nymph suspended beneath a big attractor dry can work wonders. Lightly weighted nymphs or emergers in sizes #8-18 are used, with 12 to 20 inches of 3X-5X tippet between the two flies. The indicator dry is occasionally taken too, and such a two fly rig can be very productive over the course of a day. Adjust the length of the tippet between the flies, and the weight and nymph pattern and size until the best combination is found.

Freestone rivers have a large variety of hatches, and the trout certainly get on to them. The larger varieties are usually quite obvious. Imitations can be fished from the boat blind or to sighted rising trout. The slower the boatman can maintain the boat's position in the current, the more good shots you'll have at pockets or fish. It doesn't hurt to occasionally twitch or skid larger fly patterns in swift water either. Many of the larger aquatic insects and terrestrials flop about a bit on the water before getting airborne, imitating this can bring slashing takes from big fish. Some of the larger insects you're likely to run into on freestone streams include several species of stonefly, green and brown drakes (mayflies), and October Caddis. There are many more species you can generically call medium sized hatches, and these are what attractor patterns are routinely fished to imitate.

Freestone river trout do get selective at times, and match the hatch patterns should be kept on hand for these most pleasant situations. If you have done your homework in the months before your trip you will be armed with the knowledge, and thus with imitations of the hatches. If the fish get fussy you'll be ready to get the best action of the day, a testament to your planning. Keep on hand a variety of more realistic mayfly, caddis, and stonefly patterns, in assorted sizes. Don't let a few dollars worth of flies be the weakest link in your chain of angling contentment, especially if traveling far and tapping your coffers extensively already. Having the fish rise contemptuously without you is no fun, but if it does happen take notes for tomorrow, and look around you. Swallows will likely be circling, songbirds too joining in on the feast, portly trout rising steadily and giving themselves away, and the whole river world will be alive with interest. Breathe in the fresh air and riparian scents. Gaze across the landscapes. A hatch is a time of plenty and you don't have to catch fish to enjoy it!

When it comes to freestone hatches, it is the spent wings, emergers, and miniature models that often go unnoticed. These can be tough to see among the wavelets and romping currents. Flying ants, beetles, midges, Tricos, and micro-caddis are among the most common minutiae trout may focus in on. Evening spinner falls of mayfly imagoes are prime candidates too, and are often overlooked by anglers who habitually use attractor patterns. Multiple hatch situations occur, where spinner falls of several mayfly species are mixed with emerging mayflies and caddis. Take time out every so often to see what's happening around you. Have an insect net available to strain the water, I always think of this as wildlife viewing on a smaller scale. Don't get overwrought about the bug's latin name, but be observant when it comes to insect life and trout behavior. This is what sets fly fishermen apart from many other river users, they learn to see the river in a more comprehensive way if they truly want to master the sport.

Since it can be hard to see such small fly patterns on broken waters, strike indicators or two fly systems can be employed. Hi-Vis versions of standard fly patterns are good choices too. Parachutes and Comparaduns can often be used successfully instead of actual spent wing patterns. Fluorescent wings can be used for better viewing, these are easier to see and can be just as productive. Look into the expected hatches ahead of time and go armed to meet them.

You'll want to pull the boat over and wade fish some good runs during a prolific hatch or spinner fall. Spotting rising fish might not be easy, but if you take your time, look up some slicker water, and position yourself advantageously in regards to lighting, you can find targets. Many trout move into quieter water to rise steadily, where they don't have to fight the current, especially along inside bends, quiet edgewaters, and in foam-laden eddies. Crouching down low often gives you a better view, as can looking straight upriver as opposed to across or down. Blind fish good-looking pockets while trying to spot risers. I might mention here that some freestone rivers are notoriously slippery, the streambed can be composed of large round stones, coated with algae. The Madison, for example, has perilous footing. When on the river be armed with felt-soled wading shoes, many anglers use wading staffs. Swift currents plus slippery rocks add up to frequent spills!

Freestone rivers are beautiful, lively, and perhaps the best places to learn float fishing techniques. They are often forgiving, and their trout will sometimes chase a beginner's dragging fly across gleaming riffles and churning pockets. The river's hurried currents cover many mistakes.

There are other benefits too. As the clear waters bounce, glide, swoosh, and gurgle along they mask your descent. You float up to unsuspecting wildlife busily making a living or crossing the stream. Scenes go by gracefully, in a way that is novel to daily life in our artificial world. That basic element—water—on its monumentous journey to the sea, hypnotizes us somewhere down in our primitive psyche. Our furtive, superficial grip on the natural world of mountains, forest, and stream somehow seems momentarily tighter when on the river. Once civilizations and societies were centered around rivers, they provided food, water, transportation, and inspiration. Technology has changed that, perhaps to our psychological detriment, for it seems that river and sea towns always have more coherence. Is it any wonder then that fishing is the most popular sport in the world? Perhaps it is less a sport than a seeking, a re-entry into the world which we have managed to separate ourselves from over the centuries. To me, this too is a part of float fishing's appeal, it is a chance to disconnect and re-embark, to relax and breath easier, as you reacquaint yourself with our heritage of beautiful flowing rivers.

*A Hi-Vis Parachute Adams is an excellent fish catching pattern, and can serve as a strike indicator when using a two fly system.*

*Foam-covered eddies like this trap insects, and usually have at least one trout in residence. Foam also gives trout overhead cover from predators and bright sunlight. With controlled casts, dry flies, nymphs, or streamers are likely to pull out a fish.*

*Float fishing gives you another perception of life.*

7. Tailwater Rivers

**Above:** *In low light situations, trout can be pickier, but usually take repeated casts without spooking.*

**Left:** *The big tailwater rivers fish differently than small swift streams. New tactics, casts, and flies can be necessary for an angler's success.*

Tailwater rivers differ from freestoners in a number of ways. For those not familiar with the term, tailwater is used to describe a river that flows out of an impoundment, below a dam. The lake modifies temperature extremes in the river below, and usually eliminates flood and drought fluctuations of water levels. The lake also acts as a sediment trap for incoming rivers, resulting in a cool, clear flow often high in nutrients, and thus, perfect water for trout. A Tailwater river flowing out of a lake has generally changed character from the river it used to be. Where once it was a turbid prairie stream, supporting catfish and sauger, flooding during run-off, nearly drying up sometimes in drought, it now supports large populations of trout in its steady, clear currents. Weed beds full of aquatic insects flourish. Fish populations are now higher than anywhere else in the world. This is why anglers seek the tailwaters.

Most tailwaters are larger rivers at lower elevations than the freestoners that may be their upstream tributaries. The gradient of most tailwaters is slight, maybe 3 to 5 feet per mile. In other words, they are big, moderate paced rivers that don't initially look "trouty" to small stream-bred anglers. The slower paced currents make a difference in the hatches that occur, and in the way trout feed on them. Consequently, there are marked differences in fishing tactics compared to the freestone rivers.

As you may remember from the preceding chapter, freestone rivers have a wide variety of hatches that tend to burst out for relatively short time periods. The multitude of hatches have their little seasonal niches as water levels and temperatures change throughout the year. This is why, in part, attractor patterns work so well on the freestoners. Tailwaters on the other hand, have less variety in hatches, but the hatches they have occur in huge numbers over longer time periods. Since the lake above has moderated the water temperatures, there is much less temperature change in the river. Hatches go on for months instead of weeks. The trout rise daily, in some cases almost all year long. Another difference becomes quickly evident, most of the tailwater hatches are of smaller insects. Few stonefly species are here, and none of the largest ones—salmonflies or golden stoneflies (there are some exceptions). Of the mayflies, the smaller sized ones are best represented, ranging from size #24-14. These include *Baetis, Pseudocloeon, E. infrequens* and *inermis* (PMD's), and *Tricorythodes*. They hatch from April to December, offering a high percentage of dry fly fishing. Caddis too are numerous, and midges are uncountable. Midges hatch year-round and make up a major part of a tailwater trout's diet. Some tailwaters, such as the Missouri, have plenty of crayfish, minnows, and other small baitfish that large trout can feast upon while others, like the Bighorn, don't. Fresh water shrimp and aquatic worms may also thrive among the weed beds and stones. What an angler faces then are numerous trout used to feeding steadily on profuse hatches of small insects, or underwater fare—selective trout.

Since the currents are slower on many tailwaters, this means that trout have a better chance to look over your offerings. They can also see your casting mistakes. The demands of precise imitation and presentation can be high, as can the rewards for the skilled. Much of the fishing is done out of the boat, wading to schools (yes, schools) of rising fish, or nymphing productive riffles, eddy lines, and drop-offs. The boat is used mainly as transportation by some anglers and guides. But there are excellent float fishing opportunities on tailwa-

ters, especially if the hands on the oars are skilled, and your observation keen. Schools of fish can be found rising in deep water. Some fish are easier to fool when approached from the middle of the river. There are still undercut banks to be worked, plus long weed bed runs where a deeply sunk nymph, scud, or San Juan Worm works amazingly well when drifted along with the boat. The mobility of a boat will put you into more fish over the course of a day than you would likely encounter otherwise, and many that you couldn't get to wading. Many tailwaters are crowded with anglers too, and being able to move to greater or lesser "hot spots" can be the key to success.

To get the most out of your encounter with tailwater rivers try to get your precision casting down to a delicate perfection. This is "far and fine" fishing at its best. When wading, you might be able to work yourself into a position just 15 to 20 feet behind a steadily gulping fish. On the other hand, you'll have targets out towards mid-river that call for 60 foot slack line deliveries of #22 flies. From the boat, casting to sighted rising fish will usually require 40 to 60 foot casts with long leaders, light tippets, and small flies. Good eyesight is most helpful. The boat can be slowed to a standstill or anchored, and fish can be cast to repeatedly. Since there are many natural insects on the water, the fish don't tend to go out of their way to get your fly. You have to put drag free drifts right over the fish, often enough to "intercept" them at the right moment in their rise rhythm. They may be rising once every 5 seconds, and by luck or design, your fly needs to go over them about the time they are coming up for another bite. Since trout are veterans of human encounters, your fly pattern will likely need to be small and realistic.

One facet of tailwater fishing that I notice many anglers having trouble with is depth perception across the wide open waters. They may be used to small streams where targets are close and well defined, say near a rock, bank, or ripple line. Many tailwaters present broad featureless expanses of water, hundreds of feet wide. When a fish rises, they have little to mark its position by. This is especially true when fishing out towards the middle in a wide tailout or flats. Anglers will put their fly several feet short of, beyond, behind, and occasionally in front of the trout. Much fishing time will be wasted with the fly going down the wrong feed lane. Perhaps this open water targeting can only be perfected with experience. It is something you should be aware of and concentrate on improving. Tailwater trout are less likely to move out of their way for a fly than freestone trout, so more exacting and repeated casting is called for. This takes time and you don't want to use your day up casting where there are no fish. Use the slightest surface swirl (often created by the waving of underwater weed beds) for marking your position. Pay close attention to how much line you let out. Lee Wulff noted in his book *The Atlantic Salmon*, that when anglers have a take on a cast, their usual reaction is to pull several more feet of line off the reel for the next cast to the same fish. In other words, they start casting too far, as if the fish were steadily moving away. If you get a drift right over your fish, maintain that line distance and keep working it. Human nature seems to interfere with many simple processes.

Since trout can see boats easily in these more placid waters, longer routine casts with dry flies are often called for. Well balanced high modulous rods of 8 1/2 to 9 feet are generally used, with 3 to 5 weight lines for fine dry fly work. Six to seven weight rods are brought along too, for casting hoppers, heavier nymph rigs, and streamers, especially when the wind comes up. These can throw 50+ foot casts effortlessly, turning over light leaders to 15 feet. You'll want to stay as far away from your target water as you can comfortably cast, so as not to spook the trout.

Strangely enough, trout down in the weed beds can be caught right under the boat when fishing nymphs and San Juan Worms.

*San Juan Worms have become tailwater standards across the west.*

Weight is usually added to the leader, and strike indicators employed to effectively drift fish this way. It is not among the most pleasant methods of fly fishing, but it works. Beginners can catch otherwise tough and selective trout on their first time out.

When float fishing tailwaters and casting to rising fish, small flies in sizes #14-22 can be necessary much of the day. The fly's descent to the surface should be lithe and graceful. The fly might also be required to precede the tippet if trout are to be consistently fooled. Here again, the reach cast thrown slightly ahead of the boat is the best tool for accomplishing this task. It gives you longer drag free drifts as well. Overflow populations of midges, *Trico's*, Little Blue-winged Olives (BWO's including *Baetis* and *Psuedocloeon*), Pale Morning Duns (PMD's), and Caddis grow steady rising, yet demanding trout. Some trout will be intrigued enough to pounce on a #12 Royal Wulff, but one should expect the opposite to be the case much of the time.

## Casting Downstream to Tailwater Trout

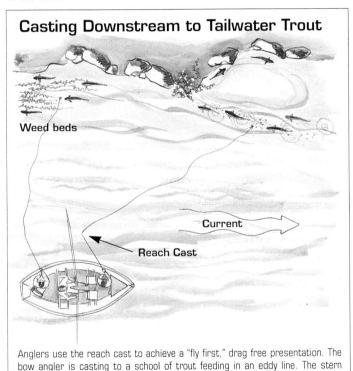

Weed beds

Current

Reach Cast

Anglers use the reach cast to achieve a "fly first," drag free presentation. The bow angler is casting to a school of trout feeding in an eddy line. The stern angler is casting to fish scattered across a weed bed flats.

There are exceptions to this small fly rule that need to be considered as river to river cases. Streamers and crayfish patterns work well on some tailwaters. Big attractor patterns like Humpies and Stimulators happen to work well on the Missouri, often being taken by larger browns in swift, shallow riffles and choppy eddy lines. Cicada patterns are popular on Utah's Green River. These fish are not necessarily seen rising routinely, but suck in these morsels anyway. Hoppers and Cicadas, plus other terrestrials work well at the right time of year, from mid-July into October. Damselfly adults are taken too, on rivers where they flourish. One day the fish will seem "easy," the next day tough as nails. Fly patterns go through constant evolutions here since the fish get so much fishing pressure. A pattern will have its moment of glory, and then seem to fade in effectiveness as more people use it. Each tailwater river will have developed its own character. Do some research, make some calls, read some books, and you can get the "low down" before you visit a particular tailwater river. As a guide, I might add that your casting skills outweigh any other factor when it comes to routinely catching fish. You can obtain flies on the spot, learn when the hatches occur, and siphon out the

hot spots, but if you can't cast well, and get long, controlled drifts, you'll spend a lot of time not catching trout.

Demanding trout fished to from a boat call for special considerations in approach and execution, compared to wade fishing. (Here again we're talking about fish that can't be easily waded to, or by preference are pursued from the boat.) I find that some anglers hate casting to rising fish from a boat, while others enjoy the singular challenges. Often it's the boatman's rowing skills that make the difference. Can or will he bring the boat to a standstill in the current so you can work on a fish? Can he routinely position the boat in ideal casting situations, without undue rocking, clunking, swerving, and swaying? In other words, can he give the angler a stationary casting platform from which he can do his part—catch the fish? This is where teamwork is essential for repeated victories over temperamental feeders; where the "far and fine" skills of the angler need to be matched by the stoic rowing prowess of a tireless boatman. Add to this the considerations of casting from the close quarters of a boat with three people, and you are on the verge of a float fishing team that fish should fear!

The boat progresses downstream slowly. Lines may be out with dries, nymphs, or streamers, but the rower and anglers scan the river constantly for risers. Multiple rods are carried by the fishermen, one for fine "match the hatch" work, plus another for larger dries, nymphs, or wets. If the trout located are wadable, the boat is pulled over and the fish stalked. If the trout are better pursued from the boat, one angler is chosen for the attack, and the boat quietly worked into a comfortably long casting range. The angle of presentation, effects of the current, hatch in progress, and wariness of the trout are all taken into consideration before the first cast. Too often anglers cast to sighted fish that are really out of their controllable range, their first out-of-control cast drags over the fish rather than achieving the drag free drift needed. Often trout are spooked by this. Wait till you are in perfect range for your cast to work. Think of trout as wild animals. Deer don't stand around while you take endless shots at them, neither will some trout. Consider your first cast to be your most likely—it should be your best, though that's not easy to accomplish. When a hatch is thick, many trout will let you take shot after shot after shot at them. The thinner a hatch is, the spookier the trout will be. This will depend on the trout's nature and the river it dwells in.

Trout have many enemies. On my home river herons, cormorants, kingfishers, osprey, pelicans, eagles, mink, and otter in good numbers keep the trout concerned. Prolonged drought (8+ years) has lowered the year-round water levels, and trout are twitchier than ever. Consequently, a flashing leader seen overhead will send them into a panic, others have learned to "duck" leaders and the flies attached to them as they go by. This situation requires that false casts are not made directly over the fish or within their vision. It may also require that casts be made downstream, with the fly approaching first. Low, high speed casts are harder for fish to spot than high lagging ones that unfurl in slow motion. On slick water, the fly might need to land 6 to 10 feet upstream of the trout if it's not to be spooked, followed by a long, controlled, drag free drift. This is easier said than done. You might think that slick water would create less drag, but the opposite effect is usually the case. Weed swirls create untold nuances in the river's surface. Unperceived drag sets in almost immediately. Trout easily detect this drag and the shadows it creates beneath the smooth surface, where it would be hidden on a choppy freestone river. A downstream, slack line cast is often the answer, something that takes practice to consistently achieve. (Refer to Chapter 3, Special Casting Techniques.) The trouble here is that if you lead them by too much, your line starts to drag excessively. If you don't lead the trout enough, they see your line in the air. It's a

*An angler has pulled over to stalk rising tailwater trout he located while floating down the river. Giant eddy lines, eddies, drop-offs, and flats are among the tailwater zones where rising trout can be sighted. Looking for them is half the battle. The "margins" of the river are the most likely spots for risers, out of the main force of the current.*

fine line, so to speak. If the fish are feeding greedily enough, you can often drop your fly closer to them, as you can when clouds, rain, and wind help obscure leader shadows. Since several of these major hatches are daytime affairs, the sun glistening on your fly line is especially conspicuous to the fish on sunny days; much more so than with an evening rise.

Another occurrence that few angler's consider, and indeed has rarely been discussed in print, is that of "spraying" the trout with your false casting. Every time you pick up your line and fly off the river, some water adheres to them. When you false cast, considerable amounts of water "spray" off your line. Get up above someone, on a hill or cliff, and watch them cast across still water. You will see what a disturbance this makes. The spray goes beyond the length of your fly line by 20 feet or more, in a swath 5 to 10 feet wide. Spooky trout in quiet water pick up on this. You can see them flinch as the spray sprinkles suddenly upon them, and become furtive, edgy feeders if not exiting the scene altogether. This is another reason to make sure your false casts aren't directly over your targeted fish. On sunny days trout may flee this sudden "rainfall" as they would an osprey, or your fly line winging over their heads. Trout can be spooky indeed.

Another trick we have found useful at times, and one that does pop up in fishing literature (yet is not put to use by many), is that of using sunlight to your best advantage. On days when the fish are exasperatingly wary to movement and casts, it can sometimes help to get the sun at your back as long as you're not actually casting shadows over the trout. When the sun is in your face, you are highly illuminated and the fish have an easier time spotting you. With the sun at your back, trout have a harder time seeing you and they can often be approached quite closely. This is like driving directly into a sunset

and having a hard time seeing details along the road ahead. Trout also seem to have a harder time deciphering the authenticity of a fly when staring up at a bright sun, but they do see the shadows cast by heavy leaders. If you really want to fool a particular fish on a sunny day, you might want to apply leader sink to your tippet, since sunk leaders cast much less of a shadow than floating ones do. Floating leaders also contort the surface of flat water, forming even bigger shadows. By having your fly floating and your leader sunk, additional fish can be fooled. Small spent wings, midges, beetles, and ant patterns eventually catch many such notorious, persnickety, infuriating, enticing, selective risers; trout you may have fished to so many times that you now feel like you're related somehow. There are several theories on how to use the sun to your best advantage. These can be applied to float fishing.

Many skilled anglers like to find rising tailwater fish from the boat, pull in below them to anchor, and disembark to stalk them. A precision caster can fish directly up and over rising trout, dropping the fly oh so lightly just a foot or two above the fish with a delicate flat finish (non-glare) tippet. His casts are under such control that ultra-spooky veteran trout don't catch on, even though the mid-day sun is beating down, casting harsh shadows. The perfect cast fools the jaded edgewater riser.

In reality, a high percentage of fly fishers spook such fish. Their casts don't land as planned. The trout sees the line in the air and flees, or the fly lands hard and drags—with the same effect. This is why I prefer to have average casters fish down and across to mid-day tailwater trout when they are at their spookiest. The same fish come autumn can be easier to fool with overhead casts. Whether this is due to a lower sun angle and intensity, or the fishes greater desire for

*Note the droplets of water peppering the surface above this ex-rising trout. Water that "sprays" off your line when casting and false casting can scare flat water fish. I took this picture from the willows as a boat went by and an angler "sprayed" them.*

less available food is hard to say.

The same often goes for late evening risers. Fish that fled glistening overhead casts on the first presentation in mid-day, will often take endless upstream presentations over them once the sunlight has dropped off the river and evening hatches or spinner falls ensue. There is, naturally, a trade-off here. Even though trout don't seem to be able to see your leader as well after the sun goes down (or at least seem to ignore it more), their vision in regards to discerning fly patterns is supposedly and evidently more acute. Low light makes it easier for them to inspect the authenticity of intended meals and fly patterns. It is easier for trout to see in low light, than when looking up with the glaring sun as a backdrop. You may well remember many occasions when rising fish at twilight were impossible to fool, even though you caught fish on a variety of non-realistic patterns throughout the day. Much has been made of this fact over generations of anglers, both here and abroad. Apparently, when looking into the sun, trout are easier to fool if you don't scare them with the cast. In low light situations, they don't scare as easily with the cast, but are harder to fool! The smallest of midges often hatch at twilight too, compounding hatch matching problems. It's hard to win sometimes!

This digression is of philosophical interest only to many float fishermen. Since hatches and fish have been encountered throughout the long day, they don't stay out till last light fishing anyway. That can be pushing 11 p.m. in a Northwest mid-summer. By then they're rolling towards the nearest bar & grill!

Another consideration when float fishing on tailwaters and anywhere that calmer waters and spooky trout abound, is the color and design of your boat. It should be somewhat camouflaged, at least blending in with general background colors. If you're not floating whitewater, a lower sided craft will be less visible to trout. For many western waters, the ideal fly fishing boat has yet to be designed. The dories commonly used catch wind, and are higher sided than they need to be. They were designed for Class IV rapids, not placid rivers with spooky trout. Most of the skiffs are too short for my liking. Rafts don't row particularly well. Jon boats are too narrow or lack the features desired. Canoes aren't wholly suitable. Those elements of practicality, rowing ease, casting stability when standing, storage room, low wind resistance, and the beauty associated with classic rowing craft have yet to be combined. Such a craft would be more than a showpiece. It would allow boatmen to position and hold the boat in

ideal casting locations longer and with less effort. This means more effective float fishing.

## SCHOOLING TROUT

Tailwater rivers can show anglers astonishing sights that they will rarely see elsewhere—schools of trout actively rising, cruising, and sipping flies. Up to 100 trout may be feeding together, rising steadily to blanket hatches of small flies. As many times as I've seen it, it still thrills me and kindles those predatory instincts lurking in every angler's soul! These formations of schooling, feeding trout call for the breaking of some traditional fishing strategies.

The classic approach to picking off a number of fish from a pool would be to start with the furthest trout downstream, catch and lead him down, then work up to the next one. With these school feeding trout, the opposite is often the case. They are feeding so close to each other, actually touching and rolling over one another at times, that it's difficult to cast to the most downstream fish without lining and spooking the school. To put the fly far enough in front of one fish, you'd have to drop it on another's head. Instead, you go for the lead fish first, or the one that's closest to your edge of the school, presuming that you're approaching then from the side, out of the boat. Often the largest fish are at the head of the school. You can see the white of their mouth as the boat approaches them. You can even hear their "gulps" as they gobble down flies at an efficient gait. You shoot a slightly downstream reach cast about 6 to 8 feet upstream of the fish when in range, feeding out more slack as necessary to achieve a long drag free drift with your fly. If a big trout takes it, give him half a second to descend before setting the hook, otherwise you'll pull it out of his still open mouth. The larger they are, the slower they tend to rise. Now set the hook firmly but smoothly, not with an erratic jerk. The water will explode and the school scatter. The fight is on! If the food is plentiful, and the hatch thick, the other fish in the school will soon be back. They want to feed, and won't be kept down for long. First you'll see a few come back. Wait till more come though, and they resume steady feeding. Now you can try again, and perhaps work on them for quite a while. Some schools will be better to pull over and wade fish to, while others are better approached from the boat. In either case, it's an exciting game, and a feature of some tail-

*In bright sunlight, casting over a trout's back will often scare it if not executed with perfection. At such times, casting down and across with a slack line reach cast can give better overall results. In low light situations, such as cloud cover, rain, wind riffles, or twilight, the same fish can be cast over repeatedly.*

*Schools of rising trout can be found in eddies, and eddy and scum lines. These trout are holding in a bank eddy and feeding off what the main current brings by, Trico spinners in this case. These particular fish rise all day, every day, from July into November, with few exceptions. This may sound like an exaggeration, but it's not.*

## EDDY LINES

The big eddy lines peeling off from bends in the river, points, and the heads of islands often contain dozens of trout. Most of these are "hot spots" that anglers pull over and wade fish to. If, however, you are making time, the shoreline is deep, or the best riffles are occupied, you will want to work these eddy lines from the boat. Some trout seem to expect danger from the shore side too, where kingfishers, osprey, heron, and eagles lurk in trees, watching for golden opportunities. These particular fish can spook more easily if wade fished to from the shore side, than they do when cast to from a boat or wading in the middle of the river. While many anglers prefer to get out and wade to all fish when possible, others like to pick them off from the boat, especially if it has been a long, full day of fishing already. I personally enjoy rowing skilled fly fishers, and the teamwork involved in picking off sighted fish from the boat. When you are both in sync, it makes for a great fishing comradery. The skills of both parties are involved in the duplicity and capture, and memorable days are shared.

Risers (rising trout) can be tough to spot in these rippling eddy lines, especially if they are mere dimples or quiet "head risers." These rise forms blend easily with the small wavelets bouncing along an eddy line. "Head and tailers" are somewhat easier to see, as more of their bodies are exposed. These fish are usually eating smaller flies, some of which are subsurface. It takes some concentration to constantly locate risers on a broad river in glaring light, but it certainly pays to do so. On the Missouri, I often spend the entire day seeking out and fishing to rising fish. Much time is spent wading, but many fish are targeted from the boat too. Often the most fish are caught after the hatch wanes and trout are looking for leftovers. Their discrimination tends to wane at this point, and a greater variety of patterns are taken. I remember two different guest anglers catching the same 23 inch brown one week along a very shallow bank. Both times the trout was making head rises to the left over Trico spinners, and both times he took much larger flies—an Irresistible and a Parachute Hopper! (In a head rise, the trout slowly sticks his entire head up out of the water to engulf a fly. It is an unhurried motion and quite exciting to see as you can usually look right down the trout's throat from the boat! Most of the fish that do it are larger ones, especially brown trout.)

We make a lot of use of the two fly system in this kind of float fishing to sighted tailwater trout, and these eddy lines are among the best zones. The indicator dry is usually a mayfly dun or Caddis, and the dropper nymph a midge, mayfly, or Caddis emerger. If fish are rising, the nymph is fished just below the surface. If no fish are rising, a heavier nymph and longer tippet between the two flies is fished deeper. Flashbacks, Brassies, San Juan Worms, Scuds, Pheasant Tails, Bead Heads and Soft Hackle Caddis Emergers are favorite wets here.

Fishing one, two, or even more nymphs under a strike indicator is productive during non-hatch periods as well. The length of leader below the indicator, fly pattern combinations, and weight added to the leader are all adjusted till consistent results are achieved. Some anglers get so caught up in this big water nymphing that they quit looking out for rising fish. I often see wading anglers out in the middle of a broad riffle, nymphing it hard, while fish rise steadily behind them near the banks. Both forms of fishing—dry and wet—take concentration and catch fish so sometimes you have to decide what you want to do and work towards that end. If you'd rather fish to rising fish, keep looking for them. If you want to catch fish at any cost, stick to nymphing until steady risers are located by the boatman. Have two

water fisheries.

School risers in big eddies and slackwaters will cruise in obvious directions, randomly switching course, and following lead fish. You can estimate their feeding path and time of arrival, and have your fly waiting for them when they get there. This way you don't have to cast right to them, lessening the chance that you scare them with a false cast, spray, or the final delivery. It's quite amusing to see the school approach your fly, hear their mouths slapping the surface, and see the white of their open maws as they chew their way across the surface to your impostor! When one takes, it'll shake its head in disbelief before tearing off and scattering the school. They'll be back though, to their eddy of plenty. It is trout gluttony at its peak!

These trout can be exasperatingly spooky and picky if the fishing pressure has been on. And the scum and floating weeds torment you and sodden your fly. The boatman may have to pursue these fish around and around a big eddy, to stay within casting range. All in all, it's an exciting game, found only on tailwater rivers and lakes with good hatches and spinner falls.

## PRODUCTIVE TAILWATER ZONES

The key to tailwater success is deciphering the fish holding water. Such zones are on a grand scale and differ from the small stream experiences many anglers are used to. The one general rule that applies to both is that trout will be staying out of the main force of the current, in positions where food is brought to them. On tailwaters this is generally slower water areas off to the side of big channel flows. Here, eyesight and taking the time to look for rising fish, hunting and stalking, pay dividends in the number of big fish hooked. For not only are rising fish to be found, but enough of them that you can wander in search of larger specimens. Though the expression is now trite, it is often said that tailwaters are like giant spring creeks. And so they are.

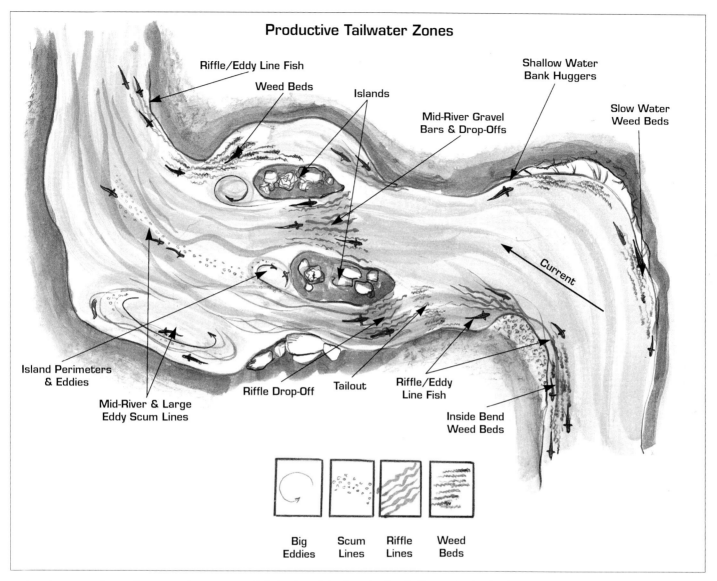

## Productive Tailwater Zones

Riffle/Eddy Line Fish

Weed Beds

Islands

Shallow Water
Bank Huggers

Mid-River Gravel
Bars & Drop-Offs

Slow Water
Weed Beds

Current

Island Perimeters
& Eddies

Mid-River & Large
Eddy Scum Lines

Riffle Drop-Off

Tailout

Riffle/Eddy
Line Fish

Inside Bend
Weed Beds

| Big Eddies | Scum Lines | Riffle Lines | Weed Beds |

rods set up, one for each use, and you can switch back and forth throughout the day. If you want to work these eddy lines quickly, as you float down the river, trying running streamers or crayfish patterns through them. Cast into the eddy and strip the fly back through the width of the eddy line. This is a classic western float fishing technique that accounts for a lot of big fish every season. As discussed previously, the two anglers in the boat can mix up techniques to offer the fish a variety and sum up their disposition. The bow man could work a two fly system, while the stern caster weilds a streamer. I often use a brown Woolly Bugger or brown mottled streamer, as I think the fish could take them for either sculpin or crayfish. If the action is slow, don't be afraid to experiment.

If you know a big hatch is coming up soon, one of these giant eddy lines is a good place to pull over and wait for it to start. Fish often line up just on the shore side of the eddy to rise when it comes off. Fish will move into the riffle itself if the hatch is thick, sometimes disregarding the angler's presence. Before the hatch, you can nymph with pre-emergent patterns, switching to emergers and dries when the fish say to. When a hatch is going full bore, fish will keep rising despite a few of their party being caught and the thrashing of an angler. This is one of the trout's prime feeding zones, and when chow is on, they'll be there come what may. Many trout learn to avoid leaders and anything suspicious while continuing to rise. Most of them make mistakes sometimes though, and many fishermen revel

in the challenge of schools of selective risers. When guiding, I'll often anchor below such a riffle line, fix up a bite to eat, and wait out the hatch for a fine session of fishing. This also gives you a chance to look over the entire scenario more closely, as trout can be found rising to leftovers throughout the day. They can be hard to spot when floating, but by stopping and walking around, some can usually be located along quiet edgewaters, eddies, tailouts, and in the eddy line.

It is noteworthy to consider how many large trout will occupy these shallow, rippling eddy lines, even in the mid-day sun. A friend of mine recently caught a 27 inch brown on a small Parachute Adams in such a location. Big trout will hang in the very shallow water inside the eddy line too, where it is quiet and less than a foot deep. Experiences in Montana and New Zealand have repeatedly shown me that brown trout especially don't seem to care about the depth of water they're laying in, if unharried. Certainly they will be flushed out, usually by anglers not looking at water before they wade through it. But left in peace, they will return to the shallows to feed and rest, where they don't have to fight the current and food is always close at hand.

Browns and rainbows in the 18 to 24 inch class are frequently caught in these eddy lies and shallows. They require cautious stalking and delicate presentations. Small match the hatch patterns are often necessary. It is amusing though, how many of them will go for big attractor patterns from time to time, especially if laying out in the ripples, when everyone else is matching the hatch. I've seen many big fish come up to blast a #12 Humpy when Tricos coated the river. Often this occurred with anglers who had poor vision. They refused to fish with minute match the hatch patterns, and were occasionally rewarded with larger than average fish during the hatch. Every river is different, but it can be fun to experiment with "non-match the hatch" tactics, just for the heck of it. The general trend, necessitated by fishing pressure, is towards smaller flies. But some fish are still thinking big when it comes to relieving hunger!

## Foam Pools and Scum Lines

"Where there's foam, there's fish," the old saying goes. This is most always true, especially on tailwaters. Huge eddies as big as ponds gather up mats of floating weeds and "scum," as river-borne foam is often referred to. Big eddy lines and converging currents can produce scum lines that wander down the middle or side of the river considerable distances.

*What looks like a big foam line here is actually a solid lane of* Trico *spinners! This is a daily occurrence from July into September, in mid to late morning. Yes, there are trout feeding on them!*

Wherever such foam lines are found, so too can trout be spotted. Often schools of fish will cruise them. Since many leftover insects, both duns and spinners, get caught up in them, food for trout is always available. There may be little rising going on along much of the river, but in scum lines and eddies, the rise still goes on.

The biggest challenge with such foam and weed conglomerations is the scum itself. Your fly gets matted almost every cast, unless a fish takes. The trick is in the timing of your cast. Ideally you want to target a fish that's out in a clear patch of water, free of weed. In many cases, trout will be cruising in and out of scum concentrations while gathering food.

What I try to do is continuously false cast until a fish (or school) looks like it's heading for a weed-free zone. By doing this with a shortened line, you'll keep your dry fly weed-free, dry, and high floating. Then, anticipate the trout's feeding path and quickly drop your fly in open water just before it gets there. At this point, a twitch added to your fly's drift will often cause the trout to pick it out from amongst the other food items riding the currents. Sometimes drop-

ping a fly very lightly in a scum line trout's field of vision will get it to pounce on the fly. Other times he may see the line in the air, or be otherwise scared off by the fly's descent. I often use floating scum as camouflage for my cast, making it while the trout ducks some floating weeds, and having the fly waiting for him when he comes up for a look in clear water.

Scum risers can be annoying if they're picky and spooky, since you'll often have to de-weed your fly and deal with contrary eddy currents. They are targets though, and ones that rise much of the day. If a hatch is on and rising fish can be found in scum-free locations, I'd rather abandon the scum risers for easier pickings elsewhere.

## Edgewaters

Very shallow edgewaters, some completely devoid of cover, are interesting holding positions of feeding trout in rich tailwater rivers. When a prolific hatch or spinner fall is on, many trout—and quite large ones—will slide over into these edgewaters to a favored feeding position. Here they have little current to fight, and plenty of struggling morsels to eat come their way. With barely enough water to cover their backs, they rise steadily, keeping an eye out for predators. These trout can be most amusing to spot and pick off from a boat, or get out and wade to. They are often very touchy about being approached from the bank side and cast to from behind.

Baetis *mayfly duns have been concentrated in this edgewater by afternoon breezes. Trout move into non-descript edgewaters like this, rising to the occasion. Wind-free banks will show you surface-feeding fish.*

These are definitely "far and fine" trout. A downstream, fly first presentation, aided by a slack line reach cast is usually in order. You'll be casting across the current into calmer, shallow bank water, to trout highly attuned to any suspicious movement—be it in the air or dragging across the water. And when you trick one as he casually sips away...get ready for a hot reaction! Good sized fish duped in the shallows can be expected to dash for cover, sizzling across the flats to deeper water mid-river. These are definitely among the most exciting trout you'll catch. Be prepared to let them run. Your reel should be able to feed out line smoothly and at a high rate. If they run right at you on their way to the depths, you'd better be ready to strip line in fast, and then prepare to feed it out again as they go by. Once out in the current, catapulting jumps are likely. Good line control through-

*A trout laying in the shallows has just taken, expect such fish to make fast runs for mid-river. Let them. Here is where good quality reels, that can pay out line fast, are a boon to the angler. Can your reel allow a big trout to run out 100 feet of line terminating in a strained and knotted 6X tippet in a matter of seconds? That is the definition of a good trout reel.*

out the fight is necessary, especially with light tippet to 7X and hot fish. Such edgewater fish can be found throughout the day by the observant, as they pick off leftovers from hatches and terrestrials.

## INSIDE BENDS

Tailwater rivers have other characteristics and zones that differ from freestone rivers. Most of your freestone river casting will be blind, and to obvious pocket water, undercut banks, rocks, and eddy lines; broad tailwater rivers have less conspicuous holding zones. Again, keeping a keen eye out for subtle risers can be the key to success.

Perhaps the first zone you'd overlook, especially if you were weaned on smaller trout streams, would be the shallower, slower, "inside" of a bend. The undercut outer bend might be more likely to draw your initial attention. While there will be fish along the cover of an outside bend on a tailwater, there will often be many more fish scattered across the inside bend—and steady rising ones too! Inside bends have slower currents, where trailing weed beds grow profusely, providing food and shelter for dozens of trout. When a hatch is on, you will see many trout working steadily. They don't tend to "school up" here, as they often do in eddies and eddy lines. Instead, they're fanned out over larger areas, ideal places to park the boat, wade and fish for extended sessions. If too deep for wading, they can be pursued from the boat. Since the current will be slow to moderately paced, the boatman will have no problem bringing the boat to a standstill to work on individual fish, one at a time. The fishermen will probably need to take turns on fish for the best results, and to keep bedlam from dominating. If there are enough fish spread around, the casters could then pick different targets and both fish at once. They won't want to both cast at the same fish though.

These trout rising among the weed beds of an inside bend can be among the most selective of the river. They will see less diversity than a bank feeder will, and will be able to see your offerings well in the slower, smooth currents. The myriad surface eddies that waving,

*The inside bend of a tailwater river can support expansive weed beds and dozens of hatch-oriented trout. These shallow, slow water areas provide classic "match the hatch" fishing.*

submerged weed beds throw off make dead drift presentations more difficult than first imagined. You'll want to have a selection of flies representing the various stages of every hatch you're likely to encounter. These are the fish that will test your patience! You'll need nymphs, emergers, duns of various types, and spinners. These trout see so many of the naturals going by, that they get into a rut eating them, and refuse a lot of imitations thrown their way. One day they can be exasperatingly difficult, and the next day semi-gullible. Thank God for the days that they're actually easy! On such days they might be fools for Hoppers, Caddis, Emergers dragged through the currents, or might just love your fly pattern. Don't let it shore your ego up too much though, for surely their simple minds will tear it down again soon!

In non-hatch periods, these inside bends and their waving beds of weeds can look barren and lifeless without rising fish. They are productive if you systematically wade fish them with indicator nymphs, S.J. Worms, and the like. When floating through them, the two fly system again works well. You might need a longer piece of tippet between your indicator dry fly and the nymph, to keep the wet fly just above the weed beds—say 2 to 4 feet of 4X to 5X. Some good

*A fisherman has anchored in an "inside bend" flats. He's wandering the weed beds in search of rising trout which are sprinkled throughout the area. The PMD's will be hatching soon!*

combinations include Caddis dries with Caddis emerger droppers; mayfly dun dries (Parachutes are good, the trout can mistake them for spent wings) with various nymphs, or even Hoppers with S.J. Worm droppers (a "killing" combination at times!). Straight forward indicator nymph or "worm" fishing is a good choice too, perhaps with extra weight added to the leader. A long drag free float can be achieved out of the boat as you travel near current speed. Beginners can catch selective trout this way. Your choice will likely depend on the current hatches, whether terrestrials are important, and what the hot patterns of the day are. The two anglers in the boat can experiment to find the best combinations. There are times when some new pattern will interest fish that have been hammered with the same old flies, these fish also eat scuds, damselfly nymphs, crayfish, leeches, and other life forms. Even after a hatch or spinner fall is over, cripples and leftovers will still be trickling down the river, getting caught up in weed beds, keeping the occasional surface-oriented trout rising. In any case, these inside bends are among the most productive areas of a tailwater river, and fish can be taken from them throughout the day, wet or dry, wading or floating, depending on what their aquatic insect neighbors are up to. In this water of 1 to 4 feet of depth, trout can sometimes be spotted underwater as well, and targeted. It is premium tailwater territory.

# Island Systems

Islands and the system of gravel bars and drop-offs often associated with them tend to be hot spots on tailwater rivers. Large populations of trout take up residence and move into feeding lies upstream, beside, and downstream of islands.

On the upstream side of an island is usually a tailout from a preceding run or pool. The river gradually shallows up as it reaches the head of the island. The current slows down to a good fish holding velocity. This often wadable shoal area can be laced with weed beds. Trout tend to be scattered widely in good numbers, and are avid risers at hatch time. As you float towards an island, especially if the river is widening, take a close look around for risers. A widening river here usually means that there will be tailout flats that are worth stopping to look at and fish. If a hatch is on, be prepared to anchor

and wade-fish to steady, selective risers. If no hatch is on, you can slowly float fish your way through this area with a two fly system, or strike indicator nymph, scud, or S.J. Worm. Streamer or crayfish patterns tempt some fish too. These weedy flats are much like the inside bends discussed previously.

As the water peels off both sides of the island, rippling eddy lines are created. These are prime feeding areas for fish and favorite stopping points for drifting anglers. Schools or individual trout are found in these eddy lines and in the eddy along the edge of the island. In non-hatch periods, they are good places to explore with nymphs and streamers. When float fishing such eddy lines, the rower will slow the boat as much as possible, while the anglers repeatedly cover the water with dry flies or wets. At the same time they should all be watching for rising fish in the eddy along the island's bank, and perhaps along the true river bank too. If some rises are seen, the boat can be pulled over below them, and the fish can be stalked.

Island systems often have gravel bars associated with them, that can run all the way across the river. Besides the eddy line peeling off the island itself, there can be a riffle drop-off running from the head of the island all the way to the shore. Fish move up into these riffles to feed during a hatch, and linger there if undisturbed. Aquatic insects flourish in such riffle water. Fish root around for the insects there at all times. Many people seem to think of riffles as being swift water, this is not really the case though. Riffles are where the main force of the current loses its velocity, slowing down against shallow gravel bars, allowing fish to hold easily and feed. Many trout feel secure beneath the broken, choppy surface of a riffle. It offers them camouflage from overhead predators like kingfishers and osprey. On broad, open tailwater rivers, this cover often substitutes for overhanging trees, boulders, or other cover anglers associate with smaller freestone rivers.

The tail of an island usually has drop-offs, converging currents, and often a large eddy behind it or along the river's true bank. The drop-off and converging currents are excellent nymphing locations when no hatch is in progress. You may need to add extra weight to get your nymph down near the bottom, which can be quite deep. The eddies behind the island might show you schools or individual rising fish during a hatch. Since leftover insects collect in such eddies, fish often rise there long after the hatch has waned. Anglers who constantly keep their eye out for risers will score on such fish throughout the day. If the eddies are deep, you can pursue these fish from the boat. They often cruise the eddies, so you may have to fol-

*Island systems present an assortment of possibilities to floating and wade fishermen.*

low them around to keep in the best casting position. If the eddy is small and shallow, and streamside foliage allows, pull over and wade fish. As twilight approaches, big eddies can draw enough rising trout to keep you busy till dark, as can the drop-offs above and around the island.

The small side channels running around islands attract trout. It seems as though trout prefer this more intimate setting when they can get it on a big river. The current is a little slower, cover closer at hand, and feeding lies are plentiful. During spawning season, these sites are used heavily by fish if they are swift, and gravelly. Anglers should be aware of spawning fish, and not walk through their redds or nests, and not fish to them. Unfortunately, many fishermen can't resist the sight of big fish lying in open, shallow water, and harass them through the day. Others with no apparent powers of observation, walk right through these redds, as fish often lay eggs in the same place you would wade through if crossing from the bank to an island. If you're fishing a river in spring or fall, and you see hollowed-out depressions, with fresh gravel showing through the algae covered streambed, suspect that they are redds. These are usually in 1 to 5 feet of swift, gravelly water, and common around islands. Leave these fish to spawn in peace so there will be fishing in the future. They are the key to maintaining the fishery, and there is little challenge or reason to harass them. Flies do cause mortality in trout, especially ones that are already stressed from spawning. If a tailwater has good tributaries feeding it, many or most of the resident fish will use the feeder streams to spawn in, rather than the main river itself. Fish and Game Departments are wising up, and closing spawning areas at the proper times to allow trout to spawn in peace.

When floating down the river and a small side channel presents itself (especially a short one), it's best to pull over and wade fish it. This not only allows you better fishing coverage, but if a wade fisher happens to already be in the side channel fishing his way up, you won't ruin it for him. Floaters need to be considerate and conscious of wade fishers, and alert to hidden spots where they could be. If a channel isn't big enough for a boat to pass a wader in comfort, i.e. without ruining his fishing and peace of mind, think twice about floating it.

# FISHING THE BANKS

Fishing to the banks on a tailwater river can be quite different than it is along freestone rivers. The currents are generally slower in a tailwater, and there can be less structure along the shores. Much of the shoreline is shallow, gravel-bottomed, and lacking in cover in the traditional sense. There might not be any rocks or over-hanging trees, and the water might only be inches deep and almost still. There can be weed beds growing here, the kind damselflies land on and trout lounge beside. On tailwaters, such banks hold fish.

Since tailwaters have prolific hatches of small flies, trout will slide over to these shallow banks to feed on them, where they don't have to fight the current. Schools of trout will even occupy these shallow edgewaters, finning under the mid-day sun, sipping for hours. It takes a lot of small flies to fill up mature tailwater trout, so they spend a lot of time rising. They're a little twitchy here, they know they're easy prey for heron and kingfishers. Poor casts will run them back out to the depths. You'll see the wakes of fleeing fish as they bolt from the edgewaters. Precision casting and delicate presentations are in order.

Some of the largest trout to be found rising will be in these shal-lowest of locations too. In many cases the larger rising trout will be in the shallowest water, and the fish will get progressively smaller as the water gets deeper, swifter, and further away from shore. This is a tailwater version of the biggest fish taking the best feeding positions, which in this case is the slow, shallow, fly-covered edgewaters.

These are the fish that newcomers to the scene wade through. They'll walk right through them without even looking, figuring all the fish are out in the middle. They'll walk up the bank causing wakes to shoot out in every direction and think nothing of it. Any shallow, calm water in a tailwater river is likely to hold feeding fish. You must use your eyes to locate them. Look up and down the banks for several minutes, regardless of how promising the water looks to you. There will likely be rising fish in view. Do this before you wade blindly out into the river.

From a boat, you can locate these open bank feeders and pick them off. Many of these fish are hard to catch from the shore. They can be right up against the grass or gravel, where it's hard to get any kind of drag free drift into them. The shore catches your fly line. Such bank huggers are very wary about any movement coming from the shore side too, that is where predatory birds are most likely to come from. You can try them from directly downstream. If that spooks them, fishing from the middle of the river into the shore can be the best route. This is yet another case where the slack line reach cast will be necessary to deceive these fish. The boatman can hold the boat in the current while you work on them. He can anchor the boat too, though sometimes the sound of the anchor hitting and grating on the bottom will scare fish. If the river is shallow enough at this point, anglers can bail out of the craft and wade to the trout from the outside. Lastly, you can pull over the boat below the fish, and take your cautious time in wading up and out to an ideal casting position. They are easily scared by waves you emit when wading and sounds your feet make in the gravel. If there is a school of trout rising, this can be your best choice. I do like picking off the odd bank feeder from the boat though, stalking them throughout the day like any other predator would.

Besides these shallow non-descript banks, there will be more traditional banks to fish also. Some will be swift and rocky, others over-hung with willows and swarms of caddis, and still others deep and lake-like. Along all these banks there will be fish that are used to routinely eating small flies, but that also dine on terrestrials, caddis, damselflies, crayfish, and minnows. All of these food items are common to the quieter water, weed beds, streamside bushes, and cover of river banks. What we do when fishing the banks of the Missouri for instance, is keep two rods rigged, switching as the situation mandates. If no rising fish are present, we might fish Hoppers or Damselflies mid-day, Caddis dries with Caddis emerger droppers in the evening, or Brown Woolly Buggers just for the heck of it. If we see some upcoming rising fish working on a particular hatch, we'll switch to a rod with a small match the hatch pattern on it, as these fish may be somewhat picky. If the hatch is on the wane, the same fish might start going for a broader variety of reasonable patterns. Though they were feeding on *Tricos* or *Baetis* steadily, they might now fall for more visible Parachute Adams or H&L Variants in the #18-14 size range. These are patterns you can see, but that still catch fish focusing on smaller flies. We might also fish a two fly system with a nymph, emerger, or second smaller dry as the dropper. Most of these fish will gladly suck in a nymph that comes within range.

The swifter the water is along the banks, the more likely trout will rise for larger patterns. We've certainly had many good days fishing big attractor patterns on tailwater rivers. But with increasing fishing pressure, this is usually less productive now than it was in the old days. Still, hungry fish do come up for Wulffs, Hoppers, and

Humpies, they continue to catch fish world-wide. Black Crickets are good choices too, few people fish them. If damselflies are abundant on the river, they add an exciting variation to your fly pattern choice. Takes to damselfly adults are often savage, even more so than to Hoppers. Cicada patterns are killers when these insects are in a heavy emergence year. Experimentation is half the fun, so if nothing traditional seems to be working steadily, try some deviant measures. Skid your dry fly across the surface. Fish two fly rigs wet that imitate a larger minnow chasing a smaller one or a crayfish. Fish emergers on the drag. The takes can be sensational.

If you have never fished tailwater rivers before, you will find them to present new and unusual challenges. The fish populations and average size are high, so too are the numbers of fishermen pursuing them on these consistently productive waters. You'll need to think small in terms of general fly patterns, and cast accurately. Your line control and ability to attain long drag free floats should be practiced to perfection. Your whole line of thinking may have to change if you are used to swift freestone rivers and trout that are gung-ho for attractor patterns. But if you're looking for good "match the hatch" action with selective larger trout, give the tailwaters a crack.

*It is better to pull over and wade fish small side channels. If there happens to be a wade fisher already there you won't have ruined their peace of mind by unnecessarily floating through "their" water.*

*Tailwaters offer year-round fishing opportunities and big trout to die-hard anglers.*

*Large capacity nets with long handles are desirable for float fishing.*

# 8. Fighting and Netting Fish

The first difference you'll notice when you've hooked a fish from the boat, is that the initial first run is often right at you. Since anglers are generally casting towards banks from the middle of the river, and since the trout are most likely to seek safety in the depths after being fooled, expect a bank hugger's initial run to be your way. This doesn't happen nearly as often when wade fishing, so you'll want to be mentally prepared to strip in line rapidly after the take when fishing from a boat. Sometimes trout will run straight at, under, and then beyond the boat. The fisherman will have to strip in line very quickly to keep up with the fish, and then feed it back out again as the trout heads out to sea.

The rower has an important part to play here, as he does in most facets of float fishing. He can make the difference between whether fish are hooked, landed, or lost. An experienced boatman will know that trout are likely to rush out towards mid-river, and will promptly pivot the craft and start backing across river after the hook is set. He will gauge the power of his backstrokes by the behavior of the fish, trying to keep the angler in the best fighting position. Since a fish running right at you and then wallowing under the boat isn't much of a fight, the rower can keep the fight exciting by keeping boat pressure on the fish. He will row away from it at just the right pace, knowing when to let up or accelerate. Another option is to quickly land the boat, and let the angler play it from shore, especially if it is a large specimen. Many fishermen prefer this when possible, as the effect of fighting a fish and the current is more dramatic than floating at current speed and fighting only the fish.

I think that pulling over to fight out the battle from shore presents a couple of minor potential problems. If the angler is agile and his line is under control, it's fine. He can leap out of the boat and not miss a beat. If, on the other hand, the angler is less athletic, encumbered by waders, and has fly line tangled about the boat, his exit might be a weak point in the battle. He might stumble out of the boat, lose total line control, or otherwise be out of touch with the fish at a critical moment. If a big fish is being fought on light tippet and a small fly, this is doubly fraught with failure. I see it as the angler's choice though. He can make his own decision after taking the boatman's advice.

I have noticed one other possible cause of fish loss when pulling over to fight trout. This only goes for cases where you land on the same bank that the fish was hooked along. Since you hooked the trout from one angle, as you floated the middle casting to the banks, and since now you have switched positions with the fish—it in the middle and you on its bank—the relation of the line pull on the hook has changed 180 degrees. You hooked it from one direction, and now you're pulling against the hook in the opposite direction. It seems to me that this occasionally causes fish to come unhooked. It's hard to verify, but I think a higher percentage of hook pull-outs occur when you switch angles of the fight 180 degrees.

If you land on the opposite bank from which you hooked the fish, there is no problem. You maintain the same angle of tension on the hook throughout the fight, or maybe even improve upon it if the boat is manipulated properly. The best angle to hook and keep a fish hooked is from across, to directly downstream of the trout. The boatman can work to maintain this ideal fighting angle when possible, following the fish downstream if necessary, before landing to finish off the fight. Wading anglers on swift rivers are often in the dilemma of having a good fish run downstream in a heavy current and then having to pull the fish back upstream, especially if they can't follow the fish down the banks. This causes the loss of many fish, as the angle of tension on the hook has likely changed, and it takes much longer to pull a fish up against the current, even if it were dead. The fly frequently pops out of the trout's mouth in such cases. The longer this kind of battle goes on, the more likely it is to occur. With a boat, you can follow a fish downstream, and pull over to fight it, if desired, from a location where the odds are on the angler's side, not the fish's.

All fish cast to aren't bank huggers though, and all of them don't race straight at the boat. Many will jump and thrash around banks and try to dive under them for cover, others will be in position to race directly away from the boat. In either case, the angler without the fish on should get his line out of the water and cease casting till the fight's over. This will eliminate possible tangles between the rods at critical moments. If the boat is anchored, you'll have to try to make sure the fish doesn't get tangled in the rope, or pull up the anchor during the fight. Both the angler with the fish on and the boatman will have to avoid getting the fly line caught in the oars, especially if a hasty maneuver is underway. I often have to pull an oar in as a fish circles the boat or races under it. Many fish seek sanctuary under the boat towards the end of a fight. Fishermen should try

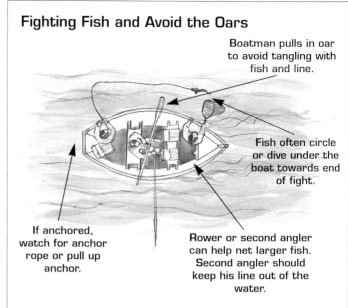

## Fighting Fish and Avoid the Oars

Boatman pulls in oar to avoid tangling with fish and line.

Fish often circle or dive under the boat towards end of fight.

If anchored, watch for anchor rope or pull up anchor.

Rower or second angler can help net larger fish. Second angler should keep his line out of the water.

The rower may have to pull in his oars when a trout gets near the boat at the end of a fight. Many fish will dive under the boat for refuge. Watch out for the anchor rope.

to get the fish on the reel as soon as possible, so as not to tangle with any equipment that might be cluttering up the boat. When a fish does rush right at the boat, you might not be able to reel in fast enough, making stripping necessary. After that though, try to wind up excess line and stay tangle free. Beware of any rough edges on the boat if the fish dives under it. In the final stages of the fight, the oars remain a concern, if the rower has to maintain a position in the river, or avoid obstacles. The trout may circle and hide beneath the boat prior to netting.

In some cases we (boatmen) even set the hook by manipulating the boat! Some anglers we guide have poor eyesight and slow reactions, especially when fishing smaller flies in quieter waters that don't set the hook for you. They repeatedly set the hook too late to engage the fish. When this happens, we carefully watch their fly, and backstroke vigorously when a trout rises to it. We attempt to set the hook with the boat's momentum, before the angler sees or reacts to the rise. It's an amusing process, but the effort is worthwhile when trying to maximize a guest's pleasure during a trip. For many people the number of fish caught is the sole gauge of a trip's success. Doing everything you can to beat the odds is part of the game.

The netting process should be simple. A long handled, large capacity net should be on hand, preferably one with soft mesh that doesn't scratch up fish. If the trout is a large and lively one, either the rower or second angler might want to net it for the fisherman. The rower can glide along at river speed (not back row) so the angler isn't fighting the current at the critical landing stage, rowing only to keep the angler in the best position to net the fish. Trout should be played quickly and effectively, and not for too long. Get them to the net with some life left in them, not belly up. The trout should be led over the net head first, not scooped up tail first. The latter method causes the loss of many fish. Nets that are too small, or that have short handles can be problematic when float fishing, making it hard to reach the fish and land it. Repeated scoops often end up knocking the fish off the line.

You can also land trout with no net. I find it best to kneel down on the bottom of the boat, lean over the side, and if possible, unhook the fish without touching it with forceps. Barbless hooks make this fish's eye level, not the angler's. The fish look bigger this way. A big fish can look surprisingly small in a photo taken at the angler's eye level. Hold the fish out towards the camera a bit, but not in an exaggerated fashion. Using a wide angle lens will exaggerate the size of the fish in relation to the angler if taken at fish eye level, and keep both in focus. Crop closely and eliminate wasted space in the composition. You don't need the angler's feet and the mid-day sun overhead. Fill the frame with the angler's face, upper body, and fish. If the angler is wearing a hat, as they usually do, use a flash. When shooting on sunny days, make sure the sun isn't reflecting off the fish's side into the lens. Light cloud cover gives the best conditions for fish photography, as glare and shadows are reduced. Take some action and scenic shots along the way too. I find that many people don't take as many photos as they intended to by the end of a trip, waiting too long for perfect shots. If you want memories, shoot along the way, capturing all the facets and elements of a trip—put-ins, people, boats, scenery, action, fish, shore lunches, still lifes, aquatic insects, and various angles of the river. In the long run, you'll be glad you shot the extra film, to enhance your memories down long fishless roads.

*When photographing anglers with fish, crop closely, and try to position the lens at the fish's eye level. Hold trout over the water briefly for photos, then return them immediately.*

*Long handled, large volume nets are ideal for float fishing. Expect trout to make last second dives under and around the boat! The rower may have to pull in the oars.*

an easier process. If you do have to touch the fish, try this. Roll the fish over on its back, horizontally while still in the water. This usually pacifies trout, making it less of a struggle when unhooking them. Handle them gently without squeezing. Let them recover for a moment before releasing.

A lot of people like to take photos before releasing trout. This can put a lot of stress on a fish, and cause injury if dropped in the boat. The best way to do it when float fishing is to keep the fish in the water until cameras are ready to shoot. The second angler who's acting as photographer and the fisherman can kneel down in the boat, leaning over the side. The fish can then be held up over the water, not over the boat, while the boatman keeps the oar out of the picture. If the fish flops free, as they often do, it will land in the water and not bounce around the boat. Do this quickly and efficiently, and put the fish back in the water to breathe between multiple shots. You could also beach the boat to take photos, keeping the fish in the net and water until you're ready. Keep the trout in the water as much as possible, and handle it as little as possible with pre-wetted hands. Take the photos while standing in knee deep water. Trout are less panicky this way, and less subject to injury if you drop them.

Here are more photo tips: Take catch and release photos at the

9. Unhooking Yourself

**Above:** *Wrapped! These float fishermen flipped a rental raft and lodged it on this boulder. If passing parties hadn't stopped to help them, it might still be there! The river applies tons of pressure to craft in this position. Be cautious when floating, especially at high water and if you don't know what your rower's experience level is.*

**Left:** *When the perfect days come, be sure to revel in them.*

Human hook-ups are common when fly fishing, and even more so when float fishing. Three people in close proximity can eventually lead to a flesh wound. I'm pretty good at ducking as I usually spot bad casts in the making and dive for cover. The wind can always buffet your cast unexpectedly though. Other typical causes of human hook-ups include starting your back cast with too much slack on the water; not making your back cast high enough and thus catching someone on your forward delivery; setting the hook violently with the rod tip and yanking your line and fly back into the boat; rushing a cast or switching casting directions radically to hurry a cast to a hot spot; and getting tired. Any time you lose sight of the special casting requirements of float fishing, tangles and flesh wounds will eventually occur.

The best technique I'm aware of for releasing a humanoid, is as follows: Get yourself a couple feet of heavy

## Unhooking Yourself

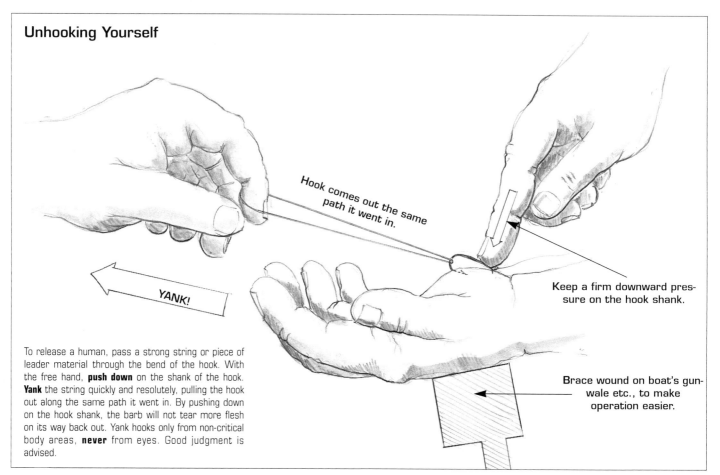

Hook comes out the same path it went in.

YANK!

Keep a firm downward pressure on the hook shank.

To release a human, pass a strong string or piece of leader material through the bend of the hook. With the free hand, **push down** on the shank of the hook. **Yank** the string quickly and resolutely, pulling the hook out along the same path it went in. By pushing down on the hook shank, the barb will not tear more flesh on its way back out. Yank hooks only from non-critical body areas, **never** from eyes. Good judgment is advised.

Brace wound on boat's gunwale etc., to make operation easier.

leader material, say 10 to 15 pound test, run the leader around the bend of the hook and grasp it firmly with one hand. You will be pulling the hook out along the exact same path it went in. With your free hand, push down gently but firmly on the hook eye and shank. The hook should remain in a vertical position and not roll over to its side. The victim at this point should be in a position to stabilize himself. If the hook is in his hand, have him put it on the gunwale of the boat. When the victim is stabilized, and the de-hooking party set, you're ready for action. If the hooked party is nervous, have him look the other way. Tell him you're going to yank it out on the count of three, but yank it on the count of two!

When the hook is yanked out, make sure that downward pressure is kept on the hook eye and shank. This forces the hook to exit by the same path it went in, instead of the barb tearing new flesh, as would otherwise be the case. When you yank on the leader which is looped through the bend of the hook, yank it fast and hard—a clean jerk. You don't want to be timid or pull it slowly.

This method is usually painless, and many of these puncture wounds don't even bleed. With small hooks, you can hardly see any damage. Compared to the old methods of pushing the hook all the way through so you can cut off the barb, or just grabbing it with pliers and slowly and painfully twisting it out, the leader yank method is a blessing. Naturally, you will want to clean the wound and dress it with an anti-bacterial cream, and a bandage if necessary.

There are situations where it's not so easy. Soft flesh like an ear lobe is a little trickier to work with. A big barbed hook stuck through the cartilage of the nose or very near the eye requires second thoughts. You might want to let a physician handle it. If by some terrible misfortune someone is actually hooked in the eye, never attempt to unhook it! Snip the leader off and cover both eyes with a sterile dressing, to block out all light. This keeps the eyes from mov-ing, which can cause greater pain and damage. They should be covered loosely so as not to put pressure on the wound. The victim should be transported on his back immediately to the nearest eye specialist or hospital. Waste no time. Nothing else matters.

Fortunately, I and no other guide I know, have had to deal with a serious eye injury. You'll notice most guides never take off their sunglasses, for the protection reason alone. Wearing hats, sunglasses, and long sleeve shirts will help deflect hooks, and the sun's corrosive rays. Using barbless hooks will make unhooking both fish and anglers easier. A First Aid kit should always be on board to handle a variety of cuts, wounds, insect bites, headaches, colds, sunburn, upset stomachs, allergies, plus any special considerations a party member might have. You can be a long way from help on some float trips and self-sufficiency is a desirable attribute. A few other safety items to have on board include matches and fire starter in case of cold wet weather and hypothermia, raingear for the same reason, food and water (especially if it's very hot and dehydrating), flashlights, and clothes to match the season. Life jackets of course are a necessity and legally required. I might add at this point, if someone invites you to float a river, and they're novices or you don't trust their judgment, think twice about it! This is especially true if the rivers are high and cold with snow melt, flooding, or if your "friend" seems poorly equipped. I know that in Montana a number of people drown every year, most of them are novices who lack good judgment, the proper equipment, or both. Many go forth on seething high water rivers without life jackets. Alcohol is often an ingredient in such disasters. Use your own judgment whether rowing yourself, or going out with someone whose skills you don't know, on a challenging river. With the price of fishing equipment these days, just the loss of that can be a disaster.

*Early season on the Madison. Though weather and water conditions are a little "iffy," good times and reasonable fishing are still to be had during the pre-run off season on high altitude rivers. Fish can be more "on/off" at this time of year. Some very good days are encountered too.*

# 10. Seasonal Conditions

When's the best time? Where's the best action? Will there be good hatches? These are among the most asked questions a guide or outfitter hears. Those unfamiliar with river and weather patterns in the Rockies can be surprised by the lateness of snow melt or "run off", and the extremes in weather. As hatches and quality fishing experiences are largely dictated by water temperature and conditions, it is worthwhile to have an understanding of the seasonal changes on western rivers.

Before getting too wrapped up in this though, bear in mind that the following information is stated in general terms. The only certainty about mountain conditions is that they'll change. It can be 100 degrees in May and snow in August. It can be surrealistically beautiful in autumn or deadly cold. As most visiting anglers have schedules and set dates for their fishing, being prepared mentally and materially for any eventuality is a must, be it sun, storm, high water, or drought. These are unpredictable and can change in a hurry. Don't take it out on your boatman. Be prepared to adjust techniques and your mental frame to suit the condition at hand. Your chances of seeing a river at its fishing best are small on a single day's excursion.

The float fishing calendar can be divided into three basic periods when it comes to the fishing season: pre-run off, run off, and low water period of late summer/fall. Float fishing goes on in the winter too, as we do get some long warm spells and trout can be found rising and feeding year-round. There is no closed season on many western rivers. Let's look at a typical year on the river.

# THE PRE-RUN OFF PERIOD

The pre-run off period begins at the end of winter, and is really a continuation of low, clear water conditions that have prevailed since the previous summer. Most serious anglers get started in March, and definitely by April. At this time the rivers are usually low, clear, and ice-free. Tailwater rivers are ice-free all winter. It is too cool in the mountains yet for much serious, sustained snow melt which results in high, muddying water. This pre-run off time usually lasts till mid-

*A beautiful pre-run off day on the Madison. Nymphs and wet flies give the most consistent results at this time of year.*

May, at which time high altitude snow fields melt in earnest and freestone rivers begin to rise. Be aware though, that any unseasonally warm period or heavy rain can bring an instant rise in rivers at any time during the pre-run off period. Temperatures can change 30 to 40 degrees from one day to the next. A good report from a couple days ago doesn't insure good conditions today.

For the most part, this pre-run off period will see good water conditions and decent to good fishing. Spring comes later to the Rockies, so the landscapes are a little bleak when it comes to vegetation. Snow-laden mountains and wind swept ranges certainly give one a feeling for the power and majesty of western terrain though. It's a quiet time on the rivers, with fewer people about, and nesting waterfowl animating the shores. In favorable weather, which is a large percentage of the time, it's most beautiful and exhilarating indeed. When the weather bears down hard, you'll feel like crawling into the nearest shelter like a marmot.

As to fishing conditions, water temperatures are low, ranging from the upper thirties to the upper forties. Trout feeding periods can be shorter, and nymphs fished on the bottom will give the most consistent results, especially in March. But western trout are adapted to such conditions, and vigorous, surface feeding, jumping trout are found even when the water is still in the 30s. Midges dominate as food items, especially on tailwater rivers where trout can be found rising in full force to them. Overcast, humid days tend to produce the best hatches and numbers of rising fish. They do hatch on sunny days too, the more humid the better. On freestone streams, little winter stoneflies sometimes bring up fish. These are smaller black and brown stones, matched by #16-10 hooks. When mixed with enough midges, trout may begin to rise. These are the only hatches of consequence until April, though I understand that *Baetis* mayflies emerge on some spring creeks in March. Much of the fishing day will be with wet flies of some sort. On freestone rivers this will include stonefly nymphs, generic nymph patterns such as Hare's Ears and bead heads, Woolly Buggers and Streamers, and San Juan Worms. Midges and midge pupae can be locally important. On the tailwater rivers, productive wets include Midge pupa, smaller streamlined nymphs like Pheasant Tails, Scuds, egg patterns, San Juan Worms, Crayfish, and Streamers. Good fishing is encountered, but there is a lingering chance that winter will roll back down out of Canada.

*A* Baetis *mayfly dun rests on a spring dandelion. These hatch from late April into June, and again from late September through November in our area. The duration of these afternoon hatches makes the* Baetis *family of mayflies (known also as B.W.O. or little Blue-Winged Olives) perhaps the most important in western waters over the course of the season.*

By mid-April things begin to happen. Swallows return to grace the scene. The first mayfly hatches begin in earnest. *Baetis* mayflies are abundant, especially on tailwater rivers and spring creeks, but occur on freestoners as well. These are locally called Blue-Winged Olives, kind of an all-embracing term for any mayfly with an olive toned body and blue, gray, or dun wings. The flies we're referring to are matched by #16-20 patterns, commonly hatching afternoons. The cloudier and more humid it is, the better they hatch. A good *Baetis* hatch can last several hours a day for over a month in the spring, with another generation hatching in late fall. They can be present on area waters four-plus months of the year, making them the top mayfly hatch when it comes to overall duration and fishability.

Not long after the *Baetis* make an appearance, *Rhithrogena*

The western march brown mayfly (Rhithrogena morrisoni) is a wide-spread freestone species, hatching from as early as late February on low altitude waters, into June in the Rockies. As with most spring hatches, it occurs afternoons. It is matched by #12-16 flies, and prefers swift waters. Some tailwaters have march browns too.

Medium size stoneflies start showing up on freestone rivers come April, and sometimes provide fishable hatches.

mayflies show up. These are swifter water mayflies, common to freestone rivers. They do occur on some tailwaters too, the Missouri for instance. This larger, grayish mottled mayfly is commonly called a western march brown. It is matched by #12-16 imitations. Like most spring and autumn hatches, it emerges afternoons, when the water and day have warmed up a bit. There is usually no hurry to get on the river early and late in the season when it comes to hatches.

Small to medium size brown stoneflies are found on freestone rivers at this time of year too. As water levels and temperatures go up, so does the size of the stonefly species emerging. The skwala hatch has become an event in the last few years. This medium size stonefly hatches in April and is the first hatch of big fly to bring up big fish. Number eight to six patterns bombed along banks can provide action similar to the famed salmonfly hatch which is still two months away. These stones aren't as numerous as salmonflies can be, but they hatch at lower, clearer water levels, when it is easier for fish to get on them.

A pre-run off day on a freestone river will feature a possibility of stonefly dry fly action, and perhaps a fishable encounter with a *Rhithrogena, Baetis*, or midge hatch. Expect to fish weighted nymphs and streamers much of the time though, in non-hatch periods. Even if there is a hatch, the fish might not rise to the occasion. Nymphs may provide the only consistent results.

Pre-run off tailwater fishing should give you consistent dry fly fishing during midge and *Baetis* hatches. These are both small flies, and match the hatch patterns plus skilled casting will be needed to get the best results. In non-hatch periods, smaller nymphs, Scuds, and San Juan Worms fished with added weight and strike indicators will be the choice of many experienced anglers. Streamers and crayfish patterns will catch some aggressive fish too. Again, the best hatches are likely to be in the afternoon of overcast days. Light rain and snow are ideal. These flies don't like clear, dry atmospheric conditions to hatch in. I've seen partly cloudy days in spring when bugs came off and fish rose whenever clouds blocked the sun. As soon as the sun peaked out though, the flies and fish disappeared. In long periods of continuously sunny weather, the insects will hatch fairly well. There's a limit to how long they can wait for preferred conditions. Many trout seem reluctant to rise in the sunshine of a spring day too, as if the low angled sun glares too strongly in their eyes, which are used to lounging in the low light depths of a long winter.

The first Caddis hatches also begin in the pre-run off season. They might start out as a sprinkling of flies, but by May larger numbers are seen. The "Mother's Day Hatch" has gained notoriety in the

last decade on a number of Montana freestone rivers, hatching out in blizzards come early May. Most Caddis encountered will be in the #14-16 size range.

# THE RUN OFF

By mid to late May, a strengthening sun begins to beat down across high altitude snow fields. Every creek and coulee is awash with migrant snow water. Freestone rivers begin to rise and sometimes flood. This is the start of the second major float fishing season—the run off.

The run off season means different things to different people. For many anglers it means salmonfly time. It can be a three ring circus on rivers like the Big Hole where salmonflies are prolific. Chasing the salmonfly hatch is such a western tradition that it probably needs no introduction, except to the unborn and urbane. Dozens of boat-towing Suburbans and pick-up trucks rumble down gravel roads, racing from stretch to stretch of river, in hopes of intercepting the hatch. The goal is one of those ultimate fly fishing experiences: large trout gorging themselves on equally huge flies—a full 2 to 3 inches in length. The chance of really hitting the hatch full on, when fish are reckless, numerous, and big, is around 25 percent. Other years see mediocre hatches, flooded rivers, stuffed uneating fish, or some other mysterious combination of elements that produce so-so fishing. Maybe it's too many anglers wanting to be at the same place

Stonefly time! This one inspects an imitation of his nymphal form while riding on my boat. These insects are a full 2-3 inches long.

*Golden stonefly cases gripped on riverside rocks. The hatch has started!*

at the same time. In any case, it's an exuberant gamble coinciding with high water on some of the west's most spectacular freestone rivers. The air is sweet, the landscape's fresh and inspiring, and the streamside greenery drooping under the weight of these lumbering aquatic insects. Salmonfly hatches occur as early as mid-May on some rivers, and run until mid-July on high altitude rivers like the upper Yellowstone.

Run off is also the time when white water enthusiasts hit the rivers running at full bore. If you're a newcomer from the east coast, you'll by now be getting the idea that things are a little different "out west." While late June might be getting into the dog days of summer back east, with its low and warming waters...out west it's more like spring. Rivers can be at their highest level of the year. The weather could be hot, cool, cold, raining, or snowing. I've found that many visiting anglers think that June will be high summer in the Rockies. It's only part-time summer. The other face of June can be temperatures in the 40s to 60s, with the occasional bone-chilling rain storms. There is a definite need to bring warm clothes and rain gear in the high country. Be prepared. If you are rowing your own boat or going out with a novice, be cautious of potentially dangerous high water conditions.

Some other major hatches occur during the run off period too. Golden stoneflies follow the salmonflies by several weeks. These aren't quite as large as salmonflies, but they are big, 1 1/2 to 2 inches in length. They hatch as the water is starting to go down, and in a low water year the river could be clear. This can give superb top water fishing. Golden stones hatch for a longer period than do the salmonflies, and often provide better fishing. They can be around for a couple weeks, where as salmonflies tend to pass in a week or less.

The western green drake and brown drake show up in late June. They can bring up freestone fish if the river's not too high. On controlled flow rivers like the Henry's Fork, the Green Drake has long been rated as one of the best hatches of the season.

A smattering of other high water species including *Epeorus, Paraleptophlebia, Heptagenia,* and *Siphlonurus* models can be found hatching afternoons. Pale Morning Duns begin their seasonal emergence in late June. These hatches can be over-shadowed by salmonflies or golden stones on freestone rivers. High, discolored water can also keep fish from rising to them. The fish may be hugging the bottom and banks, picking off the abundance of nymphs that spring and early summer have to offer. If the river is not bank full and is marginally clear, you might find some afternoon risers to stop and pursue.

Run off doesn't effect all rivers equally though. There are freestone rivers that rise moderately and fish well with nymphs and dries, even if discolored. Then there are the tailwater rivers, clearing tributaries, and spring creeks, running clear with rising fish.

On tailwater rivers, effects of run off vary. Often the river will be unchanged, and the fishing predictably consistent. If it has been a high snow-pack year, power companies may have to release more water from dams to make room for the expected snow melt to come. High water releases from the dam can continue even after the run off

is over in upstream feeders if the lake is overfull. The water will still be clear, but there will be fewer good wading areas and a boat is even more important to success. Some dams maintain steady levels as much as possible, while others fluctuate levels daily to meet power requirements. On tailwaters with steady flows, a major level change to make room for run off water will put the fish off for a day or two, as they readjust. Major releases from dams, of an unusual nature, have effected tailwaters for longer periods too. Trout in tailwaters that fluctuate daily, adjust quickly. You might want to check ahead of time to see what volume of water the dam is releasing and if it is scheduled to change. Tributaries of a tailwater river will likely be high and murky, and can disrupt the fishing from their junction downstream.

The hatches you're likely to encounter will include the midges and possibly *Baetis* continuing from the pre-run off period, plus Pale Morning Duns and Caddis. Green drakes, *E. flavilinea,* brown drakes, *Heptagenia, Siphlonurus, Epeorus,* and *Paraleptophlebia* mayfly species' are encountered on various clear flowing rivers.

*A Pale Morning Dun, (P.M.D.), one of the major mayfly hatches of the west. These are abundant in spring creeks, tailwaters, and freestone rivers. Trout can be very picky when feeding on them. Bring lots of patterns in #22-14! Hatches in most waters start in late June and carry on into July and early August. Some occur evenings too, not mornings as the name would suggest.*

In non-hatch periods, S.J. Worms, Scuds, mayfly and Caddis nymphs and emergers, midge patterns, and streamers all catch fish. Bead Heads have become quite popular as of late. Caddis dries with nymph droppers can be fished under over-hanging willows where Caddis flutter. Riffles, drop-offs, and eddies can be prospected with wets or stalked with dries when a hatch is on, as can the weed bed flats. Hatches will be more likely afternoons and evenings, with the exception of the PMD's and green drakes.

If area freestone rivers are very high and fishing poorly, the tailwaters can get very busy. Anglers flock to them for the consistent fishing, clear water conditions, and rising trout. Be sure to give other anglers plenty of room. Don't crowd in on someone who's having success. If you're moving within a 100 foot radius of another fisherman—you're too damn close! When floating, don't race around and cut off other boats. If you were last to put in, then expect to stay behind the boats that put in earlier. Ethics among fly fishermen have now become among the worst on the river, and many guides set poor examples. The idea is to relax and enjoy our diminishing natural resources, not to compete.

As the high waters of May to late June recede, the third season gets underway. From about mid-July on, all rivers are usually low and clear, and will remain that way (barring a heavy rainstorm) through fall, winter, and into the next spring.

# THE LOW WATER SEASON

The low water season begins as early as late June, but often not until mid-July (geographic location and altitude play major roles.) Water temperatures warm up into the high 50s and 60s, and even the 70s. A medley of hatches proliferate. July gives you many of those picture-perfect days. There's still a mantle of snow in the high mountains for scenic effect. The foliage is bright green, before the dry heat of August browns the hillsides.

On freestone rivers you run across a wide assortment of hatches throughout the day, attractor patterns can work well because of this. Many of the mayfly and Caddis hatches that started up in high water will continue as the river clears. Smaller stoneflies including little brown, green, and yellow ones flutter around in abundance. A potpourri of Caddis mixed with mayfly spinners dominate evening action. Swallows are busy feeding day and night, along with nighthawks and bats. It is surrealistically beautiful along river corridors throughout the west.

Clouds of *Tricos* begin appearing mornings on both freestone and tailwater rivers. This gives some of the most consistent and challenging sport of the season for two months. In non-hatch periods on the freestoners, strike indicator nymphs fished in pocket water, drop-offs, and runs produce very well. Many freestone trout move into swift broken flows as the summer water heats up to its maximum in August and early September.

Terrestrials gain importance in the fish's diet as summer progresses and wanes. Hoppers of course, of every description, cicadas, crickets, spruce and aquatic moths, beetles, and ants are found more frequently in fish's stomachs. Damselflies, craneflies, snails, and bees are consumed too. As summer slips into autumn, there are fewer hatches for trout to feed on overall, so terrestrials make up the difference.

Streamers and larger stonefly nymphs still produce too. Early mornings, during thunderstorms, late evenings, and nights can find larger trout on the prowl for big food items. Summer gives anglers in the boat plenty of opportunities to experiment with various patterns between and during hatches. Fly pattern choice might make a difference not only to the number of fish caught, but also to their average size. On Montana's Smith River for instance, more smaller fish will usually be caught if you match the hatch, while the larger specimens usually go for bigger attractor patterns and wets. Every river will have its own idiosyncrasies.

When water levels on the freestoners drop to their lowest, so does the current speed and number of miles you choose to float in a day. Wade fishing will be ideal. In many cases you won't need waders, and can fish comfortably in shorts. (Be sure to have plenty of sunscreen along plus foul weather gear also). You'll probably want to float a shorter stretch than you might have in June, and get out to wade some productive looking drop-offs, pools, and runs. This takes up more time than you think, and the river doesn't carry you as quickly downstream, so plan your mileage accordingly and have a flashlight onboard in case you don't make it till the stars are blinking around the cottonwoods and pines.

If a hot spell makes the fish sluggish in that mid-August to early September period, you'll want to get out early and fish when the water is at its coolest. Fish can be stacked in swift runs where the aerated water gives them more oxygen. You might catch a morning *Trico* fall, then follow that up with some terrestrial fishing, and deep nymphing in fast runs and pockets. Late evenings can provide another brief flurry of activity. You might experience some slow periods, but the odd fish will usually be found along the way in the heat of the afternoon. A Hopper, Cricket, or Humpy with a medium sized (#12-16), weighted nymph dropper would be a good choice here.

Such hot summer days are very relaxing. You may want to spend a little time in the shade of some cottonwood trees, watching the swallows work, daydreaming, and winding down. Many anglers enjoy an afternoon nap, especially if they're going to be fishing until dark anyway. If the fishing is dead slow, put your time to profitable use eating a long lunch, watching clouds drift over the mountains and patterns the sun creates among cottonwood leaves. Listen to the river sweep by. For a lot of people these are even rarer moments than those they get to spend fishing. Don't whine about slow fishing, enjoy the total relaxation it can provide you.

The low water period on tailwater rivers will not be such a dramatic change from the run off as it is on a freestoner. There will be less diversity in tailwater hatches, but they occur in great numbers for long periods. The PMD's that started in late June will continue into August. *Tricos* will be out in force mornings, from July into September. Caddis are abundant afternoons and evenings. Terrestrials work well here too. Deep nymphing with mayfly, Caddis, Scud, and S.J. Worm patterns produces in non-hatch hours. Come mid-

*Left: Little brown, yellow, and green stoneflies frolic along freestone rivers as water levels settle down into their mid-summer banks.*
*Below: Clouds of* Trico *spinners greet the mid-summer angler come morning. Skilled fishermen love the challenge these tiny #24-18 mayflies offer daily, for two months of the season.*

*Another trout falls for a Hopper! Don't they ever learn? Terrestrials make up a large percentage of a trout's diet in mid to late summer.*

*Putting slow fishing times to good use.*

trout can get a little more gung-ho. The cooling water temperatures jibe with their metabolism better, and there are less food items about for them to choose from. We like to think that trout know winter's coming, and that they're trying to fatten up for the long haul. I don't know if their little brains are that comprehensive, or if it's just instinct driving them on as always. Since most of the hatches are gone, and fewer nymphs available, it only stands to reason that they have to be a little grabbier come autumn. It seems as though trout become a little less selective compared to how they acted in mid-summer too. The lower angle of sunlight might have something to do with this. The shadows your casts are throwing upon the water are less intense, the fish are hungrier, and the catching often better. Many anglers choose to visit western rivers in the fall to get away from the crowds. Summer tourists have gone home, the scenery is spectacular, and the fishing good. It's almost like another whole season to look forward to. Water levels on all rivers remain low and clear. Some rivers that might have been extremely low come back up a bit as ranchers quit irrigating and a little more moisture comes our way. Fresh snow lies on the mountains, elk are bugling, waterfowl migrating through, and streamside foliage brightening. Cottonwoods and aspen glow yellow. Reds and oranges accent the landscapes. Trout take streamers and nymphs readily, and rise to hatches of Baetis, *Pseudocloeon*, midges, *Ephoron*, and *Paraleptophlebia*, mayflies, and October Caddis.

*Ephoron*, the great white mayfly, and *Paraleptophlebia* mayfly species are among the fall hatches to be found on some freestone rivers, along with the giant October Caddis. The much smaller

*Spider webs often tell what the trout are feeding on. Morning Trico spinners caught up along the banks of the Missouri.*

September, the tiny Blue-Winged Olive—*Pseudocloeon* can be important afternoons as *Tricos* wane. *Baetis* and midge hatches dominate fall dry fly fishing into December. Cloudy, humid, rainy, and snowy afternoons provide the best dry fly action in autumn as they did in spring. Many anglers go for larger spawning browns at this time with streamers and egg patterns too. Each tailwater will have some special considerations of its own as well, when it comes to hatches and dates of emergence.

Tailwater fishing will remain fairly consistent throughout summer, but even here excessive heat can slow the action down a bit. Being a skilled slow water nympher can make the difference between a so-so day and a good one. Those wide open, featureless flats and weed bed zones have plenty of fish, but they're not as interesting to fish as freestone pocket water is. This kind of tailwater nymphing is boring to some but productive for others. Staring at a strike indicator most of the day on acres of open water doesn't fit some peoples idea of fly fishing. To liven it up during the summer, try hanging a deep riding appropriate nymph from a big Hopper. Both will be taken and you can pretend you're dry fly fishing. If the action's been a little slow between hatches, try flinging something unusual out there like a cricket, damselfly dry, or cicada pattern. Emergent Caddis nymphs and Soft Hackles sunk and swung up from the bottom can turn a few fish. Brassies and Pheasant Tail nymphs are consistent tailwater producers in non-hatch periods too, as are Bead Heads.

If there has been a hot spell and slow fishing, the first big cold front is likely to invigorate the trout. I remember last August when the fishing got tough, a freak snowstorm hit, and the trout rose better that and the next day than any other day all summer. Trout rose where we hadn't seen them for weeks. As fall progresses, the

*High country rivers are most beautiful in autumn. River flows are low and the trout hungry.*

midges and *Baetis* mayflies are generally more important though. The white mayfly *Ephoron* is limited to rivers that have partially silty bottoms. The October Caddis, which approaches a #8 in size, is found on trout rivers throughout the west. Both trout and steelhead fly patterns are tied to imitate it. They are large enough naturals to bring up some big fish.

Besides possible encounters with these sporadic hatches, fishing strike indicator nymphs, attractor dry flies, terrestrials, and streamers will produce on freestoners come autumn. Many anglers stick to streamers unless a good hatch is underway, in hopes of picking up a bigger than average brown trout heading for spawning grounds. These trout can be aggressive, and pounce on well presented streamers. Low light conditions can provide the best trophy fishing, including overcast and stormy days, and mornings and evenings. If the trout haven't been getting pressured, some will take in the mid-day sunshine too. Big, heavy streamers are preferred by many, it's hard to have too big a streamer. Egg patterns are also used, and can be more effective on pressured trout. Trout that are actually on the spawning beds should be left alone to repopulate the river. In most parts of the world it's considered very unsporting to fish to them.

Tailwater rivers have a temperature lag. The water stored in the lake above has warmed over the summer. As fall progresses, tailwater flows remain warmer than those of the freestone rivers. Hatches and steadily rising fish continue longer, and are more fishable than many freestone autumn hatches. Fall *Baetis* and midge hatches on tailwaters can provide as good fishing as can be found all year. This can last well into December. Nymphs and streamers produce well too. These rivers don't freeze over, so anglers ply them all winter.

Freestone rivers on the other hand do freeze over. Most anglers finish up on them by December, after some late fall pursuit of large browns. They'll likely stay locked up with ice till March, though warm spells will open them up. Anglers fish them where the ice is open and still catch fish. Some anglers go out specifically to catch mountain whitefish during the winter too. They are populous, and good eating when smoked, many are destined for smokehouses. Whitefish rise well to midges as well, and fishermen pursue them for the sport of it. Occasional trout are taken too, though on many rivers trout lay low in mid-winter and don't surface feed as frequently as whitefish do. Fall anglers can also spend part of their day shooting ducks or upland game birds including pheasant, Hungarian partridge, chukar, and a variety of grouse. Good wing and big game hunting are often adjacent to excellent fishing waters.

That is a float fishing season at a glance. There are hatches 12 months a year, and rivers open of ice to fish in when temperatures allow. From April into November excellent fishing can be encountered somewhere, and a boat is the best way to get to many of the best spots. This eight months of quality fishing a year has become a way of life for many across the west, and for visiting anglers too. Their year centers around the river's heartbeat, the progression of seasonal changes, hatches, and trout habits. It's great to live in an area where numerous clean rivers flow, and wild trout fin. Such places become rarer with every passing year and unchecked world population growth.

Before long it will be time to varnish the drift boat again and make ready for another long season of rowing and fishing. There are flies to be tied and hatches met. There will be cold and snow to endure, thunderstorms and wind to be buffeted against, sun and heat to sweat under, and plenty of fish to be caught. One seasonal highlight leads into another so quickly that autumn seems to come more quickly every year. There is no place I'd rather be.

**Above:** *Crowds and how to mentally deal with them: A consideration to look into before arriving at a destination. If state agencies won't deal with such problems, who will? The traveling consumer can make a difference.*

**Left:** *Roadside and boat camps exist on many western rivers. Leave them clean and observe fire ordinances. Drought years in arid western states see numerous forest fires, and these days they make the instigator pay for fire-fighting costs!*

# 11. Crowded Fishing and Peace of Mind

Visiting fishermen and locals alike can be dismayed by the numbers of anglers and boats on the big name rivers. The crowds, antagonisms, and even fights have made the press in recent years. Everybody wants to be on the hot river at the same time. Perhaps the age-old question "when's the best time?" should now be replaced by "when is a good time to fish when it's not crowded?"

There are ways to avoid crowds if serenity and getting away from the rat race are among your primary goals. There are rivers that have good, if not spectacular, fishing and are largely ignored during the summer invasion. There are rivers that get hit hard during a famous hatch, but are quiet the remainder of the season. The fish are still there, as are plenty of other hatches, and they still have to eat.

If you're looking for something a little more adven-

*Getting ready to pack rafts "over the divide." Wilderness float trips on state and federally regulated rivers offer memorable "get away from it all" adventures.*

turous, there are wilderness rivers where 2 to 7 day float/camping trips are available. Many of these are tightly permitted by the Forest Service, so relative serenity is insured when compared to rivers like the Green and Big Horn.

If you are hiring a guide, be sure to tell the outfitter just what you're looking for. If you don't mind the company, and you want to fish a big name river at prime time, that's fine. But if you want a quiet "get away from it all" type trip, where solitude and scenery are as important as the fishing, tell the outfitter so. He can offer you some options within his realm, and his guides will probably enjoy getting away from the stressful guide scene they endure on crowded waters. Consider the experience you really want and take it from there. Do you want to fish small exacting patterns to large selective trout, or is casting a Royal Wulff upon bouncing mountain riffles more to your liking? Will you be shocked if 25 other boats are on the same stretch of river jostling for position, or does this mean nothing to you as long as you catch fish? Ask whether there are any good stretches to fish that aren't as popular.

There are a few time periods many experienced anglers avoid. Memorial Day, Fourth of July, and weekends in general have been times that studious fishermen shy away from. Partying floaters, inner

tubers, and weekend fishermen often make the river a little boisterous for serene fishing. (Sometimes a reverse psychology takes place, and weekends and holidays end up with less fishing competition.) As an example, if you wanted to float the Big Hole River when it is uncrowded and the wade fishing is good too, you wouldn't want to go during the salmonfly hatch. At that time the river is bumper-to-bumper boats, and the water will likely be high with run off. Yet if you were to ask when the best time to fish it is, you may very well be told "during the salmonfly hatch." You can't expect to have rivers all to yourself anymore. Even the most remote ones are popular. The growing popularity of fly fishing and other river sports has seen to that. You can however figure out ways to escape the most crowded periods and rivers.

Naturally the fishing traffic on western rivers is at its peak from June to September. Families are on vacation, Yellowstone Park is overflowing with human wildlife, and R.V.'s are rolling across the landscapes in every direction. There is good fishing to be found, and out-of-the-way places that are quiet, but you'll have to do your homework to find them. It's not just the famous waters that have fish. Most every mountain river, stream, and lake does. Explore a little and fan out. If you've heard a certain river is the new hot spot, it's probably already been beaten back into mediocrity by the time you get there. The mobile fishing public has the numbers and willingness to do it these days.

If your schedule allows, you might want to consider fishing outside of the busy summer season too. September to October is quite popular with many experienced fishermen. Most of the summer tourist traffic is rumbling off into the sunset. The fishing is good too. Fall is a scenic and quiet time on the river. Many locals now divert their energies to the world class hunting that's available.

There is something about autumn that makes an angler want to linger a little longer by the river. Those Indian summer days, golden cottonwoods and aspens, and fresh snow on the mountains are exhilaratingly beautiful. Trout rise to the last hatches and pounce on nymphs and streamers. An image of Joe Brooks working a Platinum Blonde through some big pool on the Yellowstone River somehow comes to mind. Plenty of my own images from spending autumns camping on Montana's Smith River and having browns to 24 inches slam Hoppers and streamers come to mind too, browns as colorful as autumn landscapes and the spectacular canyon that surrounds them.

You might consider the pre-run off season if you have the time or are in the area on business. Late March into May can provide rea-

*Packing into the Bob Marshall Wilderness in Montana. Most western states have wilderness areas. Many, such as "the Bob," have floatable rivers.*

*Out-of-the-way rivers are there for the adventurous. Here, rafts are being readied for a multiday float trip down Montana's South Fork of the Flathead.*

sonably good fishing and hatches. You'll want to check, but most rivers should be low, clear, and fishable. There is little traffic on the river, except on warm weekends. That special feeling of being on a stream again in the freshness of spring is always exhilarating. Budding foliage, greening hillsides, returning swallows, nesting geese, plus the first hatches and rising trout get the blood flowing. You're gambling with the weather a little more, as you do in late autumn, but the rewards on a good day are worth it.

These are just a few ideas on escaping crowded situations. But if you do float fish a big name river at prime time, make an effort to enjoy it despite the presence of others on stream. Joke with passing boats and anglers. Ward off that competitive feeling that creeps up. Enjoy your fishing and try to see the river for what it is. Wrap yourself up in your own world of flowing water, riverside landscapes, hatching insects, and rising trout. There is an art to dealing with crowded waters, of seeing the qualities a river possesses, even if it isn't fishing well. Considering how short life is, you'd do well to take everything in appreciatively. To everyone else on the river, *you're* the crowding party.

## FLOAT FISHING ETIQUETTE

Let's face it, the days of having a river to yourself are slipping away. A growing enthusiasm for river sports, diminishing quality waters, and spiraling world population growth can only mean increasing competition for diminishing recreational space. As our economy flounders in a new global market of cheap labor and stiff competition, natural resources will likely be sacrificed to the want of jobs. Modern conservation practices and pollution control may not be able to keep up with urban sprawl, and agricultural and forestry needs. What does this have to do with float fishing etiquette? There are more and more people on the good rivers that remain, and there will be many more people in the future. We must try to insure that the experience can still be a pleasant one. These are "the good old days" compared to what our great-grandchildren are likely to endure if we keep breeding faster than trout can in their polluted waters.

So it's up to us to act judiciously on stream, and not let "fish lust" unbalance our consideration for others. As a float fisherman, you have a number of responsibilities to assume.

Starting at the beginning, there's launching the boat. If you're using a busy public ramp, it's essential to unload your boat and equipment, then promptly move your vehicle and boat away from the ramp so others can use it. You can rig rods, drink coffee, and idle in low gear after you clear the ramp. Don't block it if others are lined up to put in.

If you're not using a public ramp, make sure you're not trespassing. Some people seem to think that any large houseless tract of land next to a river is fair game for access. It's not. With the increase in fishing, hunting, and boat traffic, and the serious grass and forest fires that have plagued the west over the past eight drought years, most ranchers are very sensitive (to put it mildly) about their rights being violated. Twenty years ago float fishermen were novelties,

*Public access points are numerous in most western states. Don't trespass on private land.*

today ranchers feel invaded as dozens of fishermen and boats lurk around their property, many throwing rubbish and using private land as campsites and outhouses. In Montana, you must stay below the high water mark. It may be easier to walk up through the rancher's fields, but it's not acceptable. The current liberties floaters have in some western states depends upon their respecting private property.

Now that you're afloat, you'll need to give wading anglers and other floaters wide berth. There is a first come-first serve rule that generally governs angling behavior. Many wading anglers feel that they have first rights to the water, since float fishing is a relatively new intrusion and since float fishermen can easily float somewhere else. There is some truth to this. If you're approaching a wade fisherman as you float downstream, leave him plenty of untouched water. Boats often look closer to a wade fisherman, than floaters perceive. If the river is mostly empty, pull to fish the other side as soon as a wading angler comes into view. There are fish everywhere, and it's better for everyone's peace of mind. If the river is more crowded, give the wading angler at least 100 yards of clearance. Don't cast into his water. Put your rod down and wave, or head for the opposite bank. This is especially important on smaller rivers. Give a wading angler at least as much room as you'd want to have.

It's hard to figure what goes on in some people's minds though. I've had float fishermen cast within ten feet of me when I've been wading, on a river where they could easily stay 100 yards away. I've had other guides pull in within a rod's reach of my boat and actually have their clients sneak up between two of my clients to try to pick off some fish we were casting to! These guides belong in amusement parks, not on rivers. I sometimes find myself guiding a client on a small river who keeps casting right at a wade fisherman, even after I've told him to pull in his fly while we pass. I guess they figure they're paying good money for the trip, and they're going to get every cent's worth. This kind of behavior is very exasperating, and has no place on the river.

There's another side to this story. I've often been floating down a smaller river, in an especially narrow spot, where someone happens to be wade fishing. My usual response to this situation is to slow down or bring the boat to a stop if the guy looks like he's on a good rising fish or in mid-fight. I like to have him see me, make a few more casts, and if he's not at a juncture of success and failure, signal me to float by. Then I hurry by, doing my best to stay out of his best fishing water. Often I'll yell to him in advance that I will float right next to him so as not to disturb the fish in his area. (If you don't tell them this in advance, they'll naturally think you're a moron who's

about to run them over, instead of someone who's trying not to disturb their fishing.) At first, most wade fishermen don't grasp that I'm going to float within a rod's reach of them to avoid spooking their fish on a small river. But after you explain it to them before you float by, they're usually very gracious about it and thank you for considering their fishing—since most floaters don't.

But every once in a while you run into an obstinate wade fisher who after seeing you, refuses to move from the only channel of passage on the river! Perhaps he's just had a run-in with some other senseless floater, or he thinks float fishermen are ruining "his" stream. Perhaps he thinks you're going to evaporate and disappear. I've passed guys like this who actually make you drag your boat over rocks to get by, rather than moving. It's a good thing I'm mild mannered! I almost never argue with or yell at what any sane person would consider completely unreasonable behavior, though many anglers and guides do. If you're wade fishing and a boat has to go by, wave him on if you're not dueling with a fish. If you are, tell the floater what the story is and ask him to hold up or float where he'll least effect your fishing. Any conscientious floater will be glad to pull over and wait a moment. Mindless recreational floaters who think fishermen are just standing in the river for fun, and that trout are just

*Solitude, beauty, and fast fishing; what every angler hopes for in a fishing trip. A lovely run on Montana's South Fork of the Flathead.*

fish in a bowl, should be politely educated as they go by (or run into you) as to how they should act. Bellowing at them may or may not achieve your goal, and might rile some big beer-sodden fellow to knock your lights out. After all, he might be a local and you are perceived as one of those "out-of-staters" who are ruining everything. Communication on a benevolent level is the key here to keep everyone's experience pleasant.

Both floaters and wade fishermen should feel comfortable backing off in an encounter, and still be able to get a good day's fishing. An exchange of information at this point might benefit both parties. Boats don't scare fish for long, and sometimes not at all. Trout engaged in a hatch will resume feeding quickly. The floaters can take this moment to enjoy the scenery, something they tend to overlook when that competitive fishing urge besieges them. Wade fishermen can take time out to search the water for naturals, look under rocks to sum up the local nymph population, retie a frayed leader, or eat a snack. There's always something beneficial to be done. It takes work and consideration to keep the river pleasant for all. Float fishers must do their part, and see themselves from the position of a wade fisherman, perhaps one who has fished the river all his life and has seen an infusion of boats in the last decade. If floating anglers keep a polite distance from waders, a relaxed harmony can be achieved. That's what we're out on the river for in the first place.

One strategy wade fishers use on rivers that are popular for float fishing, is to fish upstream from boat ramps. On many rivers a series of ramps offer floaters a variety of stretches from which to choose. If a wading angler works upstream from a ramp in the morning, he should have the river more to himself, as boats that put in at the next ramp above won't get there until the afternoon or evening. If the wading angler goes out in the evening, he might want to fish downstream of the ramp, as no more boats will likely be launching, and boats floating down to the ramp may be stopping above it to wade fish before they call it a day. Many boat ramps have very busy periods during morning and evening, and will be quiet mid-day. I know many boat ramps that have excellent fishing adjacent to them, fish that floaters pass by in their eagerness to get down the river in the morning or pass by to call it a day in the evening. If the wading angler considers boat traffic in this light, he can find more solitude and quiet water to fish. These days, such strategies can make a big difference in your overall fishing experience. Avoiding angler traffic can be just as important as locating fish.

When it comes to other float fishing parties, space out, resist that competitive feeling, and don't get into racing matches to hot spots. On crowded rivers racing syndrome rears its ugly head like a serpent from the depths of human nature. Boats jostle for the advantage of being first. Boatmen race by, rowing like mad men, and pull right in front of you. Guides are among the worst in this category. Not all of them of course, but too many. There's something about human nature that doesn't allow us to stay in place, take our turn, and enjoy a hard-earned day on the river without competitiveness creeping in. It manifests itself in some by a total loss of etiquette and consideration. Others hit the river earlier and find ways to avoid crowds. What seems to be a minority have trained themselves to enjoy whatever the day shows them, focusing only on the pleasures of the fishing possibilities at hand. If they put on the river later than other boats, they don't feel amiss at staying behind them as logic dictates. Finding ways to catch fish that boats in front of you couldn't is real sport! Racing around them and cutting them off is being an ass!

A last point is that of littering. You wouldn't think you'd have to tell someone who enjoys the beauty of the river not to litter. Alas, that's not always the case. While most people have gotten past the stage of throwing beer cans and food wrappers in the water, cigarette butts, monofilament, strike indicators, and leader packaging are still common sights. For some reason, cigarette smokers have never grasped that everyone else thinks that cigarette butts are litter. Carry a small container to put your butts in. Most boat owners don't want them on the floor of their craft, and nobody wants them in the river or along the banks.

Strike indicators are common sights these days, littering streams everywhere. There seems to be one for every worm container found along the bank. When you peel one off your leader, stuff it in a pocket. Don't cast them into the breeze because they're small.

On wilderness and easy access rivers, and wherever camping is popular, toilet paper is an eternal problem. Some river managers and Fish & Game departments have even built outhouses along remote rivers to alleviate this problem. It's up to float fishermen to bury their human waste and toilet paper. Keep the river presentable for those following in your wake.

Some fly clubs and local organizations have river clean up days. Participating in these is certainly beneficial to your favorite river, and can be fun as well. Many groups have big clean up parties afterwards, where old and new fishing liaisons are made, and fishing information exaggerated. When you're fishing, stop to pick up a piece of garbage here and there. The effort adds up in the long run. It's amazing how many rivers are relatively litter-free these days, compared to what they were 10 years ago.

*These float fishermen are working the cliff walls in hopes of catching trout that are into the salmonfly hatch. The nymphs crawl up the cliff walls to emerge, and some fish learn to wait for them there. Other trout in the run off period might move into slower shallow eddy waters, where the sun warms them up in the afternoon.*

**Above:** *Full time local guides know where the fish are. A nice dry fly double on Montana's Missouri River.*

**Left:** *Guides on Montana's Smith River get ready for another day's work. This scenic 60 mile, 5 day float trip offers a great camping/fishing experience. There are many different types of trips to choose from across the Rocky Mountain states.*

# 12. Guides

Many visitors to western rivers invest in a guide to maximize their chances and enjoy the benefits a drift boat offers. Having someone else do the work of manning the oars and positioning the boat appeals even to those that fish these rivers on a regular basis. The scenic qualities of our rivers are best enjoyed from the tranquility of a drift boat or raft too, as the panoramas sweep by, wildlife is surprised, and out-of-the-way reaches of water are fished. There is no trudging and sweating for miles in waders, crashing through brush or crossing barbed wire fences, and no canopy of foliage to reach out and grab your back cast.

Your choice of a guide can depend on many things. A personal reference is among the best. You might write several outfitters seen advertised in the fishing periodicals or write the state licensing agent for a list. You might want to see how long an outfitter has worked on the river and ask

*Guides are available for most quality fishing waters. Shop around for the experience you desire, and for the best local talent.*

maybe the river is too crowded already and you should think about going somewhere else, for your and the river's sake.

The consumer can make a difference when it comes to crowded fishing. Consider that every time you travel to fish, you're impacting someone else's home turf. We like to pretend that the economic gain that area pockets somehow replaces the once uncrowded, untrammeled sporting opportunities that may have previously blessed those residents. The local who fished all his life in peace, now sees dozens of fishermen in "his" hole. Many quit in disgust. If you're planning to fish a river, at least have the courtesy to hire well established local talent. For many resident sportsmen, even this is little compensation for what they see as a ruination of the resource by an overwhelming travel industry, all at the expense of their future recreational opportunities. Sure this is a touchy subject and a two sided coin, but tread lightly in somebody else's back yard.

One thing worth inquiring about when researching or booking a trip is the type of fishing to be expected. If you only want to cast to selective rising fish, or throw big attractor patterns out on the waves, be sure to ask if this can be expected. In some cases, at certain times of year, there might not be much dry fly fishing. Instead, you might be heaving big streamers and nymphs, or staring at a strike indicator all day. Shop around for the kind of angling experience you're after or think about trying something new. Many well established outfitters have newsletters and videos which give you a run down of their season. Most will be straight forward on the phone, as honest dealings will insure the best long term repeat business. If you talk to an outfitter that promises you everything in any situation, chances are he's exaggerating or worse. Most outfitters will supply references upon request as well. The best ones will go to good lengths to match you up with the kind of fishing experience you're looking for.

On the other hand, be mentally and materially prepared for any situation. The river you plan to fish could be affected by a sudden storm or drought. While June might be hot and sultry back east, it could possibly snow and flood out west. Water and wind conditions can reduce dry fly fishing time, as can a lack of hatches. If circumstances force you to fish in a way you don't prefer, go with it. Don't get huffy and childish about it. You may or may not be able to switch dates and locations. Outfitters book many trips well in advance, and can be booked solid in the main season. They can't shift trips around at will. Scheduling doesn't always allow it. Outfitters govern neither the weather or fish. You just have to take what Mother Nature deals out to you and do the best you can at enjoying it. Many of the best fishing days will occur in inclement weather. Rain and snow can bring on tremendous hatches and get big fish feeding aggressively. Often those who tough out bad weather are rewarded with super fishing experiences. And then there are the inevitable days of mediocrity.

If you do hire a guide, listen to what he has to say. Different rivers grow trout with singular feeding traits. Perhaps you have fished everywhere in the world and undoubtedly know 10 times what your guide knows. At least follow his suggestions part of the time. If a guide feels like you're listening to him, he'll try his best to get you into fish. He may be working 12 hours a day, 7 days a week so humor him a little. If you ignore all your guide's suggestions and just treat him like a rowing machine, he may soon give you a minimum of fish finding services. Many guides have spent years and decades learning the river. They don't consider themselves slaves, but as knowledgeable professionals. The amount of information and service you get out of your guide can depend on the level of respect you show them when they're trying to do their job. There are good guides and bad ones of course, ones that take their job seriously, and some that don't know much about fishing that are after a quick buck. I realize that in other parts of the world where guides are required by

for his most experienced guide. (In many states an outfitter is the business owner. He may or may not guide routinely. He will hire additional guides as his business grows, and might retire himself to the fly shop or office, only taking the occasional guiding job himself.) It makes sense to hire long-time guides who are year-round residents on that particular stretch of river.

By hiring local guides you're also helping to minimize crowding. Too often these days, if a river happens to be particularly good, guides from out of the area and out-of-state will bomb it at the same time. Some are legal, some not. The rivers get beaten into mediocrity by anglers and guides who all want to be in the same place at the same time. The locals' peaceful fishing is ruined. This is something that is often forgotten and really is a shame. By hiring out of area guides to fish a river, you're probably abusing someone else's resource. More and more out of area guides promote and "sell" the river further and further afield, resulting in more traffic than an unregulated river can sustain. By hiring local, on river guides, you're generally getting the best, most knowledgeable talent available, and people who are committed to that river, unlike hit and run operators who often give nothing back to the resource in terms of time or money for conservation projects. If the local guides are all booked up, law for any sporting outing, the quality can vary from drunken and dismal to the hardened professional. In the Rockies, where competition is stiff and guides aren't required by law, a high level of competence now exists, best utilized by shopping around. Some are too eager, some too laid back. Some are friendly, others a little abrasive. Some are excellent teachers, others have a short fuse. Don't hesitate to ask an outfitter about these qualities in a guide either. Matching up the right guide and preferred fishing experience with the right time and place can make all the difference in the world to your float fishing trip.

There's another side to a guide's sense of knowledge that I enjoy and stay open to. It's easy for guides working the same river everyday to get into pattern ruts, saying only this or that will work. But I've seen fish caught on such a wide variety of flies that I seldom say no when a guest asks me if I think a certain fly will work. I've seen selective fish take #8 White Wulffs and Hoppers during *Trico* hatches, and the most peculiar patterns produce well. I'm always curious to see what a new or old fly might do in a variety of situations, to the point that sometimes I probably appear indecisive. After all, some people expect a guide to tell them every move they should make, while others expect me to show them where the fish are, give some suggestions, and let them take it from there. Many a time a skilled visitor's new pattern will outproduce regional favorites. This may be in part because the fish haven't seen it before, especially if they receive a lot of fishing pressure. Sometimes it's just better, and the guide absorbs it into his ever-changing arsenal of knowledge. An exchange of knowledge between guides and guests benefits all. Guides who don't get to travel much because they are always busy on home rivers get to learn new tying styles. Guests get to pick the brain of a boatman who may be spending 100 days a year observing trout, hatches, and their inter-relations. Be sure to get your money's worth out of a guide by learning what you can from him. He'll be glad to hear about your personal fishing experiences too, as most every fishing encounter will have some usable bit of knowledge worth extracting. Don't be afraid to suggest ideas to your guide, or to listen to his. You both have something to gain.

Let me go into guide/guest relations a little further. These vary as much as people's personalities do. Some guides are extremely flexible, and go out of their way to please. Some expect anglers to do what they say, when they say it, and can be pretty gruff about it. Some guides are even known to be mean, skilled and extremely knowledgeable, but antagonistic when guests don't immediately follow their instructions. I know some guides in the Rockies like this, and have heard that it's a trait some Florida tarpon guides have made an art of.

Most guides however, are there to please. They see themselves as ambassadors of their state, as well as rowers, fish finders, teachers, entertainers, conservationists, meal preparers, and often friends. Each guide has his own approach. Some lean over guests shoulders all day long, telling them every move to make. Some people like this, some find it a little unnerving and even annoying. My personal approach is to do the work, put them over fish, help people when they need it, lean over their shoulder occasionally, but to also leave them alone at times to relax, fish, and look at the scenery. Some guests have a hard time relaxing with a pro guide hovering over them, critiquing every move. They breathe a little easier when they are given some instruction, then left alone for a while to put new knowledge to work at their pace. I try to balance these facets throughout the day. After all, the main reason people fish and float rivers is for fun. Sure they want to learn and catch fish, but I don't think most of them want to feel like the pressure is on all day. Guides feel like they have to produce results, even for beginners, hence they often feel pressured to keep efforts up to a peak for hours on end. Anglers who like to have a guide at their elbow constantly, may feel neglected if a guide wanders off for too long. I try to judge a person's character and skill level quickly, and be as attentive or laid back as seems appropriate, while still doing my job. I'm sure I make mistakes in judgment along the way, but overall I think it insures a successful day.

Feel free to tell the guide your skill level, what you'd like to get out of the day, and if you'd like constant attention or time to fish by yourself. If there is a certain way you prefer to fish, tell him that too. It might not be the most productive method on a given river, but if that's what you want to do after listening to your guide's advice, that's fine. Don't forget to tell him if you have any medical problems, food or other allergies, deadlines to meet, or you need any equipment like rods or waders. Some guides provide these, others rent them.

Guides should tell you what they have in store for you, when it comes to time on the river, types of fishing to be expected, equipment preferred, and any business ends that need to be tied up. Some guides will bring a large supply of flies that you can pick from throughout the day and pay for at the end of the trip. Others carry a smaller variety and prefer that you purchase flies at the fly shop in the morning. Many outfitters require a deposit to hold a trip date, and expect the balance to be paid the morning of the trip. The shop

*Choosing the right fly pattern is important, but how well it's fished will determine the catch rate. There are rivers that are easy on beginners, and others that test even the most skilled. Practice casting before visiting a river if catching fish is your goal.*

might not be open when you return in the evening. You may also have to fill out some minor paper work of a bureaucratic nature, such as release of liability forms and Fish & Game Department river use records. Look into all of this ahead of time, so there are no surprises, and so you don't waste time at the fly shop in the morning when you could be out early on the river.

Different guides in different areas have their own peculiarities when it comes to hours and manners of guiding too. Some guides work a pretty straight 8 to 5 on the river, as you might on your job. This might miss some of the best hatches of the day, but western rivers do have daytime hatches and feeding fish throughout the day, more so than some eastern rivers. Other guides work from 8 till dark, which is around 9 to 10 p.m. This means a 12 to 14 hour day on the river plus his set up time, morning or evening fly tying needs, clean up, and the time it might take to run you to a hotel or to breakfast. From personal experience, I can tell you that many good guides work these hours almost seven days a week for months on end. This is very grueling and leaves him with very little time on his own to wind down. The money has to be made while the summer lasts.

Ask what hours you can expect to be on the river, where you should meet, if there are restaurants around that can serve early breakfasts and late dinners, and if accommodations are available nearby. Tell the outfitter what kind of day and experience you are looking for. If it doesn't jibe with your expectations, shop around.

If your guide busts his butt on the river till dark, gives you flies, drives you around, mails your photographs, or has been especially attentive to your needs, tip him well. It's easy to forget when you're

*A lunch stop on the Missouri. Rowing is hungry work!*

*Guiding with wooden boats requires more maintenance work, but has that special appeal on the river, like a prized bamboo rod or classic reel. Here an angler prepares for the morning* Trico *spinner fall.*

enjoying a vacation that this is work for a guide, and guiding till dark is unpaid overtime with no company benefits of any kind. Time flies by for an angler into an evening hatch, while his guide is starting to think about his usual late dinner and that first cold draft beer!

If a guide gives you a short day, doesn't seem to know his stuff, or gives an overall poor performance, don't feel obligated to tip. Tips as I see it, are to be earned.

Another thing to ask an outfitter, if it concerns you, is how much time will be spent fishing from the boat, and how much wading. Some anglers prefer fishing from the boat all day. Others dislike it, and look at the boat as only a means of transportation to the best wading spots. Different rivers have varying degrees of good wading water. Since the purpose of this book is to help you get the most out of float fishing, especially if you have never tried it, be sure to give it a good chance. I like both methods, as best fits the situation. Very selective fish in shallower water are better fished to wading, as you have maximum control. Many other situations favor float fishing though, not just for access reasons, but for presentation as well. You probably won't master float fishing in one day, though some beginners do. Many of the skills need plenty of practice before they become second nature. You may have to unlearn temporarily some of your wade fishing habits when in the boat and think out your casts more carefully.

Perhaps it would help you better understand a guide's psyche if I describe a day in the life of a guide. I can't presume to say that my day is typical of other guides, but it is of some.

I usually get up at 4:30 or 5:00 a.m. make a pot of strong coffee, and tie flies for 1 1/2 hours. Since we have a lot of selective trout these days, a constant evolution of fly patterns seems necessary to routinely fool fish. I'm always nervous about not having the right fly for every fish in the river. I usually eat a bagel for breakfast while I'm tying, to save time.

At 6:30 I start preparing lunch and clean out my boat from the previous day. When the summer is rolling we sometimes work 20+ days in a row, have a day off, and work more long stretches. Most guides here look at hitting the river around 8 a.m. The *Trico* hatch gets under way around 9 a.m., so there's really no great hurry to be on the river at daybreak. I like to have my boat ready to go no later than 7:30, in case the guests are up and ready early. If the guests were here the day before, they may have bought the flies needed and taken care of any paper work, so they don't have to waste time in the fly shop the morning of their trip. I like leaving a little early to miss the boat launching traffic at the ramp. If it's very busy, you might have to wait in line to launch otherwise. The fly shop takes care of shuttling our vehicles during the day. Once upon the river, it's time to size up the guests personalities and casting skills. Fishing the *Trico* hatch for instance requires practiced finesse and good eyesight. It will soon be obvious who needs extra instruction. I like working with beginners, but of course it's hard for them to catch many trout during a *Trico* spinner fall since the fish are so picky. A guide must have plenty of tricks up his sleeve to help the novice catch tough trout. Strange as it may seem, I'd estimate the percentage of really good casters we guide in a busy summer to be less than 5 percent. Casting skills are the most important attribute an angler can have; that and a good-natured disposition. There's nothing that will make a guide's day like having a super caster in the boat, especially if he is by himself.

One of the main things we hope for at the beginning of the day is calm to moderate breezes. If the wind gets strong, which isn't unusual, fewer fish will rise, and it's a real workout positioning the boat properly. Drift boats sail in the wind, since they have no keel to prevent side slipping. If the wind's up early, the hatch can blow away, and a hard day's work is in store. Fish can certainly be caught nymphing, Buggering, and with Hoppers, attractor patterns, and with two fly set ups. In lee or windless spots along the river, rising trout can still be found. Most anglers however, are not very practiced at casting in the wind. It takes a rigid rod and the proper technique (see "Wind Casting," Chapter 3) to beat the wind. It also takes a positive frame of mind. Some anglers are defeated by their attitudes before the first cast is made. When the day is really windy, some anglers opt to get off the river early, and eat dinner at a normal time. Others figure they'll tough it out and hope the wind drops by the time the evening hatch comes off. Sometimes it does, sometimes not. Unless the angler wants to quit earlier, I usually stick it out till near darkness.

Another thing we wish for is an uncrowded river. When it's really busy, all the wade fishing hot spots can be taken if you're not out early. Dispositions and competition can get ugly. It's stressful as a guide to deal with much of this. The trick is to find little pockets of fish that others don't see or know about, and have a series of these spots down the river to count on. Guides have to think up strategies when it comes to put in spots and times, in order to miss the crowds. Some guides who have spent a lot of time on crowded rivers, like the Big Horn, will have developed crowding habits and tolerances that are out of place on more pacific rivers. They'll race for spots, cut other boats off without a thought, land just yards from you, have their guests fish antagonizingly close to you, and otherwise make the river a less enjoyable place to be. Such guides are still in the minority, but competition for space and poor state regulation on numbers of guides makes it a growing minority. Certainly I've raced for spots from time to time, especially since many out of area guides have invaded local rivers in recent years. It's a chore to keep that competitive side of human nature from taking over. If you happen to be with an overcompetitive and thoughtless guide, be sure to straighten him out a bit.

Somewhere along the river, we pull over for lunch. I like to make up a lunch from scratch everyday and make a nice presentation of it. Many guides will have a brown bag lunch from the local cafe. It can be hard to keep good meal provisions in stock when you are working most every day. My wife makes the 110-mile round trip every few days to keep me stocked up. I also maintain a nice looking cedar boat I built, since I think anglers like that effect when they visit western rivers. A beautifully-kept wooden boat has more character, it has the look a tourist likes to find in a certain region, to set it apart

*Fishing till dark? Not all guides do it. Hatches and fish are encountered throughout the long day. What time is dinner served?*

from the commonplace. When a guest knows you built and maintain your boat well, they tend to think that you're serious about your guiding. Anyone can go out and buy a shiny new plastic one. Since I have no other life, it's worth the little bit of extra effort.

Afternoons are when the wind often comes up. Some days exciting Hopper fishing takes place. Other days nymphs, S.J. Worms, or Buggers produce better results. Sometimes you just battle the wind and cuss under your breath till your arms cramp. One summer we had a thunder storm with 90 mile an hour winds! I'm glad I wasn't out there, but several of our boats were and had a scary time of it. They hid behind the boat on shore, hanging on to it to keep it from blowing away and to ward off the white caps slamming into the banks. Powerful thunderstorms and hail are common on western rivers in summer, accompanied by high winds. In lightning storms I still haven't decided whether it's safer to be out on the river or huddled under cover. The tree-clad mountains take most of the blows. I've heard of people along the banks getting hit by lightning, and people out on big open lakes, but I haven't heard any first hand experience of floaters on mountain rivers getting struck so I usually keep on floating. We have had trees half chewed down by beavers blow down almost on top of us, and have had some very cold experiences on five day camping trips. Plenty of people get hooked with wayward flies, but we've never had a heart attack or other serious occurrence in the 18 years I've been guiding. I suppose it's a matter of time though. We take first aid classes every year in hopes of being ready for emergencies. We have had a couple of hairy experiences during white water trips. Many folks think a whitewater trip is like a carnival ride until you flip a boat in ice cold water at flood stage. Consider what it would be like to swim in a raging torrent before you float a river with someone whose skills you're not sure of, and never take your life jacket off in dangerous water.

As afternoon heads into evening, guides on some rivers customarily finish up for the day around dinner time, 5 to 6:00 p.m. In many places you can easily go back out yourself to fish the evening rise, putting to use new knowledge you picked up during your guided day. Some guides on other rivers stay out till dark, providing a 12-plus hour day on the water. Some fishermen desire this, others are good and tired after 8 hours of fishing, especially if they're not used to it. I usually stay out till 9 p.m. or so. In my area on the Missouri, you can't get dinner after 10 p.m., so that's my bottom line. I can't hit the ramp any later than 9:30 and still get dinner. I don't feel like making it for myself after being up and at it since 4:30 in the morning. A 16 hour work day has already gone by, and I'm ready to relax! My free time allotment per day is very small, and I don't like to waste a second of it.

There are several things that bug me when guiding. Wind of course is a major pain. Getting on the river late when it's busy can make it hard to get to many good untouched spots. Anglers that constantly tangle are an annoyance, since I undo many of the tangles, but I've gotten to the point where I actually find that kind of relaxing. Fishermen that don't learn to use reach casts, and other techniques that I might clue them in on dozens of times throughout the day, begin to frazzle your nerves, as do anglers who don't strike at the right moment habitually. This is often a result of poor eyesight. Fishermen who don't stand in the center of the drift boat, making it lean continuously, are particularly annoying. It's hard to properly row a tilting drift boat. Anglers who don't cast quickly and efficiently when I'm rowing my guts out to hold them on rising fish really bug me after a while. If I'm rowing as hard as I can to put them on a sure target, I don't expect them to sit there drinking a beer for 5 minutes, before picking up and unstringing their rod. Cast, let the second rod cast, or there's no use in me putting out an extreme effort. I can float with the current and blow off rising fish if that's what your responses to prime situations tell me. Usually when I approach a hot spot with active fish, I'll row harder and my voice will have a decidedly different tone. The fishermen on board know something good is coming up. Of course most of them are eager to get their flies to the spot. Human nature however, often leads them to cast too soon, so that instead of getting a good drag free float over the fish, their fly drags at the last second and at the worst moment, right in front of the fish! This happens so often, it's like clockwork. Wait till that perfect moment to cast. I don't want to give you the idea that I'm in a bad mood much of the day, I think I'm one of the easier going and mellowest guys on the river. I'll put up with most anything. These are just things to think about, since some guides are more volatile!

As the day reaches an end, the late sun is going down, thoughts of dinner are sizzling in my brain and the restaurants are near closing their kitchens, I do get fidgety about making it there on time. I'll get inwardly annoyed if fishermen won't quit when the deadline is near, if the boat ramp is blocked by some unthinking sportsman, or if my anglers dink around forever before hopping in the vehicle so we can head for home. One thing that particularly bugs me at this point is if they want me to drive them to some out-of-the-way hotel. If I know it ahead of time, that's fine, I'll get off the river a little earlier to make up that time. It should come out of their fishing time, not my tiny bit of relaxation time. Suburbans use a lot of gas too, so I'd expect a couple of extra bucks for gas, but wouldn't say anything about it. Same with flies. I tie and give away a lot of traditional and experimental

flies during the course of the day. I don't keep a record and ask for payment either. I expect anglers to consider that fact in the form of a tip though, especially if it's been a typical 12+ hour day on the river, which is above and beyond a reasonable work day for anyone. Outwardly, I try to remain calm and smiling. But inwardly I'm psyching out if I'm getting close to missing dinner.

Often guests will invite you out for dinner as a tip or a tip in part. Guides will generally take them up on this to save money. Most guides are relatively poor. Occasionally I'll turn down dinner offers from guests, not because I don't like them or wasn't having fun with them, but because often I feel like having time to myself, where I can stare into a cold beer mug and not have to respond politely in a social situation. Many people, like myself, ended up being guides in part because they're loner types. Working on the river is more compatible with my psychological make up than is office work. I hated being in rooms full of people in school when I was a kid, and still don't like it. If I've been guiding for long periods, I like sitting by myself or with other guides to discuss happenings on the river. I don't have to respond to anyone reasonably, as I would a guest, and I can wind down. After working since 4:30 in the morning, I need at least a good hour and a few beers worth of wind down time before hitting the sack. Normally I'll get to bed around 11 p.m. This gives me 5 1/2 hours of sleep a night, which is enough for me when the season is busy.

As I mentioned previously, all guides don't work the same hours. Some need 8 hours of sleep to perform well. Others can carouse past midnight and still carry on fine the next day, and the days after that. There's a little bit of the "wild west" syndrome still flowing through some guides' veins. They would have been buffalo hunters if born 100 years earlier. Others are very business-like at all times, beacons of respectability on the river who have families they want to get home to at civilized hours. Individualism is certainly a guide trait, and all manner of humanity can be found behind the oars.

Many guides judge their guests on two basic levels: casting/fishing skills, and personality. Whatever else a person might be in the non-reparian world, he's either a good, average, or lousy caster when in a drift boat. One can also be a good or poor learner. A beginner that learns quickly rates higher than an average one that has mental blocks. Every guide hopes for that rare "super caster," as that's how fish are caught. The guide can tell and show you every trick in the book, but if you can't make exacting casts in critical situations, you won't catch as many fish. Casting is everything. Fly fishing techniques are simple if you think about the mechanics involved, look for your own mistakes, and try to solve them. Watching another skilled caster to analyze his style is a good way to learn. Your guide can pull over and show you how to do it, but you'll need to listen and watch the fine points of his casting demonstration. I've had beginners who learned to cast like pros in an hour, and mid-level casters who couldn't break old bad habits after 5 days of instruction. You'll get the most out of your trip if you practice at home in advance instead of waiting for the moment of truth on the river.

Personality is the second trait a guide has to deal with, and so judges in a guest (and vice versa). A fisherman can be a C.E.O. of a top corporation or a movie star, but if he's a jerk in the boat, then he's viewed with some disregard. Anglers who whine about problems, the weather, poor fishing, or whatever else might come your way on a less than perfect day, are viewed as childish. Of course if your guide is an ill-prepared, unknowledgeable joker, you have reason to be annoyed. Guides cost good money these days. But if a problem is beyond the guide's control, such as weather, lack of fish cooperation, or an unusual equipment breakdown, take it in stride. Wind, tangles, and broken fly rods are among the common problems encountered on stream. Poor fishing occurs from time to time for a variety of reasons. How an angler reacts to these problems is what a guide takes notice of. Does he grin and bear it, as the saying goes? Or does he complain and cuss all day. Complaining tends to cut into your problem solving abilities, which you'll need to catch fish and enjoy the trip. An angler that faces problems and cheerfully looks for the best ways to overcome them will be viewed with more respect, regardless of his fishing skills or social position in the "real world." Some fishermen have problems learning to fish with others from a boat and constantly tangle. Quickly unlearning old habits and concentrating on new float fishing techniques will help make the day more enjoyable for all. If the fishing is slow, make a point of enjoying the scenery and habitat, make the most out of the situation. The fishing may not live up to your preconceived notions, but you don't have to make it worse by complaining instead of adapting. A guide will put himself out for fishermen of any skill level who try and have a good time of it.

Naturally, you're going to judge your guide as well. Does he know his stuff? Does he talk too much? Is he working hard throughout the day? Guide personalities vary greatly, but it's their job to please, educate, and put you over fish. Since tips are part of a guide's income, they generally try hard to excel, hoping for that extra few bucks in their pocket come sundown. The best way for you to get the most out of a guide is by treating him with respect and by prodding him on in a congenial fashion. I know I'll put out an extra effort for anglers who are good natured and who are trying their best to catch fish. Remember that it is a team effort when float fishing, and both parties can spur each other on to greater successes.

On long days, expect your guide to take a few coffee breaks too. If he's putting you on the river 10+ hours, he's going to need some moments to relax if he's to keep his concentration up. It does take concentration and energy to position and row the boat properly, look for fish, duck bad casts, plus take care of all the other odds and ends of a guiding day.

Some guests ask the guide to fish along with them. I think this is OK to a limited degree, for instance if the guest wants to see a technique demonstrated. But there are guides who get carried away and will go off fishing by themselves

*Skilled casting is what catches fish. "Oh, why can't they cast?"—the lament of fly fishing guides worldwide!*

for large parts of the day when wade fishing. I don't think guides have any place fishing in competition with their guests. Personally, I don't even take a rod of my own with me, and don't fish unless asked for a demonstration. I think the fish don't need to be caught any more than necessary, and guides shouldn't harass the same fish day in and day out. If nothing else, it makes the fishing harder for their next day's clients or the next boat down the river. I've caught enough fish and don't need to be fishing when I'm guiding. Having a guide fish often ends up with him neglecting his real duties. There are guests who cheerfully insist though, and if you want your guide to fish too, so be it. But as a guest hiring a guide, I certainly wouldn't expect him to take out his rod and fish in competition with me without being asked.

The only other time I'll fish for a moment, is to show anglers that the fish can be caught. A fisherman might not be fishing a fly correctly, especially a nymph when no fish are visible, and think that there are no fish around. His lack of success may soon have him doubting the river or your wisdom. At this point I'd ask to take his rod and try to turn up a few fish so that he knows it's his fishing style that needs attention, not a problem with a lack of fish. This needs to be done occasionally to keep an angler's spirit up and urge him on to greater learning efforts.

I hope this gives you a little insight into a guide's day so that you can get the most out of your trip.

# 13. Hatches and Trout Fare

**Above:** *The object of so much attention—a salmonfly (*Pteronarcys californica*) lumbers along fresh streamside foliage. Everything seems to feed on them, fish, raccoons, robins, even gulls that fly in every year from distant lands just for the occasion.*

**Left:** *A studious angler examines the hatches with a pocket screen. Fly fishing takes you into a deeper understanding of river life than other forms of fishing are likely to.*

A complete treatment of hatches is beyond the scope of this book. The following charts and information however, should give you a workable starting point for contemplating basic hatch scenarios on different water types throughout the year. This is a very general presentation though, and actual hatch dates for specific rivers will vary with altitude, weather, water levels and temperatures, dam influences, winter snow pack, and a host of other influences that have a bearing on a stream's life.

We are talking about a vast area here, and there's no substitute for up-to-the-minute reports from local experts. There are usually fly shops near most rivers that can be called for updates and information on hatches and fishing techniques common to your river of choice. Weather and water conditions, and consequently fishable hatches can change quickly here though, so travel with a pocket full of fly patterns and an open mind!

If you have a latent interest or burning desire to further understand aquatic insect hatches of the west and their relation to trout, Frank Amato Publications has a number of volumes on this subject available. A list of books can be obtained by writing them at P.O. Box 82112, Portland, OR, 97282, or by calling 503-653-8108.

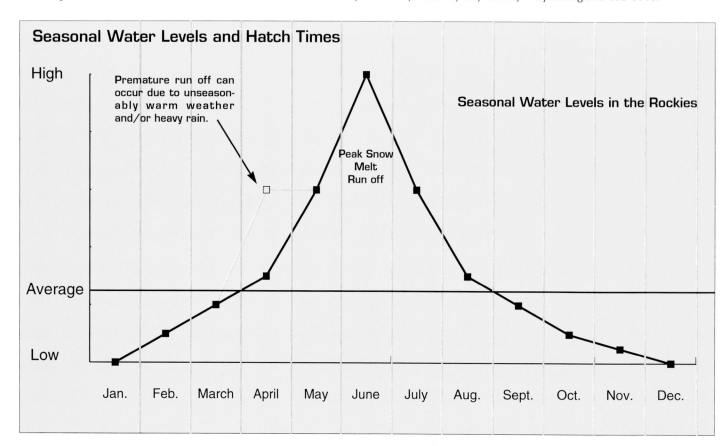

## Seasonal Water Levels and Hatch Times

Seasonal Water Levels in the Rockies

Premature run off can occur due to unseasonably warm weather and/or heavy rain.

Peak Snow Melt Run off

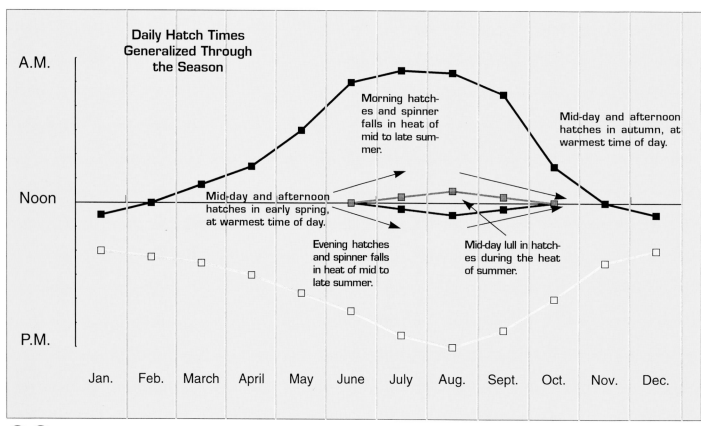

Daily Hatch Times Generalized Through the Season

Morning hatches and spinner falls in heat of mid to late summer.

Mid-day and afternoon hatches in autumn, at warmest time of day.

Mid-day and afternoon hatches in early spring, at warmest time of day.

Evening hatches and spinner falls in heat of mid to late summer.

Mid-day lull in hatches during the heat of summer.

## Tailwater River Hatches and Trout Fare (A general seasonal overview)

| Month | Jan. Feb. March | April May | June July | August | Sept. Oct. Nov. | Dec. |
|---|---|---|---|---|---|---|
| **Primary Hatches and Surface Fare** | Midges, sub-surface pupae little winter stoneflies (black and brown) | Midges, pupae little Blue-Winged Olive mayflies (*Baetis*) possible march brown (*Rhithrogena*) mayflies first caddis possible stoneflies | Midges, pupae BWO. (*Baetis*) Pale Morning Dun mayflies (PMD's) caddis possible *Callibaetis* other mayflies beetles & ants | Midges, pupae *Trico* mayfly spinners PMD, mayfly spinners PMD mayflies numerous caddis beetles and ants hoppers, cicada damselflies, craneflies *Callibaetis* & other mayflies | Midges, pupae little Blue-Winged Olive (BWO) mayflies *Tricos* end caddis some October caddis hoppers, cicada beetles, ants, bees | Midges, pupae |
| **Primary Sub-surface Fare** | Midges, larvae, pupae scuds, cress bugs small mayfly nymphs & caddis larvae aquatic worms & leeches sculpin, minnows crayfish | Midges, larvae, pupae *Baetis* mayfly nymphs other mayfly & caddis nymphs, larvae & emergers scuds, cress bugs aquatic worms & leeches sculpin, minnows crayfish fish eggs | Midge larvae, pupae *Baetis* mayfly nymph PMD nymphs & emergers caddis emergers damselfly nymphs scuds, cress bugs aquatic worms & leeches sculpin, minnows crayfish | Midges, larvae pupae PMD mayfly nymphs & emergers caddis emergers damselfly nymphs scuds, cress bugs aquatic worms, leeches sculpin, minnows crayfish | Midges, larvae, pupae *Baetis* nymphs caddis emergers scuds, cress bugs aquatic worms, leeches sculpin, minnows crayfish fish eggs | Same as Jan. through March |
| **General Fly Patterns to Have On Hand** | Midge dries & pupae #26-18 small mayfly nymphs Pheasant Tail Nymphs #20-14 (P.T.'s) Bead Head & Brassies #20-14 Scuds, cressbugs #18-12 San Juan Worms #10-6 Woolly Buggers, leeches #8-4 Streamers, crayfish #8-2 | Midge dries & pupae #26-18 Blue-Winged Olive 'match the hatch' dries #20-14 March Brown dries #16-14 Stonefly dries #8-6 Caddis dries #16-14 *Baetis* nymph (P.T.'s) #20-16 caddis emergers & soft hackles #10-14 scuds, cress bugs #18-12 Bead Heads & Brassies #20-14 San Juan Worms #10-6 Buggers & leeches #8-4 Streamers, crayfish #8-2 egg patterns #14-10 | Midge dries, pupae #26-18 BWO and PMD nymphs & emergers #20-14 caddis dries & emergers soft hackle #18-14 beetles & ants #20-14 BWO & PMD 'match the hatch' dry flies #20-14 scuds, cress bugs #18-12 Bead Heads, Brassies #20-14 San Juan Worms #10-6 Buggers and leeches #8-4 Streamers, crayfish #8-2 Damselfly nymphs #12-8 | Midge dries & pupae #26-18 PMD dries, emergers, nymphs & spinners #20-14 *Trico* spinners #24-18 caddis dries & emergers #20-14 hoppers and cicadas #8-4 Damselfly dries & nymphs #10-8 Parachute Adams #20-14 Attractor patterns (Stimulator, Humpy, Wulffs, Trudes, H&L variant) #20-12 scuds, cress bugs #18-12 Bead Heads, Brassies #20-14 San Juan Worms #10-6 Buggers and leeches #8-4 Streamer, crayfish #8-2 | Midge dries & pupae #26-18 BWO dries, emergers, nymphs #20-14 caddis dries, emergers #16-8 hoppers cicadas #8-4 Parachute Adams, attractors #20-14 scuds, cress bugs #18-12 Bead Head, Brassies #20-14 San Juan Worms #10-6 Buggers, leeches #8-4 Streamers, crayfish #8-2 Egg patterns #14-10 Egg Head streamers #6-2 | Same as Jan. through March |

**Abbreviations:**
BWO   "Blue-Winged Olive" *Baetis* mayflies
PMD   "Pale Morning Dun" *E. Infrequens* and *Inermis* mayflies

# TAILWATER NOTES

• Hatches are less diverse than in freestone rivers, but occur in greater numbers and for longer seasonal durations.

• Temperature changes in tailwaters are modified by their dams. Hatches and fishing conditions are more consistent than on freestone rivers.

• The majority of these aquatic insects are small, requiring #26-14 fly patterns and precise, repetitive casts.

• Tailwater trout eat midges year-round, perhaps their single most important food item.

• Fishing indicator nymphs, scuds, cress bugs, and San Juan Worms is a good bet any time.

• Rising fish are usually located first, and then stalked. Fishing the water blind with dries is less important than it is on freestoners, but does still catch fish.

*Stonefly shucks are seen gripped on to streamside rocks by the hundreds after a hatch. These big insects crawl out of the river, usually at night, to shed these skins and emerge as adults.*

## Freestone River Hatches and Trout Fare (A general seasonal overview)

| Month | Jan. Feb. March | April May | June July | August | Sept. Oct. Nov. | Dec. |
|---|---|---|---|---|---|---|
| **Primary Hatches and Surface Fare** | Midges, sub-surface midge pupae little winter stoneflies (black and brown) | Midges, midge pupae little winter stones medium size stoneflies little Blue-Winged Olive mayflies western march brown mayfly other possible early season mayflies first caddis | Giant stoneflies salmonflies golden stones brown and green drakes assorted fast water mayflies PMD's caddis | Golden stoneflies little yellow & green stoneflies Trico mayfly spinner falls PMD mayflies assorted fast water mayflies evening mayfly spent wings abundant caddis beetles & ants Hoppers & cicadas | Hoppers, cicadas beetles ants and bees little Blue-Winged Olive mayflies some larger autumn mayflies some caddis giant October caddis midges, pupae | Midges, pupae last little Blue-Winged Olive |
| **Primary Sub-surface Fare** | Midges, larvae, pupae mayflies stonefly and caddis nymphs sculpin, minnows crayfish leeches | Stonefly, mayfly & caddis nymphs sculpin, minnows leeches midge larvae, pupae | Large stonefly nymphs a wide assortment of mayfly and caddis nymphs and emergers sculpins, minnows crayfish leeches | Medium size stonefly nymphs assorted mayfly nymphs caddis emergers sunken terrestrials snails sculpin, minnow crayfish leeches | Assorted mayflies & caddis nymphs & emergers some larger stonefly nymphs sunken terrestrials snails sculpin, minnows crayfish leeches fish eggs | Midge larvae, pupae assorted nymphs sculpin minnow crayfish leeches fish eggs |
| **General Fly Patterns to Have On Hand** | Midge dries & pupae #22-18 Dark stonefly dries #16-12 weighted nymphs #18-4 weighted streamers, Woolly Buggers, crayfish #8-2 | Midge dries & pupae #22-18 little Blue-Winged Olive dries #18-14 March brown dries #16-12 dark stonefly dries #14-6 Attractor dries (Stimulator, Humpy, Wulffs, Trudes) #14-8 weighted nymphs #14-4 Streamers, buggers crayfish #8-2 soft hackle wets #14-10 San Juan Worms #10-6 | Big stonefly dries salmonfly & golden stone #6-2 brown & green drake mayfly dry flies #14-10 Attractor dries (Stimulator, Humpy, Wulffs, Trudes) #14-8 caddis dries #16-12 large weighted stonefly nymphs & rubber legs #8-2 weighted mayfly nymphs #16-10 soft hackle wet flies #14-10 Streamers, buggers crayfish #8-2 San Juan Worms #10-6 | Golden stone dries #8-6 Hoppers #8-4 Attractor dries (Stimulator, Humpy, Wulffs, Trudes, Parachutes) #16-10 Trico spinners #22-18 caddis dries & emergers #14-16 PMD dries and emergers #18-14 beetles & ants #18-14 tan & rusty spinners #16-14 weighted nymphs #16-4 streamers, Buggers, crayfish #8-2 | Hoppers, cicadas #8-4 beetles, ants, bees #18-14 attractor dries #16-10 caddis dries & emergers #16-14 October caddis #10-6 BWO dry flies #18-14 weighted nymphs #18-6 Streamers, Buggers, crayfish #8-2 egg patterns #14-10 "Egg Head" streamers #6-2 | Midge dries & pupae #22-18 BWO patterns #18-14 weighted nymphs #18-6 Streamers Buggers crayfish #6-2 egg patterns #14-10 "Egg Head" streamers #6-2 |

**Abbreviations:**
BWO — "Blue-Winged Olive" *Baetis* mayflies
PMD — "Pale Morning Dun" *E. Infrequens* and *Inermis* mayflies

# FREESTONE NOTES

• Bushy attractor patterns are likely to work, since the trout see a wide variety of hatches in swift, choppy water.

• Temperature changes in freestone rivers are more pronounced than in tailwaters, and can cause noticeable on/off feeding periods.

• Larger nymphs, sculpins, and crayfish are available to trout throughout the season. Big trout like them!

• Freestone nymphs are generally wider, with more obvious gills, than those in slower tailwater rivers. Consequently, such scruffy patterns as Hare's Ears work well and imitate many freestone nymph species.

• Freestone trout get highly selective at times, but are often omnivorous. They'll eat whatever washes by them.

• Much time is spent "fishing the water" with dry flies on freestone rivers to pockets that look like they should hold fish and often do.

Fishing to steady risers happens less in a day than it does on some tailwaters.

# RANDOM NOTES ON HATCHES

• Midges can hatch any time of day throughout the year. They prefer humid, windless conditions.

• Aquatic flies tend to be darker colored spring and fall, and lighter colored in mid-summer. Consider this in terms of the sun's radiant heat, and of the heat absorption qualities of dark vs. light colors.

• Many of the largest aquatic insects hatch at the highest water flows.

• Mid-summer, low water mayflies tend to be smaller than spring and fall flies.

• Spring and fall hatches tend to occur during the warmest part of the day, noon to late afternoon.

• Mid-summer hatches (July through early Sept.) tend to occur at cooler times of day, either mornings or evenings.

• Many aquatic insects prefer humid and/or overcast weather (or low light situations) to hatch in, as it is easier for them to molt their final skin. Light rain or snow is ideal.

• The smaller the aquatic insect, the more numerous it tends to be, hatching over longer seasonal periods at lower water levels. Consequently, trout rise longer and more steadily when eating them, (it takes a lot of small insects to fill them up) but they can be in a rut (i.e. selective). Precision casting skills can be essential. Using the correct sized fly to match the natural often outweighs the importance of having the exact color.

• The larger the aquatic insect, the shorter its seasonal hatch duration and overall numbers tend to be. Many large species hatch at high, less than optimal water/fishing conditions. (There are exceptions in both spring and fall low water flows.) Fishing opportunities tend to be short and "iffy," but exciting when everything goes just right. Trout can get reckless for brief, gluttonous periods.

• Different insects become available to trout in different parts of the river, i.e., along banks, in swift riffles and runs, or in quiet tailouts and edgewaters. Trout may move into the best locations as daily or seasonal feeding opportunities present themselves. Watch and be alert to the location of hatches and rising fish, and to where and how your successes occur.

• During profuse hatches, mature trout will move into slower water to feed, including tailouts, shallow edgewaters, upstream of river obstructions, and in eddies.

• Unmolested trout like shallow water, where they can feed off the surface, or on nymphs with little effort from the same feeding station.

• Indicator nymphing will generally catch more trout than any other technique, day in and day out.

• When float fishing, precision casting and line control are usually more important than exacting fly patterns.

**Above:** *What looks like smoke here is a cloud of* Trico *spinners. These tiny mayflies hatch by the tens of thousands every morning for almost two months, from mid-July into September, and provide the greatest of sport to skilled dry fly fishermen.*

**Left:** *Fishing the water with attractor patterns is an excellent way to hone your casting skills and practice new techniques.*

There are certain fly patterns anglers cherish and feel naked without on stream. These are usually success-imprinted patterns, ones he has fooled fish with, successes that have since stuck in his mind. Perhaps only one truly fine specimen was caught, a personal best. Or, such a pattern may have deceived hundreds of trout over the years. Memories of fish, places, seasons, weather and water conditions, and companions all orbit around that fly pattern. He seldom goes afield without it and others of its kind, at least not with the same plateau of confidence.

Looking through an experienced fly fisher's vest opens a Pandora's Box of angling tales and memories, giving a good clue as to the rivers he has met around the state, country, or world. No two fly boxes are the same, as no two angler's fishing exoduses have followed the exact same woodland paths.

*An Egg Head Woolly Bugger fools yet another big brown. This is one of my favorite streamers these days.*

When float fishing rivers in my area, there are patterns I always have on board, unless I've been delinquent at the vise. Since my time is pretty well divided between guiding multi-day fishing/camping trips on Montana's Smith River—a spring-rich freestone stream, and day trips on the Missouri—a superb tailwater fishery, I pack different fly boxes for each type of water. There are similarities between all streams, of course, and marked differences. What matters most is how the trout in a particular stream manifest these differences as proven through their feeding habits. No two rivers are the same. Fly patterns and boxes in different areas have gone through different evolutions. What is interesting are the various routes traveled by regional anglers and fly tiers in achieving the same ends—deceiving the trout. Fly patterns also change as decades and generations pass. You can often tell an angler's age and experience by peering into his fly box. Mine is middle aged.

On freestone rivers there are old standards I'm never without. Stonefly nymphs are well represented, with such proven veterans as Montana Nymphs in sizes #14-2; Bitch Creeks, those perennial favorites on the Smith and other rivers; different forms of Girdle Bugs; and the now universal dead drifted Woolly Bugger. There are more realistic stonefly patterns around, but they haven't proven to be any more effective on big trout than some of these gaudy rubber leg nymphs on local waters. Those high contrast colors attract trout in high water flows. Usually weight in the fly, casting skills, and especially line control are more important factors in getting these big #8-2 nymphs in front of hungry trout.

During run off high water periods, (a good, big fish time of year) we spend a good deal of time stripping Buggers. One can feel confident about fishing Woolly Buggers almost anywhere. Sometimes the trout go for the extra large, extra heavy models best, especially when turbid water conditions fill the valley. Black, brown, olive, yellow, Flashabou, and other tier's fancies all work well. Many anglers, myself included, also tie the egg head variety—a Woolly Bugger with a fluorescent pink egg for a head. These are highly visible in the water, especially when contrasted with dark bodies, and are often used during spawning seasons. Others add rubber legs for even more movement and visibility. Brown Buggers work especially well for us. Trout can take them for crayfish, sculpin, stonefly nymphs, leeches, or what have you. Anytime I'm indecisive, I'm likely to tie on a Bugger.

In shallow reaches of freestone rivers, the Muddler remains a favorite. This fly pushes water, something trout can feel and perceive as wounded, vulnerable prey. As soon as big fish sense a small fish is

*A typical fast water nymph like this* Heptagenia *mayfly variety, is well imitated by the standard Hare's Ear. Note the curled up salmonfly nymph in the lower part of the picture. This is what they do when drifting in the currents by accident. This one still has a lot of growing to do.*
**Inset:** *Flashback nymphs catch the eye of many trout, as do the now popular Bead Head varieties.*

in trouble, it turns it from a neighbor into dinner. I've seen it happen numerous times on stream. The Muddler can also be floated downstream as a Hopper in summer, and then stripped in sunk at the end of the drift, retrieved as a Streamer. This covers a lot of water and catches fish.

At lower freestone flows, when numerous medium to small nymphs are populating swift runs and drop-offs, I'm likely to pick out a weighted Hare's Ear type or Peacock Herl nymph in sizes #14-10. I'm sure Bead Heads will be more dominant in some fly boxes, especially those of young anglers, since they work so well. Traditional nymphs still dominate mine, simply because I have lots of them. Small black nymphs work well too. Trout like them, being easily visible to fish in swift water feeding stations. I've had some fun drifting cased Caddis patterns along the bottom to sighted fish at very low water levels, when the abundant naturals are crawling all over the streambed. Come evening, when Caddis are emerging, I'll pull out a Soft Hackle wet and swing it down and across sunset reflecting currents. As deepening shadows march across the landscapes and twilight colors soften, my mind often wanders and my eyes tend to roam. A sudden lunge on the Soft Hackle fly by an eager trout quickly awakens you to the task at hand!

I enjoy working a self tied nymph through sparkling freestone runs, fished with or without an indicator. Sometimes a strike indicator feels like training wheels on a bicycle. Achieving that elusive sixth sense of nymph strike detection, staring into the illuminated depths for that flash of a plump trout leaning over for your nymph seems more fulfilling. It is a game of mental imagery, where you picture the bottom configuration and forms of hovering trout. With a weighted nymph and good line control you will your fly to dance naturally through that deep unseen arena, staying alert to any leader movement or gut feeling, however fleeting. Such signs spell trout.

I love being on a Smith River run in mid-summer, no one else around, just thousand-foot cliffs and golden eagles for company, with pine forests and cottonwood trees swaying in sky blue afternoon breezes. To unhurriedly work a run, swimming your favorite nymph around this rock and under that, plucking out trout with a regularity that matches the promise of the water is pure delight. The trout don't have to be large. I love little brown trout for their varied colors, eagerness, and the graceful place they've etched out for themselves in nature. But sooner or later that big fish comes. When you can distinctly feel their head shake slowly yet determinedly back and forth, you know you have a trout!

In my freestone dry fly box are many of the now classic attractor patterns: fanciful Stoneflies, Wulffs, Trudes, Humpies, Hoppers, and as of late, Stimulators. All are patterns you can see when popped upon succulent trout pockets and feed lanes. They bob and spin, and fool trout routinely with their high floating, hackle dancing antics.

When fishing the water with them, you can push your casting into new dimensions. There are no obvious risers to put down by bad casts, just a parade of opportunities made to be dry fly landing pads! You can tuck, haul, curve, and reach with abandon. You can "slack" them, "skid" them, and twitch them out of hopper-infested grasses. You can cast a mile or dap, as fancy dictates. This is where you gain casting skills and have fun doing it between fish!

A mid-summer trout inspects a beetle, just before he eats it.

Certainly there are freestone moments when waters are very low, slow, and clear, when stalked trout are twitchy, and able to discern fraud under the mid-day sun. This is when another section of my freestone fly box comes into play. Stored here are small black Crickets which trout love, Beetles and Ants, miniature Wulffs and Humpies down to #20, slim-bodied Parachutes, and tiny *Trico* and Rusty Spinners. Now a different emotion possesses you—that of the hunter. The trout fins, weaving slightly in easy summer currents, in an obvious "I'm looking" mode. Hopefully your carefree fishing the water practice has fine-tuned your casting arm! These trout won't stand much line abuse, and can see you if tactful precautions aren't taken. You might take the time to lengthen and slim down your tippet, and make that first cast count. From a chosen concealment, you might have to cast up and over the trout's back, across a heavier current into a bank eddy, or feed line out downstream. If said trout starts leaning upward towards your fly, be joyously concerned. And should he swing open-mouthed towards your surface dimpling impostor, steady the nerves for the set! You have won the game, which is in the fooling. The rest is just icing on the cake. Such summer stalkings are there for the keen sighted and observant.

There are match the hatch freestone moments too. These might

A freestone trout rises to an evening spinner fall. Look closely and you can see the fly between its jaws.

include *Baetis, Paraleptophlebia,* and *Rhithrogena* mayflies in spring; followed by salmonflies and golden stones. Then come brown and green drakes, followed by PMD's, *Epeorus, Heptagenia,* and other fast water mayflies. *Tricos* show up mid-summer, in smoke-like morning swarms, along with the colorful and active little yellow and green stoneflies who seem to enjoy summer as much as anyone. All manner of Hopper imitations are splatted down in bankside eddies, and along grass-shaded shores. Caddis too are plentiful, and twilight finds hordes of them hovering over the riffles. In quiet evening tailouts and edgewaters, trout sip spent mayfly spinners, while other mayflies still swarm above, rising and falling in a graceful and ancient ritual, their glassy wings catching the last rays of a sinking sun. Freestone species new to the angler pop up too, every time he thinks he's getting a grip on the entire stream life scenario. This keeps it interesting, and gives him yet another pattern to tie.

There are other flies in my freestone boxes, hundreds of them. But like many anglers, I tend to fall back on that handful of proven patterns, and trust that the casts will make them work.

My tailwater fly boxes are smaller, but have just as many if not more flies. Trout there play more games with the angler, and not always games of his liking. Consequently, you end up with many tiny experimental patterns, some that collect more dust than fish.

The smallest and perhaps most useful of these tailwater patterns are the Midges, tied down to size #26's. One should go smaller yet at times, though repetitive casting with what you have on fools a good percentage of fish. I've plenty of the now popular Griffith's Gnats and sub-species thereof, plus Parachute Midges, miniature Elk Hair Caddis, and an array of Midge Pupae. The latter is perhaps the tailwater trout's main diet over the course of the year. I often fish midge pupae as "droppers" a foot or so beneath a midge dry or *Baetis* mayfly pattern. Many trout prefer the pupa over the dry. On those lovely still, gray days in spring, fall, and winter, trout dimple to midges for hours. It takes a lot of them to fill up, requiring an afternoon of surface "grazing." If one looks at the duration of small insect hatches, you'll find that they offer the most rising fish/dry fly angling throughout the year, especially on tailwaters. In late fall and winter a midge pupa that works well for me consists only of a black thread base, ribbed with white thread for the body, and a slightly enlarged thorax of black or gray mixed dubbing. These, tied down to the smallest sizes and fished just sub-surface, take many trout routinely, trout that inexperienced anglers consider nearly impossible to fool. Patterns like this have been used since the turn of the century by British and American anglers.

The next big group of fly patterns for tailwaters falls under the Little Blue-Winged Olive grouping, which includes *Baetis* and

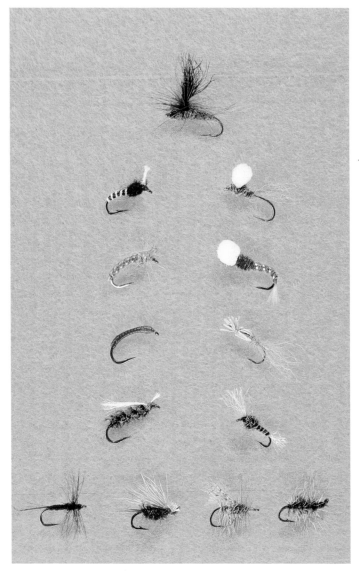

*This midge has just crawled out of his pupal shuck. Trout often target emerging midges for long feeding sessions on tailwaters.*

black wing shows up as a bold silhouette, very visible, and is apparently appealing to trout. Black is closer to the medium gray wing of the natural, than is the normal white wing, and displays a strong wing silhouette to the fish. It has long been assumed that the wing is the key factor a trout looks for in identifying mayflies as food items, and the first thing he sees as the natural drifts into his field of vision. As a California angler recently recited to me: "They eat the wing."

Using a gray wing on a big tailwater river makes small Parachutes hard to see. White is the most common wing color and shows up well against dark bank reflected backgrounds, but not so well against open sky reflected waters where black is superior. Some

*Here is a* Baetis *nymph, classically matched by #20-14 Pheasant Tail nymphs. These are populous in rich tailwater rivers and spring creeks, and are also found in freestone streams. In tailwaters, they are available to trout throughout the season, as they have multiple generations in a year.*

anglers use florescent red wings, but I find fluorescent yellow and chartreuse to be more visible, especially on choppy water and in mixed light situations. Parachutes tied with half black, half fluorescent yellow wings are good all around flies for visibilities sake.

Such Parachutes in sizes #22-14 are personal tailwater mainstays. The usual Adams gray body seems just as, or more effective, than trying to match the *Baetis's* natural body color. *Pseudos* on the other hand can call for closer imitation, as the trout get very picky on them. Fly size is usually the over-riding element of success here though, as *Pseudos* are as small as *Tricos,* down to #24.

Other B.W.O. patterns (Little Blue-Winged Olives) I carry include Comparaduns and the now popular Sparkle Dun, which are easy to tie and durable. This point is important to me, as I tie a lot of flies for immediate practical use. Some of the showcase no-hackle

*Here is an assortment of midge pupa and dries, with a black wing Baetis Parachute I use at the top. Midge patterns in sizes #26-18 are tailwater mainstays.*

*Pseudocloeon* mayflies, and some smaller *Ephemerella*. These are populous on tailwaters, and hatch up to four months or more of the fishing season. The best *Baetis* hatches here occur from late April till June, and again from late September into early December. The tiny *Pseudocloeon*, usually a bit lighter and brighter green colored, are most important locally in September, just after the morning *Trico* hatches wane for the year. Both "*Pseudos*" and *Baetis* are afternoon hatches, occuring during cool months, at the warmest time of day. They prefer humid, overcast conditions to hatch in, light snow or rain can show tremendous hatches and hundreds of rising fish.

Since this mayfly group provides the most classic dry fly fishing in terms of seasonal duration and abundance, I have quite a few flies in my box to represent them. First among these are Parachute Adams and variants thereof. I like them because they're easy to tie, durable, and trout like them. They are also taken for mayfly spinners, and are especially good as the *Trico* spinner fall wanes and trout become a little less picky.

Parachutes are easy to see on the water too. I tie the wings in a variety of colors, designed to show up well against different lighting and background situations. I use black wing models when fishing in wide open waters where the sky's reflection is your background. The

*A Baetis mayfly rests atop my fly rod. This is perhaps the best hatch in the west when it comes to seasonal duration and widespread availability.*

*"P.M.D." nymphs are populous in tailwater rivers. Trout often target the "emergers", just as they reach the surface to hatch.*

patterns are beautiful to look at and realistic, but don't stand up to repetitive abuse by hungry trout! There are also a variety of *Baetis* emergers in my box, but I don't tend to use them much, except on the odd exasperating fish. Most trout seem to favor duns.

Caddis are next to come into play on the seasonal scheme. Both dry fly patterns and emergers see a lot of summer use. I carry both elk hair and feather winged dries, plus the odd Parachute and Goddard's Caddis. These are in sizes #20-12. I'll tie tiny Elk Hair Caddis, from #20-24 to use over midge-sipping trout. Caddis start coming off well in May, and can provide very good fishing through October.

*An October caddis pupa just about to emerge. These are the largest caddis in western waters, matched by #6-10 imitations.*

Perhaps more tailwater fish are caught on Caddis emergers than on dries. Naturals can be seen popping from the river morning till evening. Even during the morning *Trico* spinner fall, you'll see Caddis hatching and trout thrashing them. This is often a sparse occurrence, but one trout are aware of. When guiding, I'll often have novice anglers swing small Soft Hackle emergers in front of rising fish or known holding positions. This is frequently rewarded with solid, self hooking takes. Such Caddis emergers fished beneath Parachutes or Caddis dries make a good fish nabbing team. There is

*A Pale Morning Dun (P.M.D.), one of the top hatches across the west.*

also a mottled white aquatic moth whose spent forms dot the surface mornings, mixed in with *Trico* duns and spinners. These are shaped much like Caddis, and Caddis dries take some fish during the *Trico* period. This can be a blessing for anglers with poor eyesight.

The emergers I'm currently using have an abdomen of dubbed Antron (various colors), a thorax of peacock herl, and thin gold wire ribbing. I use a variety of soft hackles and also pheasant tail fibers. I weight the fly lightly. Many of the fish I'm dealing with are in the shallows. In deeper runs, weight added to the leader increases your odds. These patterns are in sizes #20-12. Takes on them are decidedly bold. Fish often move out of their way to grab them. They sometimes break the tippet as the presentation is fished on a taut line, down and across, with a slight swing calculated to pass in front of fish. It is an excellent float fishing technique on the Missouri, the tailwater river I spend the most time on.

*A mid-summer afternoon finds these anglers casting along the edge of exposed weed beds. This is where damselfly dries can bring smashing takes from tailwater trout on some rivers.*
**Inset:** *Freshwater shrimp inhabit spring-rich waters across the west, including lakes, tailwaters, and spring creeks. "Scud," and Cress Bug patterns are popular producers on Montana's Big Horn.*

PMD's (Pale Morning Dun) start hatching in late June, and carry on into early August. This is an important hatch throughout the west on spring creeks, tailwaters, and freestone streams. Some big browns get into surface feeding on this hatch, which happens to occur evenings here, not mornings. It is a hatch that is not always easy to imitate. Some days you do well. The next day fish become very difficult to fool consistently. Many, many experimental patterns are tied: nymphs, emergers, cripples, duns, and spinners. They all work sometimes, but none work all the time! When the "big heads" are rolling though, you're willing to spend hours "not catching" them. We get some beauties, on those days when the trout are cooperating. A big pattern lately has been pale orange-bodied Sparkle Duns, Cripples, and Parachutes. Sparkle Duns are Comparaduns (the Caucci/Nastasi patterns) with trailing Antron or Z-lon tails that are supposed to represent trailing emergent shucks, though in reality look nothing like them. Most anglers' PMD boxes are ever-changing, as is mine, in an attempt to once-and-for-all solve (slim chance) that hatch puzzle. I suggest you obtain every PMD pattern you see in sizes #22-14, and keep them handy!

*Some tailwaters and spring creeks have thousands of damselflies, as do many trout-filled lakes. Wherever they are encountered in good numbers, trout will be taking both the nymphs and occasional adults.*
**Inset:** *Trout love crayfish! In my area they are a dominant food source for larger fish.*

Many anglers spend hours of their tailwater days blindly indicator nymphing. This doesn't appeal to me much, I'd rather go looking for rising fish. But when drifting down the river between rising fish locations we often indicator nymph or use two fly rigs. In my tailwater nymph box are staple patterns that can be depended on to routinely turn up fish. Pheasant Tail Nymphs are among them, in sizes #22-14. This pattern originated in England, tied to imitate British *Baetis* nymphs. It's a small world. The Flashback and Bead Head varieties work as well and better at times.

Quick-sinking Brassies are productive and imitate midge pupae. I keep some on hand in sizes #24-18. Scud and cress bug patterns are popular, especially on the Big Horn. Many scuds are tied in bright oranges and pinks, a hue they only achieve when deceased, or cooked up for tiny shrimp cocktails. The naturals vary from tan, to olive, to gray. Little cress bug patterns have been popular lately, tied in the light grayish-olive color range. Both these patterns are tied in sizes #18-12, and usually fished deep under indicators, often while floating mid-river.

San Juan Worms created a storm with their appearance some years ago, and have since settled in as steady tailwater producers. Anglers tie them in a variety of colors, mostly from the browns, into the reds, and on into the hot pink color spectrums. We find them particularly effective in early summer, when less tailwater hatches are catching the fish's attention. They work on freestone rivers as well, and we used them with success on various New Zealand rivers. These are tied in sizes #10-6, and dead drifted near the bottom under indicators. A lot of extra weight is often added to the leader to get them down. For me, they fall under the last resort category, only because I like to strip in streamers and crayfish patterns and feel those heavy takes! On my local rivers, crayfish play an important role in the trout's diet, especially with big fish. The Big Horn on the other

*This is an Egg Head variation of a more traditional tying style. This has been one of my favorite patterns over the past ten years. Trout can take it for a sculpin or crayfish.*

hand, has lots of worms in submerged weed beds, and fewer crayfish.

Damselfly dries are an interesting addition to your arsenal whenever they occur in good numbers on a tailwater. Trout jump on them as they lay eggs in streamside weed beds, and often get blown into the water. I see trout occasionally trying to grab them out of the air too. Rivers with populations of naturals can also fish well with damselfly nymphs that are "hand twist retrieved" over and around submerged weed beds and near the shorelines if emerging. This is something interesting to do when hatch action is at a lull and fish have to look for something else to eat.

I always have the usual array of streamers on hand including Buggers, Muddlers, Zonkers, and more traditional ties. I also have crayfish patterns. These seem to work well, perhaps for two reasons. First, trout here eat a lot of them. The second reason could be that very few fishermen use crayfish patterns routinely. The trout see all manner of Buggers and Streamers, but rarely if ever see crayfish imitations. It's hard to say whether they work better than brown Woolly Buggers or Streamers, which can certainly be mistaken for crays, but the closer imitation of the real thing certainly works!

It sometimes seems that when trout are turned on to eating Streamers, most any kind will work, and at any depth. Recently on such a day, trout repeatedly hit crayfish patterns that were stripped in near the boat, dragging near the surface just prior to recasting. One trout went after the fly four times, slashing back and forth, before finally hooking itself. This is an exciting aspect of Streamer fishing. Trout hit to disable them, fast and hard!

In the terrestrial realm, Hoppers are still number one, but steadily rising trout will often take ant or beetle patterns more consistently. Beetles can be found on the water from April on, and the Hi-vis foam models fool a lot of fish. Crickets are excellent too in sizes #14-6.

In a good cicada year, trout will be on the watch for these large terrestrial beasts. You won't see many on the water, trout grab them quickly. I remember a banner cicada year on the Smith River when the big fish were gorging on them. It was perhaps the best big fish/dry fly year we ever had there. We had to tie patterns on the spot, as it isn't an occurrence that happens often. I still have a few of these patterns lingering in my fly box ready for their next emergence! In the last decade, Utah's Green River has become known as a notable cicada fishery. I try to keep a variety of all these terrestrials on hand. They play a large part in a trout's diet, especially as the hatches fade in late summer.

One thing I've noticed over the years with Hoppers, is that the cork-like deer hair ones (Dave's for instance) seem to have a lower hook-up success ratio than the hackled models do (like a Joe's, or more recently Parachute Hoppers). That cork-like buoyancy sometimes seems to make it harder for the trout to get hold of them. Water, on the other hand, passes right through the hackled patterns, and trout don't seem to push the fly away from themselves when rising to them, as happens more often with the deer hair models. The result, in my less-than-scientific observation, is that the hackled mod-

*Hoppers are abundant in streamside foliage come late summer. Anglers enjoy fishing Hoppers because they're easy to see on the water and bring bold takes on the surface. Hoppers fished wet work well in broken freestone runs too.*

A mass of Trico (Tricorythodes minutus) *mayfly spinners get held up in streamside grasses. These hatch in incredible numbers every morning from mid-July into September, and bring thousands of tailwater trout to the surface.* **Inset:** *Trico duns appear on the water at 7-9 a.m., and then quickly molt, mate, and die. The spinners cover the water in flotillas.*

els achieve a better hook-up percentage. This might be offset by the sometimes greater fish-attracting powers of the super realistic deer hair models, though the Parachute Hopper comes close to achieving that realism. This is a small matter. I've no statistical proof, and they both work, as the trout have often testified!

From mid-July to mid-September, *Trico* spinners dominate morning fishing. These tiny mayflies hatch by the millions every morning, molt, mate, and then fall dead to the water, all between 7:00 and 11:00 a.m. Hundreds of fish make a habit of rising to them daily, providing anglers with the most consistent match the hatch rising-trout

action to be seen anywhere. The naturals are matched by #24-18 flies. The duns are of an olive and gray cast. Spent wings which litter the river in the thousands are gray to black, with the usual transparent wings found in most spinners. (Spinners and spent wings are common terms for mayflies that have laid their eggs and died with their wings spread out to the sides, flat on the water.) Since *Trico* spinners are small, numerous, and motionless (dead), exacting and repeated casts with accurate imitations are usually needed for success. Many consider this to be one of the toughest hatches to fish, while polished casters revel in the challenges. There are other notable spinner falls on tailwaters including PMD, *Psuedo*, and *Baetis* spinners, which can hit the water both mornings and evenings. I keep some tan, olive, and rusty spinner patterns on hand in sizes #24-16, plus a good stock of *Trico* spinners and Parachutes.

This is just a sample of a somewhat typical Rocky Mountain fly box. I certainly have my own pattern ruts, and I am not as experimental as I could be. I find when guiding that casting skills (or lack thereof) and conditions usually have more effect on the day's outcome than having this or that fly pattern. As one of our guides has been known to reply when asked what he caught a fish on, "a drag free drift in their face." I keep on tying new flies and patterns anyway, as all addicted fly anglers do.

**Below:** *An angler works soft-hackled wet flies through a run where trout are taking emerging caddis.*
**Inset:** *Other spent wing mayflies are important to tailwater anglers, including those of P.M.D.'s, and Pseudocloeon. Pictured here is a* Callibaetis *mayfly spinner, these are usually associated with lakes, but hatch out of slower, rich tailwater rivers and spring creeks as well.*

The Perfect Day

**Above:** *A memory released.*

**Left:** *The river never stops calling.*

The Suburban rumbled to a halt, steeply angled at the boat ramp. Feathered riverside inhabitants began chirping again as the dust settled. I stepped out into a different world than the one I left earlier at the Wolf Creek Cafe.

It was one of those still, perfect spring mornings we hope for. A gray, cool, dank cloudiness enveloped the valley, with the kind of subtle moisture aquatic insects prefer hatching in. The sensuously pleasing humidity gathered and enhanced the earth's scents and amplified riverside sounds. The musty odor of rushes, willows, and river water invigorated the angling impulse. Raucous redwing blackbirds called from cattails, perched at angles on their vertical stems. A flock of waxwings made upward sweeps to intercept wayward Caddis. Swallows perched together along telephone wires, knowing a good day was in store for their lucky species. Somewhere down the river geese honked from preferred island nesting sites. I stopped to

*Wood on water, a beautiful sight.*

breathe all this in, in a sense of passionate renewal.

On the smooth tailwater currents, rafts of midges slid on downstream, black squirming dots on a liquid field of gray. I knew the *Baetis* and *Rhithrogena* mayflies would show up on schedule come afternoon, and in force. Already the quiet bulges of trout, and splashy tail flips of whitefish were animating the smooth flow, interrupting peaceful reflections of streamside rushes, and making swirling circles among the somber yellows, reds, and browns they laid out across the water from the river's edge. Swallows fidgeted, flapped, and bobbed on the wire, making occasional sorties to scoop up midges. They too knew that larger and more plentiful fare would soon be at hand.

The squeaks and rattles of my boat trailer disgorging its load gives way to a more pleasing sound of water lapping against the wooden hull. Ribbons of cedar shimmer on the river, circling and dancing around the boat where wood meets water. It's an often repeated ceremony I enjoy.

Finally the duffel is stored, rods rigged, last inspiring cups of coffee consumed, and obligatory small talk and joking consummated. The rig is clankily removed from the ramp, and the river is now ours—a rare day with no one else in sight. Every bulging trout can be allotted its due amount of time, and parlayed with on its own discriminatory terms!

The first casts feel good. With no wind or even a breeze, the rod tracks true. Line shoots effortlessly. On some days I cast better than others. Today is a good one. My deliveries are light, reach casts smooth, and the fly cocks beautifully downstream of the leader.

We drift on downstream with creaking ash oars dipping and dripping. Hayfields, cottonwoods, and pine forests slip by, their colors subdued in the gray haze, but exuding richer scents in the still morning air because of it. Ahead a bank riser feeds at a leisurely pace, in a shallow featureless, midge specked edgewater. The slow swells emitting from his arching torso attest to his plump maturity.

The fly gliding towards him at current speed disappears in a swirl and the tippet is brought to a sudden stop by a trout going the opposite way. A boil of astonishment is followed by a fleeing "V" wake and leader slicing the water towards mid-river. I strip in line rapidly and feel the fragile graphite flex and vibrate under its living load. It is one of many fish pursued that day, with a primitive hunter's instinct that lingers, an instinct disguised by hi-tech gear, but as primeval and heart-felt as ever.

Other greater and lesser trout are duped, jumped, netted, and released, all admired for their spotted beauty, grace, and power, regardless of size. But a particular bank hugger etched a more permanent place in memory.

He rose repeatedly beneath a willow, his entire head surging up and out of the water, though only eating midges. The rower dipped the oars quietly and cautiously, keeping me in perfect position. The steely gray currents kept a parade of food supplied to the confident trout. He rose beneath the bough with little fear of apprehension.

Many casts were put over that fish. A dozen or so just to compete with the naturals. A dozen more to decide if a pattern change was in order. From a Parachute Midge to a smaller Elk Hair Midge to a tinier yet Griffith's Gnat I switched. The rower worked masterfully and tirelessly. The tailwater current was easy, as the valley was wide and gradient slight. It took only wrist strokes of the oars to smoothly keep the boat in place willowside. A dozen casts more and I added a Michelle's Midge Pupa dropper. My wife learned to fly fish over *Trico* and midge feeding trout—no easy matter—and this midge pattern I named after her.

On the third cast the dry fly pulled under as the trout took the dropper. The trout boiled and shook, wallowed and rolled, then fled for mid-river. The boatman backed off the bank to keep pressure on the fish. The fight was determined if not spectacular, but the beauty of the brown made up for any aerial deficiency in this fight. The oranges, yellows, and reds were striking. Framed in the net, it was a picture of artwork as brilliant as any in nature. The large gasping brown with the midge pupa at the tip of its snout begged to be released, and soon was. "Your turn to row," I said, needing no more at present to be content.

A great tailwater day was under way, risers were there to be spotted and fooled, and the real hatch had yet to come. Soon swallows would be circling and dipping in gray skies and water, flotillas of midges and *Baetis* would be sailing, and trout contorting the surface everywhere.

There are many other perfect days that come to mind, surely a small percentage of total time spent fishing and guiding, but dream days nonetheless. Bluebird summer days under azure skies when freestone trout attacked flies recklessly. High country rivers flowed clear, through dramatic mountain valleys and canyons. The trout were not selective, just hungry and numerous. They flushed from pockets to attack Goofus Bugs, and Joe's and Letort Hoppers, before the days of Whitlock's realism. They seized Montana Nymphs boldly in broken runs where colored stones reflected the mid-day sun. The attire was shorts and tennis shoes. No pretense of style was evident, and none needed to achieve 50 fish days. This was honest fun on remote backcountry rivers that you had to yourself.

Even the most accessible rivers have their banner days too: fantastic Caddis action on the magnificent Yellowstone; salmonfly heydays on the Big Hole, Blackfoot, and Madison; casting to schools of risers on the Big Horn and Missouri when they were more innocent; and days when browns slammed streamers viciously when cast

*All are admired for their beauty, grace, and power.*

*High summer on a hidden freestone river.*

*A perfectly calm and overcast day, laden with the type of moisture insects prefer hatching in.*

to bank cover. Great days occur every season for those lucky enough to spend many days on stream. Great days of every kind, on every type of water. Days when you can lean back in the boat in total contentment and watch the mountains glide by.

Camping along rivers adds another dimension, and many, many days have been spent under canvas along Montana rivers. There's a lot of hustle and bustle and damn hard work by the gear boaters to get a big camp set up. Meal planning and preparation is a big thing, with victories and defeats at the stove. But rowing up to a scenic campsite at the end of a good fishing day is a refreshing change from urban life. Fish tales are compared, big meals engulfed, and evening fires lounged beside. For the unquenchable angler, he can go back out for some good evening action. The darkening river valley can be alive with dancing mayfly spinner swarms and frolicking Caddis. Nighthawks and bats soar overhead too, gathering in the feast. Swirls of trout are everywhere, materializing where none seemed to be before. The twilight river world is in full motion. It is a moment you wish could last longer, that you can't quite wholly grasp, and soon flees into darkness. Then the campfire illuminates tents, trees, and faces. Worn-out fishermen joke and begin nodding in their fireside chairs. Bottles of good wine and scotch are less full than a little while ago, and sleeping bags and cots will soon be bulging. Snores emit from tents to mix with calls of owls, under a sky of brilliant and uncountable stars and silhouettes of pines. Come dawn, a big pot of camp coffee will start off another long fishing day spent traversing miles of beautiful high country river.

Not all days are so blessed. There are storms, wind, drought years, and poor fishing to endure at times. For most of us, we have to put in time and pay our dues to get those few perfect days. I've seen plenty of novices luck into real banner days, and seasoned veterans stoically endure a week of poor conditions and fishing. One has to go out with an open mind and moderate expectations. But when the perfect days come, be sure to revel in them!

I am ever ready to launch again, on any river across the west.

Landscapes, clean rivers, and trout beckon. Good days are ahead. Seasons will pass, hatches proliferate, and fish rise. The morning sun will warm up frosted tents, and activate high country trout. Peaceful lunches under cottonwood and pine groves give time to watch water flow and clouds pass over mountains. Sunsets color mountain vistas and bring on evening hatches and jumping trout. Twilight will see the drift boat winched up on the old trailer again.

For the float fisherman, the river keeps running towards spectacular unfished horizons, and never stops calling.

# Index

## A
Ants, 53, 77, 97, 98, 103
Attractor Patterns, 51, 52, 65, 77, 97, 98, 103
Aquatic Moths, 77, 105
Aquatic Worms, 56, 97, 98

## B
*Baetis* Mayflies, 39, 46, 50, 56, 62, 74, 76, 78, 79, 97, 98, 103, 104, 110
Bank Feeders, 39-42
Beadhead Nymphs, 97, 98, 102
Beetles, 53, 77, 97, 98, 103
Big Horn River, 56
Bitch Creek Nymphs, 102
Boat Fishing Skills, 11-28
Bow, 8
Brown Drake Mayflies, 52, 76, 98

## C
Caddis, 49, 50, 75, 77, 97, 98, 103, 105
*Callibaetis,* 107
Camping, 10, 80, 82, 83, 111, 112
Casting Downstream, 15-16, 57
Casting High, 13
Casting Safety, 13
Casting Zones, 16
Cicadas, 57, 66, 97, 98
Clothing, 10
Covering the Water, 37-43
Craneflies, 77, 97
Crayfish, 56, 97, 98, 102, 105, 106
Crickets, 103
Crowding, 80-83

## D
Damselfly, 65, 66, 77, 97, 105, 106
Depth Perception, 56
Dory, 4
Drift Boats, 7
Dry Fly Fishing, 51-53
Duffel, 10

## E
Edgewaters, 62, 65, 110
Egg Flies, 97, 98
Egg Head Streamers, 98, 102, 105
Entering Boats, 8-9
Epeorus Mayflies, 49, 76, 103
*Ephemerella flavilinea,* 104
*Ephemerella inermis,* 56, 76, 97
*Ephemerella infrequens,* 56, 76, 97
*Ephemerella* Mayflies, 104
Etiquette, 83-85

## F
Fall Hatches, 78, 79, 97, 98
Fighting Fish, 67
Fishing the Banks, 37, 39, 65
Fishing the Middle, 42-43
Float Fishing Tackle, 29-33
Float Fishing Tactics, 35-43
Foam Lines, 53, 62
Freestone Rivers, 44-53, 98
Freshwater Shrimp, 56, 97, 105, 106
Fly Patterns, 60, 74, 97, 98, 101-107

## G
Girdle Bugs, 102
Golden Stoneflies, 48, 76, 98
Green Drake Mayflies, 52, 76, 98
Green River, 57
Guides, 86-93
Gunwale, 8

## H
Hare's Ear Nymph, 49, 98, 102
Hatches, 46, 50, 52, 53, 74, 76, 77, 94-99, 102, 103
Hatch Charts, 97-98
*Heptagenia* Mayflies, 76, 102, 103
Hoppers, 77, 97, 98, 103, 106, 107

## I
Indicator Nymphing, 42
Inside Bends, 41, 63
Island Systems, 64

## J-K
Knee Braces, 9

## L
Leaders, 31-32
Leeches, 97, 98, 102
Lines, 30-31
Line Control, 14
Little Winter Stoneflies, 74, 97
Little Yellow & Green Stoneflies, 77, 98
Low Water Season, 76-79

## M
Madison River, 44, 53, 73, 74
Mayflies, 52, 97, 98
Mending Line, 21-22
Midges, 39, 50, 56, 59, 74, 76, 78, 79, 97, 98, 103, 104, 110
Missouri River, 56, 57, 60, 65, 78, 87, 90, 105
Montana Nymphs, 102
Muddler Minnows, 102

## N
Nets, 33, 67
Netting Fish, 68-69
Nymphing, 47, 50, 56, 60, 75, 77, 78, 102

## O
Oars, 13-14, 68
October Caddis, 50, 52, 97, 98, 105
Outfitters, 87-88

## P
Parachute Adams, 53, 97, 104
*Paraleptophlebia* Mayflies, 50, 76, 98, 103
Parallel Casts, 12
Photographing Fish, 69
PMD's (Pale Morning Dun Mayflies), 56, 76, 77, 97, 98, 105
Pre Run-Off Period, 74-74
*Pseudocloeon* Mayflies, 50, 56, 78, 97, 104

## Q-R
Rafts, 4, 7, 10, 71
Raingear, 10
Reach Cast, 16, 20, 57, 59

Reels, 30
Releasing Fish, 69
*Rhithrogena* Mayflies, 74, 75, 97, 98, 103, 110
Rise Forms, 60
Rowing, 14, 67
Run-Off, 73, 75-76, 102

## S
Salmonflies, 48, 51, 75-76, 95, 98
San Juan Worm, 56, 97, 98, 106
Schooling Trout, 59-60
Scuds, 56, 97, 106
Sculpin, 50, 97, 98, 102
Seasonal Conditions, 73-79, 96
Serpentine Case, 21
Side Arm Casts, 24-25
*Siphlonurus* Mayflies, 50, 76
Sitting Entry, 8
Skid Cast, 23
Skipping Flies, 25
Skwala Stoneflies, 75, 98
Slack Line Reach Casts, 20-21, 57
Smith River, 19, 45, 85, 86, 103, 106
Snails, 77
Soft Hackle Flies, 50, 97, 98, 105, 107
South Fork of the Flathead River, 46, 82, 83, 84
Special Casting Techniques, 19-28
Speed Casting, 36
Spent Wing Mayflies, 53, 60, 77, 107
Spotting Fish, 43, 60
Spaying Trout, 58-59
Spruce Moths, 77
Stack Mending, 22-23
Stern, 8, 13, 14
Stoneflies, 49, 52, 75-76, 95, 97, 98, 102
Streamer Fishing, 40, 50-51, 77
Strike Indicator, 47, 48, 77
Sunlight, Effects of, 58, 59, 78

## T
Tailwater Rivers, 54-66, 97, 103-107, 110
Tailwater Zones, 60-66
Taking Turns, 12
Tangling in Oars, 13
Terrestrials, 40, 77, 97, 98, 103
Thwart, 8
*Tricos* (*Tricorythodes* Mayflies), 53, 56, 60, 62, 77, 78, 97, 98, 107
Triple Haul, 26-27
Trout in Shallow Water, 61
Tuck Cast, 23-24
Two Fly Systems, 38-39, 60, 63, 64, 78

## U-V
Unhooking Yourself, 70-72
Unsnagging Roll Cast, 28

## W
Waders, 10, 33
Weather, 10, 73-79
Wind, 10, 13, 25-28
Wind Casting, 25-28, 91
Woolly Buggers, 97, 98, 102

## X-Y-Z
Yellowstone River, 6, 110